# Joy Comes in the Morning

### Kimley Dunlap-Slaughter

CREATION HOUSE
A STRANG COMPANY

Joy Comes in the Morning, But Not Before Peace
by Kimley Dunlap-Slaughter
Published by Creation House
A Strang Company
600 Rinehart Road
Lake Mary, Florida 32746
www.creationhouse.com

Unless otherwise noted, all Scripture quotations are from the King James Version of the Bible.

Scripture quotations marked NKJV are from the New King James Version of the Bible. Copyright © 1979, 1980, 1982 by Thomas Nelson, Inc., publishers. Used by permission.

English definitions are from *Merriam-Webster's Collegiate Dictionary*, 11th Edition, Springfield, MA: Merriam-Webster, Inc., 2003.

Hebrew and Greek definitions are from *Holman Illustrated Bible Dictionary*, eds. Trent C. Butler, Chad Brand, Charles Draper, Archie England, Nashville, TN: B & H Publishing Group, 2003.

Design Director: Bill Johnson
Cover design by Jerry Pomales

Library of Congress Control Number: 2008936177
International Standard Book Number: 978-1-59979-480-8

First Edition

08 09 10 11 12 — 987654321
Printed in the United States of America

*And he brought forth his people with joy, and his chosen with gladness: And gave them the lands of the heathen: and they inherited the labour of the people; That they might observe his statues, and keep his laws. Praise ye the LORD.*

—PSALM 105:43–45

# DEDICATION

*Make a joyful noise unto God, all ye lands: Sing forth*
*the honour of his name: make his praise glorious.*

—PSALM 66:1–2

A S ALWAYS, I GIVE God the glory, honor, and all the praise
for this opportunity to minister and be a witness to His
people for such a time as this. Through my personal
affliction and trying health, God has delivered me from all infirmities, giving me a heart to look beyond my personal needs to
think of those who are really suffering for Christ's sake and in
His name.

God has given me a wonderful family who has been praying
for my endurance and longsuffering so that we could overcome
various trials and tribulations. Regardless of emotional barriers,
mental hindrances, physical obstacles, or spiritual roadblocks, we
are more than conquerors through Christ who strengths us. To my
dear and loving husband, Donald, and my two amazing daughters, Kayla and Dominique, for having confidence in mommy:
Thank you for never doubting what God could do in me. Through
your prayers, love, hope, patience, and understanding, I was able
to endure the persecution and rejection that came along the way.

And I thank you, the reader, who have chosen to take a journey
along with me on this ride called joy and peace. My hope and
prayer for you is that you reach an emotional, mental, physical,
and spiritual victory in obtaining and maintaining unrestricted
joy as well as sustaining everlasting peace.

God bless you.

# CONTENTS

# PREFACE

THIS BOOK WAS WRITTEN to encourage those who are suffering from low self-esteem or lack of confidence, particularly individuals who have been psychologically and spiritually injured or attacked by the satanic forces or those who are under demonic influence.

For years I have observed people in the local church, in my family, in my community, and within the work force that are devoid of the presence of joy and peace, as well as incapable of articulating and expressing the freedom in having these two wonderful gifts given to God's peculiar and special people. I had a lot of difficulty in perceiving how anyone could function day to day without the spiritual confidence and courage that comes from the indwelling power of the Holy Spirit, when surrounded by so much depression and unhappiness. For a true believer the traits of joy and peace seem to be the easiest attributes of the fruit of the Spirit to have, without requiring any strenuous efforts or aptitude testing on the part of the recipients. Nonetheless, the majority of people I encountered daily with these alarming predispositions were fellow believers, who were lacking the foundational source of faith, because they had not truly accepted Christ as Savior and allowed Him to be Lord over their lives.

They were overwhelmed with stress, fretting over how they had no genuine freedom from challenges or concerns that stem from independent circumstances of the past brought on by outside incidents or situations. Suffering from apprehension, they were feeling like life was passing them by, and that they were just suspended in midair or drifting like a wayward boat without a sail. This was dreadful sight to see, since so many were following the lead of egotistical, overbearing, and prideful leaders who would abandon members at the drop of hat if they did not obey their commands or follow their the traditional guidelines. These congregates and co-laborers who go week after week sitting on pews, sitting in choirs, and sitting in pulpits as well as serving all around the sanctuary, have indirectly, confidently, and explicitly stated that their existence was meaningless and they were useless to the kingdom of God. They lead, serve, and volunteer, but their homes have much disorder and turmoil.

These individuals struggle with self-identity issues or from low self-esteem, as a result they are interacting with dysfunctional people, connecting with unhealthy social crowds, or seeking help from unwise counselors, looking to receive validation. Frequently, they are befriended by individuals who later become envious of their achievements, so once again they are trying to manage concealed insecurities alone, again dissatisfied with self. Without prayer, you will listen to that inner voice that will misdirect you to take another leap into the pit of the confusion, only to find yourself back in the same position, betrayed by a supposedly close friend or favored companion because you put more faith in man rather than God. Misery steps in to give false comfort, depositing irrational and negative satanic thoughts within the component that controls your individual feelings, perception, reasoning, thoughts, and self-will. Meanwhile, these individual continue to seek after the majority social unit for encouragement and reassurance, and as a result will continue to suffer from lack of self-identity in Christ until they decide to allow the Spirit to be their guide and instructor.

All believers must understand why it is vital to have the spirit of exceeding joy and immeasurable peace while taking this tedious voyage, because this world is not our home; we are pilgrims in a foreign land. Without joy and peace one will not know when to call on the name of Jesus in the midst of crisis, persecution, and tribulation. Those that are born-again believers in Christ Jesus will find that the oppressor, Satan, will work especially hard on his attack, now vengeful that you no longer part his team. So remember, he will do everything in his restricted power to subject you to self-indulgences, which are manifested from unrestrained gratification that has emerged from selfish ambitions, desires, or urges to do what pleases self. Consequently, your explanation or motivation for existing has nothing to do with your professional yearning, emotional desires, occupational needs, vocational wants, or personal urges, but from the establishment of the kingdom of God here on earth. You have an earthly representative, capable of providing you with comfort and encouragement during times of despair, the Holy Spirit or the Comforter, who will not abandon you in your hour of need.

This book is a collection of thoughts from Old and New Testament to inspire the body of Christ to endure against intrusive invaders of secular and satanic principalities and rulers in dark places while sustaining one's perpetual joy and peace. I thank God for releasing divine revelations and sacred enlightenment of His fruit into my life so that can help others preserve and sustain these two fruitful elements given to the church—joy and peace—after Christ's ascension.

My prayer is that every steward of the sovereignty of God, who reads this book, will walk away with sustaining power against the evil one, whose goal is to deprive you of your daily dosage of joy and peace. In addition, I hope to show you how to have true and perpetual joy with internal and external peace. I hope that this diary of joy will encourage you and take you to a higher level in God.

## ENTER INTO HIS PRESENCE WITH EXCEEDING JOY

### BY KIMLEY DUNLAP-SLAUGHTER

I rise early with praise and worship as the fruit comes
    from my lips.
As I bring forth optimistic prayer and supplication,
I am a free-will agent who is thankful and celebrates
    my victories by giving God all the praise, honor, and
    glory.
I may sometimes become depressed or oppressed by the
    world's light affliction, but the Spirit of the Lord comes
    in and provides me comfort.
Although enemy may come in like a flood,
I believe the Lord will position a standard against him,
    therefore he is unable to destroy my purpose, stop my
    destiny, or hinder my fortitude.
This current moment, I realize I can do all things
    through Christ that strengthens me, for God has given
    me the ability and authority to stand on His Word.
I will not be afraid for the terror by night or the arrows
    by day while I rest in the arms of
the Almighty God as He takes me to a place of complete
    happiness and the
profound peak of serenity.
Lord, I need you to give me a new heart, to aid me in
    overcoming the miseries and sorrows of life in which I
    must learn how to cope.
The love I have for You gives me reason and reassurance
    not to lose hope.

At the present time, I understand that I can enter into
   your presence with exceeding joy,
Maybe not under the moonlight, but certainly when
   the reflective sun begins to shine throughout every
   adverse or obscure situation in my life.
As the true Son comes shining from terrestrial
   extremities of my mental and physical experience,
Today, I realize that there is immeasurable peace upon
   the horizon, as well.

# INTRODUCTION

*For his anger endureth but a moment; in his favour is life:*
*weeping may endure for a night, but joy cometh in the morning.*

—PSALM 30:5

IF YOU HAVE PURCHASED this book, then you have taken your first step to wanting to know more about how to receive the gifts of exceptional joy and indefinite peace, which both come from the Father, the true Vine, the Son, the Branch that is connected to stewards of God, and the Holy Spirit, the Sustainer who is responsible for equipping you with the instructions on how to effectively obtain joy and peace in your daily endeavors. Joy is the secondary agent that comes after love that produces unanticipated or unexpected results to create the element of peace within one's collaborating social arena; there are many who do not possess theses attributes. Whether they may be rich or poor, young or old, educated or inexperienced, man or woman, or boy or girl, many have not figured out how to receive the gifts of joy and peace. Neither are they consciously aware who is the giver of these gifts. As believers we know that all good and perfect gifts come from above (James 1:17). In other words, those who have been transformed by Christ can resist the test or temptation that God allows to come your way in order to produce more fruits of faith and draw you closer to Him; since His character is unchanging so are His gifts. God, the Father, through the mediation of Jesus Christ, the Son, and through the aid of the Holy Spirit, the Comforter, will provide mental and moral development to equip you with three natural

1

faculties to help you get and keep perpetual cheerfulness and harmony when you have to face discouraging situations or fall into various trials.

First, you must have *peace*. Without it, you cannot experience the true essence of joy, for without peace it is impossible to have any means of communal delight granted by the Father so you will have solitude in the midst of harsh conditions, iniquitous ordeals, and upsetting predicaments. Joy is the supernatural quality that supplies the state of happiness and resource of gratefulness, which builds one's character and preserves one's inner being during spiritual warfare. Joy is not an emotional attribute; rather it is a spiritual peculiar and essential character that comes through the Spirit, although it can affect one's mental reactions through physiological and behavioral changes.

Second, you must become maturely sufficient to possess *unconditional love* for others before the overflow of unchanging joy can take root into a regenerated mind and renewed spirit, which goes beyond all human perception or psychological explanation and reasoning. Without God's love, you will be unable to recognize what is obvious or apparent, and what is beyond the visible or observable. For example, if a brother or sister in Christ offends you, the characteristic of unconditional love and unchanging joy will allow you to resolve difference in the spirit of forgiveness without having feelings of uncontrolled rage, settled dislike, or mutual ill will. The rudiments of love, joy, and peace can help you combat against offensive forces, even when they may be coming from others who are struggling with internal issues, family and marital problems, or occupational crisis. These fruits of the Spirit will help you discern what is going on within your unified body of worship, residency, and workplace.

Keep in mind that many people have not received this fruit of the Spirit because they are not willing to let go of unsettle past events, cope with present inflictions, and surrender personal injustices. When you can use what was meant for evil and turn it around into something good, you not only maintain peace between followers of Christ but also can reconcile someone back into the Ark of Safety.

Third, you must have factual evidence of *faith* before the materialization of unending joy can function as supernatural differentiated structure, and not as a fleshly or shallow formation of fundamental physical senses apart from any particular deliberation, emotion, or perception. Now you are experienced and knowledgeable to accept Hebrews 11:1 and 6 as absolute and true, which says:

> Now faith is the substance of things hoped for, the evidence of things not seen....But without faith it is impossible to please [God]: for he who cometh to God must believe that he is, and that he is a rewarder of them that diligently seek him.

Faith requires fervent anticipation and zealous expectation, which was offered from the Old Testament saints who were found submissive as they experienced physical punishment while trying to accomplished God's will. They obtained gracious kindness and partiality from God through their exceptional testimony and faithful witness of integrity. There where tremendous miracles performed such as separating of the Red Sea, which allowed them to travel to safe land, a pillar cloud by day to lead the way, and a pillar of fire by night to give them light—symbolizing His presence with them.

There are two types of faith operating within the life of the believer to help us prevail over the complicating, perplexing, or trying affairs of this world system.

1. Believing faith, which is having confidence in the statement or promise that God has spoken over your life and believing and accepting His Word, creed, and revelation without limitation, restrictions, or reservations.

2. Saving faith, which is compensating and redeeming grace that gives you hope and reliance without any exemption or explanation. It is the thing that empowers your will to resist dejection or despondency, even if all things appear or seem to be hopeless.

You must become like the marathon runner who concentrates only on the finish line, so focus your intellectual actions and qualifications, physical stamina and conscious principles on Jesus, who has crossed the finish line with prevailing courage, potency, and tolerance. Prevailing courage, potency, and tolerance are crucial qualities needed for a life-span marathon.

However, it is the nature of humans to disobey and misbehave to tempt to become entangled in sin, which will prevent us from making progress in holiness and righteousness, producing unsound actions coming from faulty judgment, inadequate knowledge, or unintentional mistakes. The Father loves us in spite of our frailties and shortcomings, and Christ continues to stand before Him arbitrating on our behalf; His arms are always open to accept our appeal of repentance. Despite the fact that there will be some repercussions and chastising for immoral and unlawful conduct, Hebrews 12:11 says, "no chastening seems to be joyful for the present, but painful; nevertheless, afterward it yields the peaceable fruit of righteousness to those who have been trained by it" (NKJV). In other words, God's chastening comes not as a sign of His displeasure but because He loves us and desires us to move on toward perfection. So keep in mind, that practice does make perfect, and discipline makes greater warriors in the army of the Lord. The faithful and steadfast stewards of the Lord know that they can continuously depend on the Lord's straightforwardness, which is unlike man, who can never decide what is merited and unmerited or what is reasonable or unreasonable.

Jesus, the inherited Son of the throne of grace, has entered into the very presence of God and provided an entrance for us as joint-heirs, so we must never give up our faith in Him. The Spirit of the Lord has facilitated a way for us to rise above the structural blocks of earthly strongholds and stumbling blocks of transgressions. Keep in mind that Christ overcame every form of temptation by standing on the spoken and written Word of God. There is a universal place to go to when we are in need of physical escape and spiritual healing, the throne of grace, where undeserving people of God can receive His goodness. This is the place were we can find mercy, forgiveness for all iniquities, and grace to assist us with uncontrollable temptations. Christ has given us permission to come bravely before the throne of God in prayer, and expect to receive what we need in times of physical disorder, emotional grief, and spiritual turmoil.

Only the Word of God can penetrate the forces of hopelessness that go into the core depths of the human personality, for He stands to redirect our hesitant thoughts.

Today is the day to allow your intellect, physical, and inner being to become cultivated with exceptional joy and peace, so that you can have a more proficient life, productive ministry, and successful destiny.

May God bless you with bountiful joy and keep you in perfect peace.

# 1
## WHAT IS EXCEEDING JOY?

*Then he said unto them, Go your way, eat the fat, and drink*
*the sweet, and send portions unto them for whom nothing*
*is prepared: for this day is holy unto our LORD: neither*
*be ye sorry, for the joy of the LORD is your strength.*

—NEHEMIAH 8:10

ONE DAY AS I was sitting at my desk looking out an open bay window, I begin to ponder on the goodness of the Lord, after all the physical suffering, emotional hurt, and spiritual restlessness. I still had joy, not just average joy but exceeding joy—the joy that comes from knowing Christ as my personal Savior. What is God's exceeding joy? Is there really a way to attain unwavering joy? What gives us peace in the midst of adversity? There must be away to explain this in layman's terms so that those who are facing provoking ordeals, disputing confrontations, or violent oppositions will begin to gravitate to this supernatural resource. It is somewhat like Superman's cape, which he uses to help him leap over tall buildings and fly above the city. Bear in mind that this is the day the Lord has made; you can stand and rejoice in it with confidence of knowing that you too can have unwavering joy in the midst of the storms. This is the thing that helps you battle against the villains of life, such as depression and oppression, the strong powers put here by the Devil to cause you to fall back into your old nature. Yes, you can have the same power as Superman, and be able to leap tall buildings with a single bound and soar above the cares of life without vacillating or hesitation because the joy of the Lord is your strength.

This type of joy cannot fluctuate because it comes from a supernatural representative far greater than any demonic force in the universe, for its belief is more powerful than tangible correspondence and less dependent on earthly knowledge. You will always have entitlement to this inherent character as long as you have firm conviction and follow the guidance of the Holy Spirit with assured reliance on the ability, character, strength, and truth of the Lord. You must learn how to set aside all objective and passive emotions, so that you can get off the continual roller coaster ride of extreme anxiety and self-assertive pride. As long as you are in this earthly body, you will have to deal with joy as a emotion that is connected heavenly realm or spiritual powers with many feelings, such as happiness, understanding, love, and peace; but never forget that it the Holy Spirit that will keep you.

Holman Illustrated Bible Dictionary defines *joy* as "state of delight and well being that results from knowing and serving God." The words *joy* and *rejoice* are the words most often to translate into English from the Hebrew and Greek words. *Joy* is found 150 times in the Bible; if such words as *joyous* and *joyful* are included, the number increases to over 200. The verb *rejoice* appears well over 200 times. I found and documented that the words *joy* or *joyful* appear nearly 102 times in the Old Testament and 63 times in the New Testament. The word *joy* is found about 158 times in the New King James Bible, *joyful* or *rejoice* is written fifty times, *praise* appears about 153 times, *glad* or *gladness* are in there twenty times; *peace* is written sixteen times, *delight* five times, and *happy* appears seven times.

Joy is the fruit of a right relation with God; it is not something people can create by their own efforts. Joy is something that gives you great pleasure and makes you feel content in what you do, such as giving God all the honor, praise, and worship. It makes you feel overwhelmed with enthusiasm and gives joy even when things do not feel enjoyable and pleasurable. Enjoy being in the presence of God daily and you will experience or have joy in the middle of your circumstance, knowing that you will benefit from a greater reward. Joy puts the pep in your step, the bend in your smile, the rhythm in your praise, and the love that flows from your heart to others.

No matter what you may go through, there are no real superheroes that exist today who do not have any frailties or weakness; even Superman had to have his kryptonite. The comic book writers understand that all of these paranormal heroes must have a weakness and then something with which they must be equipped to overcome challenges that face them: Superman his cape, Wonder Woman her strong cord, Spiderman his web, Batman his science and technology, and Wolverine his metal claws. Even so some of these heroes were captured as they choose saving a life over apprehending evil criminals, so cunning foes set up a situation to entrap them. Eventually circumstances would allow them to escape. Denial of one's weakness is an inefficient means of attacking and subduing oppositions from evil forces, since we cannot block them without our sword of protection, the Word of God. Any vulnerable area in our lives can become a weapon used against us, such as unreasonable views about life challenges that are independent of our strength, Christ Jesus.

On the spiritual side, Christ had the cross, Paul had the thorn in his flesh, and you have Satan and his fallen angels, so as a believer you must not be deceived that there is someone on the earth that has the ability to be supernaturally faultless. Some of these animated superheroes from the sixties and seventies, brought to life again today on the movie screen, remind us that limitation, whether physical, physiological, or emotional, does not necessarily have to be an outside element that affects our ability to fight against evil forces or powers, but more how we fight. The Father will eliminate what is not yielding valuable results, viewed as unfruitful, so that we can produce wholesome fruit, so that our fruit bearing life can produce more Christlike character and witness. Daily our life is being shaped by obedience while we have total and complete dependence on Christ, which is the only way to grow in Christian love to birth more joy.

In front of others you maybe able to spin an impressive web of positive themes, including social responsibility, standing up for what is right, and being single-minded about your calling; but if Christ is not the center of your purpose, you too will fall into various snares and traps like these animated superheroes. For the most they did not take the call to be in the lime light or on front stage in front of hundreds or thousands of people; they were not trying to draw crowds, for they had a sharp contrast between loving, supportive family relationships and destructive ones. Joy keeps the mind from interference or conflict and helps you resist being overcome by the cares of the world during great times of persecution. Your occupation in furthering the advancement of the kingdom of God should be observed in the spirit of praise and worship, not necessary with intellectual endorsement but to incorporate an unconventional portrait of Christ's righteousness into your inherited, established, or customary patterned of way of life.

## JOY IS MY INNER COMFORTER

Joy is the inner comfort given to you by the Holy Ghost that will give peace, strength, and endurance to guard you when everything around is going amiss. In addition, no man can expunge that joy that is given by Jesus, since it is a permanent joy. This world is full of unpleasant things as well as good. Unfortunately, you mostly hear of the hideously evil news from the media and newspaper; yet Jesus said that He would not leave the believers comfortless, for He left the Comforter to bring the truths of Jesus back to your remembrance. "These things I have spoken to you while being present with you. But the Helper, the Holy Spirit, whom the Father will send in My name, He will teach you all things, and bring to your remembrance all things that I said to you" (John 14:25–26, NKJV). The Comforter will show you how to endure and bear confrontations, insults, ridicule, and exile. The Holy Spirit is your Comforter when you feel there is no place to safely retreat, and if you walk in the fear of the Lord all your days, He will edify your work in due season. The Holy Spirit, the Comforter, has a duty to continue the work of Jesus as a teacher and a warehouse retaining memories that can only come when you submit to the indwelling presence of the Spirit of God now that Christ has ascended to the right hand of God. He sits there intervening and mediating for all humanity until His Second Coming; there is a persistent fortress of joy and peace available for the children of God.

In the Old Testament, the children of Israel were in need of comfort, so God sent consoling words through His great prophets—Isaiah, Jeremiah, Ezekiel, and Malachi. However, the Israelites rejected the messengers on numerous occasions because they enjoyed serving multiple gods and living in a state of sinfulness. God made a promise to Isaiah that He would deliver His people, His chosen servants, from results of their sins from which now they were prisoners in Babylon. He would provide them with pardon from their iniquities, encourage and strengthen them in their days of captivity (Isa. 40:1–11).

The children of Israel were content to be disobedient to the Word and will of God, which broke God's heart and caused His Spirit to fill with grief. He looked for someone to take pity or have mercy on man, or stand in the gap for man's unrighteousness and immorality, but there was none qualified. He called for someone to have sympathy and to intervene for mankind, for the purpose of producing compassionate rapport between Him and man, but no one was worthy (Ps. 69:20, NKJV). This is an open display of the need of faithful and loyal messengers of the gospel to stand in the gap for corrupt evildoers, immoral and unrighteous individuals. Acts of humility before God often brought ridicule from the community and leaders, even from outsiders. Like David, many who suffered great persecution wanted God to bestow divine judgment and administer punishment for their enemies, for their suffering was not merely personal, but their followers would be punished as well. There were many petitions to God for relief and rescue from their atrocious opponents (Ps. 70:1–5). Finally someone answered the call to at least acknowledge the responsibility as a leader the need of bringing God's people back to repentance. Isaiah accepted his call, which consisted of a visualization of God, a revelation of need, a visualization of judgment, and an image of hope for the people of God. He told the Lord, if you need someone, send me. I will go: "Also I heard the voice of the Lord, saying: 'Whom shall I send, and who will go for Us?' Then I said, 'Here am I! Send me'" (Isa. 6:8, NKJV). Isaiah knew that preaching God's message to insensitive and rebellious people confirms the imperative need for a Savior. The Father was aware that this task was not going to be trouble free for any ordinary man. Although Isaiah had good intentions, he could not perform this task alone. This was a task that required supernatural agents, forces, and elements to work together simultaneously and systematically in order defeat the powers of sin.

After many attempts to reach His people, God decided to send a true Deliverer to bring us out of spiritual bondage. That true deliverer was Jesus Christ, the Son of the living and mighty God, who was an example of perfection and submission, walking in the flesh. Jesus completed His assignment and left the world a survival tool, the Holy Spirit. The Holy Spirit is man's comforter, security blanket, friend in the midnight hour, and aid in distress.

One cannot have joy without peace; peace and joy go hand and hand. Peace was the angelic promise at Jesus' birth in Luke 2:14 where he promised peace on earth to the people He favors. Consequently, the world cannot achieve or provide this peace because is refuses to deal with the problem of sin. Only God's peace can guard heart and mind against the wiles of evil. On the other hand, the peace that Jesus said He left transcends above all human plausible facts or occurrences. Joy is the inner quality, which distinguishes a vital functioning element from dead dependent cells that cause abnormal growth to your objective goals and incentives, no longer reproducing enthusiastic motivation. The Spirit source of happiness is the supernatural substance that is responsible for changing the energy level in dying and living cells by which vigorous application of power is provided for vital progression and succession of assimilating new thoughts. Jesus' peace is forever and timeless; no one in this world can take it from a child of God. The world peace is inferior, for it orbits around controlling circumstances and manipulative people who offer conditions and prerequisites that are dissimilar in association and influenced by earthly fate. The soul of man has a God-conscious and moral awareness of good and evil. Joy and peace endear ethical uprightness and encourage us to be reliable servants of the Lord, for the peace of Jesus is self-possessed without regulations and demands; it is indispensable and no man can take it away. Christ's fundamental entity of peace does not bring excessive suffering or hardship. It conveys love and intense enthusiasm, for if you rely on God's wisdom, it adds beauty and honor to your life. His joy is unconditional and without reference; it is ready to guide and sustain the grief-stricken and inconsolable at all times— when hopelessness has come in like a flood and put you in a disembodied state of unconsciousness that is full of storms and unpleasant changes. This will shift you from having extreme satisfaction in kingdom building to your former state of wretchedness or sordidness.

Today you can have the tranquility that the Lord pours out with His benefits on those who seek Him with perpetual joy during every trial and adversity. Holman Illustrated Bible Dictionary defines peace as "a condition or sense of harmony, well-being and prosperity." Throughout history, humanity has always desired long lasting harmony, yet since the earlier era, the world has seldom had a long period of unbroken peace. Over centuries, people of faith and non-faith have probably exhausted as much time at war as at trying to preserve or uphold harmony among men. History records peace treaties that date as far back as the Ancient Greece and Rome era, while in the Middle Age period, Christians became the greatest force for peace. There was a church ruling called the

"Truce of God" which prohibited warfare on Sundays and holy days. Another ruling, known as the "Peace of God" forbade fighting in holy places such as churches and shrines, but the church allowed what they defined as "just wars" that were in the defense of Christianity or a communal homeland.[1] Peace should be viewed as an undisturbed mental state of the mind, for it is the thing that determines when to take fight or flight. The biblical concept means more than the absence of hostility; it is more than just a psychological state, but is a covenant agreement between God's people and the world. Furthermore, God made a covenant of peace with His people that would involve the oath of an enduring relationship with Him, granting sufficient peace and making a pledge to protect the welfare of His children. Moreover, He will profusely bless those who by His excellent compassion, understanding, and power continue to bring about harmony and reconciliation where there is hatred and enmity. There is a promised blessing for peacemakers, and they are declared as His children, who work for peace and share in Christ's ministry of bringing peace and reconciliation. Christ made peace between believing Jews and Gentiles by making them into one new man in Him (Eph. 2:14–16). Now we have a state of physical and spiritual well-being in the Lord, who is the source that supplies our strong power in any given battle and is durable enough to withstand anything. The Scriptures states that since you have been regarded as virtuous and worthy of deliverance from the power and effects of sin through faith, you will persist to have abundant peace with God by way of Jesus Christ (Rom. 5:1–2). Entering into God's exceeding joy offers your justification that brings unmerited favor with God and men with grace in present living, assurance in present trials, hope for the future, and victory in tribulations along with the assurance brought by God's peace put in your hearts by the

Holy Spirit. The covenant of peace with the Lord has cancelled out His hostility toward you, for all sins have been removed so we should no longer fear His wrath. By God's help, you can endure tribulations; this work begins with conversion and reaches its fullness when you see Christ face to face on the Day of Judgment. God is your anchor.

When the world is launching missiles of condemnation and cessation on your ship, you are to stay steadfast and unmovable with vigorous force to resist tension and stress. When you do not allow God to be your anchor, it allows the enemy to come in and convince you that what you believe God for or that the answer you are waiting for from the Lord is not going to come. If you learn to offer a sacrifice of praise in the middle of rigorous tests, it shows God that you believe that He has already worked the situation out on your behalf.

## PEACE IN TIMES OF TROUBLE

What is joy? It is having peace in times of trouble, having gladness in times of copious suffering, and learning to keep your eyes on heavenly things. It is crucial for infants in Christ to be weaned away from milk and called to mature behavior, rather than competition, defensiveness, and hatefulness toward each other. As maturing men and women of God, desire to have discretion with the others who are working side by side with you in order fulfill the Great Commission; discord will surely devour all peace, happiness, and joy.

Only when you become free from insignificant experiences that can affect your character, conduct, or ability, can you move on with what you were called or chosen to do. You must never give the enemy the opportunity to hold you hostage because of things that happened to you or because of past decisions you made due to inexperience or ignorance. The peace of the Lord should flow from your heart to refresh and strength others, to help others extinguish attacks from those who are scornful, proud, and arrogant and full of insults, hatred, and strife, as well as resisting correction. Those who locate peace locate life and blessings; considering they were once alienated from God and His promises, they do not triumph over other's infractions. Instead, they seek to restore the brother or sister by extending favorable support and comfort, remembering that they can easily fall under the entrapment of temptations. Therefore, the person proud of spiritual attainments does not understand his or her dependence on God. Comparing oneself with the weakness of another is not Christlike. God is a forgiving and loving Father who is not concerned about your past or present. He just cares about your future with Him and with your bridegroom, Christ Jesus. There will be no happiness or joy in your lives until you understand and surrender your well-being over to the Lord. Then you may see that the hardships you endured can serve as a testimony to others who are weary and frail in the adventure of life. Jesus instructs the journeymen to take rest in the arms of God, far away from all heavy loads of work, responsibility, sorrow, and cares. The Father's burden will teach you how to relax and be stress free instead of weigh you down. God's yoke is easy and His burden is light (Matt. 11:28–30).

The book of James says a lot about God's long-lasting joy and peace. James tells us to consider everything that we may go through as joy, even when you fall into difficult situations or temptation (James 1:2). The flesh wants to resurrect the old man and pull you back into his old nature, habits, practices, and customs. Faith is the key to helping you persevere with focus, endurance, and patience. If you keep letting God work perfect patience in your lives, then you will not have to want for anything. You must have the patience to wait on the Lord for your blessing and promise.

First, you must show your genuine and unconditional love for Him by doing the work of the ministry. Blessed is the man that endures temptation, for when he is tested and tried, the crown of life is his reward. This is the promise of Lord to those that love and trust in Him (James 1:12).

Second, you must repent and show godly sorrow for all your sins. Repentance and remorse over your wrongdoing will bring peace to you. God has made a covenant of peace with His people, a treaty or agreement that will reconcile and remove you from sinful and destructive behavior. The fruit of peace is sweet and savoring to the soul; it is appetizing, and there is no need to look for anything else to quench your appetite.

## STILL SEARCHING FOR JOY

Are you still asking, what is joy? Joy is unending peace with God, which was released by Jesus when He made intercession on your behalf. It gives power through the help of the Holy Spirit here on Earth. It exists to help establish holiness in men's hearts and unify you with the Lord. It is what keeps you from feeling troubled when everything else around you is in turmoil. This is when I began to understand that God has complete control over the situations in my life and I have no cares or worries.

Humble yourself in low profile in the presence of the Lord, coming before the Lord with a meek spirit. While going through your trial, if you keep a lowly and docile spirit before your foes, the Lord will elevate you in season. No matter what kind of stress or pressures you are under, take everything to the Lord in prayer, for He cares about your basic needs. You must stay alert and attentive because your enemy is lurking around waiting for the opportunity to harm or dissolve his prey. The enemy has one agenda and that is to defeat or overturn the kingdom of God. Always be attentive to his presence in the atmosphere, be firm, fixed, and established in your walk and belief, unyielding in knowledge that the Lord has all power. Never forget that you are not alone and the Lord will not forsake you. There are other believers who are facing the same satanic threatens and injurious plots, therefore be compassionate of others pains and suffering.

In the Scriptures it is repeatedly emphasized that we are not to be weary, tired, or jaded in doing well—in actions focused around the work of the harvest. Have patience and tolerance in your laboring in the vineyard; do not get bored in toiling to produce the reward. You will receive strength and enthusiasm, while receiving a blessed harvest from sowing love and courage in season (Gal. 6:9).

My brother or sister, grab hold of joy! Remember that God has your back, front, and middle protected by grace and mercy. For joy in the Christian life is in direct proportion to a believer's walk with the Lord. They can rejoice because they are in the Lord (Phil. 4:4). Joy is the fruit of a Spirit-led life. On the other hand, sin in a believer's life robs contentment and happiness. When a person walks with the Lord, that person can continue to rejoice even when troubles comes; it enables us to enjoy all that God has given. As a believer, you are to share with other believers the joys and sorrows of life. "Rejoice with those who rejoice, and weep with those who weep. Be of the same mind toward one another. Do not set your mind on high things, but associate with the humble. Do not be wise in your own opinion" (Rom. 12:15–16, NKJV). It is the believer's duty to rejoice in the hope of eternal life with God, being patient when you are tested and living always in the attitude of prayer—all as a testimony for the nonbeliever. In order for you to effectively relate to non-Christians, you are to correspond with them in unconditional love, even to your intimidators and oppressors. Live in peace with unbelievers and do good to those who treat you unfairly.

## JOY COMES FROM TESTING

The joy of God came to refocus humanity to Jesus Christ's sacrifice; the representation of joy and exultation runs through the entire biblical account of the coming of Christ. You should never employ retaliation to encumber evil; only love can do that successfully, so always be concerned about what is good and acceptable unto the Lord. You are to be fair and considerate. When you avenge yourself, you are taking God's place. He has reserved this for Himself—the right to repay evil. The spirit of joy does not offer a false sense of security from the dangers of life, for knowledge in the Lord brings prosperity. Those who know the Lord and the wisdom He offers will know what paths of actions to pursue that provide prosperity and happiness. You must choose to commit your ways to the Lord and serve Him with wholehearted devotion. He can remove destructive obstacles and hazardous stumbling blocks from your interconnecting course and lead you to your appointed goal.

The Old Testament book of Esther is just ten chapters and tells a story about a young woman who was chosen by God to accept the call of mediator and stand on the behalf of her people, the Jews. On the last day of the great feast, King Ahasuerus of Persia became drunk and summoned his wife, Queen Vashti. However, Vashti thought that her husband, the king, was making a public spectacle of her in front of the other royal guests and servants. When she did not report to King Ahasuerus when he called for her, he became enraged and infuriated. Consequently, he issued a proclamation that she could no longer come before him and would give her position as queen to another. So the king held a beauty contest and many women came from India to Ethiopia to become the next queen.

Esther, the heroine of the book that bears her name, was a Jewess named Hadassah, meaning myrtle. After she entered the royal harem she received her pagan name, Esther. The *Merriam-Webster Dictionary* defines a *heroine*, as a mythological or legendary woman having the qualities of a hero; a woman admired and emulated for her achievements and qualities; the principal female character in a literary or dramatic work; and the central female figure in an event or period.

Esther resided with her cousin, Mordecai, who held a position in the household of the Persian king in the Shusan palace. The king appointed Haman, an Agagite, as prime minister, who would have power and authority over all the Jews throughout the Persian Empire. After the divorced Vashti, he selected Esther to be his wife and new queen. Even though there were many other befitting maidens that pleased him, Esther obtained singular benevolence from the king. Along with this title role, came seven attendants from the castle that were to grant her every need and the best room in the house where his wives and concubines lived. She was regarded as a woman of deep piety, loyalty, bravery, patriotism, and wisdom. She was the dutiful daughter of her adopted father, Mordecai, who was also her cousin. She was submissive and obedient to his recommendation, and was not fearful to go to King Ahasuerus on her people's behalf. She was full of beauty, charm, and grace through which she found favor with the king. She was aware that she was sent to the palace for such a time as this as an honorable vessel of God to avert the destruction of the Jewish people, and the have the king grant protection and preserve their wealth and peace.

When King Ahasuerus chose Esther from among all the

young women of his realm to be his wife, he gave her every-thing that she needed for her cleansing and purification. She was beautiful to the king, and he was kind to her. During the time she was in the palace, she never told anyone that she was a Jew or that Mordecai was her guardian. Her cousin commanded her not to tell anyone of her lineage.

The Lord will teach you how to keep your peace and joy while your endurance is tested. In the end, the Lord will give you favor. God will prompt others to be generous and kind to you, just as the Lord gave Esther divine favor with the king and everyone in the king's household. Esther was given her own butler and maids that were loyal and faithful stewards. As you receive undoubting favor from the Lord and experience joy, do not think less of or mistreat those who are less fortunate.

Everyone will receive their reward in due season, rich with the things of the Lord and often when least expected. When you are in submission to the will of God, blessings are going come. You will experience the following:

- Freedom from physical disease or pain—good health
- Freedom from disquieting or oppressive thoughts or emotions—peace of mind
- Marked by success or economic well-being—a prosperous spiritual life
- Continued without intermission—eternal life
- Perception of obvious and superficial—spiritual discernment of good and evil
- Abundance of material possessions or resources—riches and wealth of the land

All these things come from a life that has submitted itself to

God's wisdom, because your joy in the Lord will become worn if you permit callous people to push you to commit acts of disobedience. Esther was attractive and fascinating to the king, and he was taken with her charming personality. Unlike Vashti, Esther was cordial and pleasant in the eye of the king. She was a humble and unpretentious, unlike Queen Vashti. In addition, the king loved Esther above all the women, and she obtained grace and favor in his sight more than all the virgins. Lastly, the king placed the royal crown on Esther's head and made her queen instead of Vashti (2:17). Her quiet and meek spirit caused her to possess higher honor and courtesy from the king, which made him crown her queen.

Then King Ahasuerus held a special feast in honor to all his family and servants in recognition of his new queen, Esther. He proclaimed their marriage and showered the land he ruled over with gifts. The king was pleased that he finally had a queen that gave him the utmost respect and honor. Many times in your lives, God will bless you with a rank of superiority. As kings and queens in the kingdom of God, there is unmerited favor bestowed upon your life.

There was plot to kill the king, and Mordecai gave warning to the king about what was going to take place. Mordecai could see things that were happening since he was always outside the king's gate doing business or keeping a watchful eye on Esther. He heard about the plan to assassinate the king, orchestrated by the king's two evil stewards, Bigthana and Teresh (6:2). The two men were the king's doorkeepers, guarding the entrance of the king's house.

Esther had not uncovered or revealed her family lineage. Oftentimes, the Lord is not ready for you to tell everyone the purpose and destiny for your life, since many are not able to receive with sincerity and joy what the Lord has in store for you. Do not be deceived—there are many in the family who are not spiritually mature enough to rejoice with you when the Lord has given you things that you do not deserve. The Lord is able to make clear what true joy is and how to maintain it when the opponent is waiting to see if you are going to slip up or fall prey to his lures or temptations. He will tell you who you can confide in to tell what the Lord is doing in your life that brings you joy and excitement.

## TRUE JOY

The book gives an account of a crisis in the history of the Jewish people, since a decree was sent forth by the king that every Jew in his kingdom should be put to death on a certain day. The circumstances that led to the issuing of the decree, and the measures by which the calamity was averted, constitute the objective matter of the book, and it represents a most incredible series of divine providences. Although the name God is never mention in this book, you can clearly see God's hand in every account of this story, from the beginning the king showing favor to Esther due to her distinguishing beauty, which can be considered as the providence of God in this story as her incredible beauty must be seen from the hand of God. Then Mordecai's entreaty to the Lord, Esther's earnest request and physical abstaining of food, and the Jews abstaining from food and addressing God with worship, confession, supplication, and thanksgiving for their deliverance from of execution, all in line with Mordecai's instruction, which clearly comes from divine intervention.

As a volatile human being, you will be unable to escape the snares of the evil one without a detection agent given by the grace of God. Individuals whose hearts have disowned their purpose and God's will have become the puppets of conceited and evil puppet masters of this world. Christ has to be the head of your joy if you are going too efficiently and productively complete your task. The joy in the Lord must become your weapon of defense against all forms of darkness. Only the Lord's joy can keep you from yielding to the example and urgings of the evil, malice, and wicked forces.

After four years since Esther was selected as queen, Haman, the king's chief advisor, let his position in the king's staff go to his head and wanted everyone under his authority to bow before him. Haman was ranked above all men in the royal family, he became angry and despondent merely because Mordecai would not show him obeisance and entreat him with reverence that he thought he was due because of his title.

The same is true today. There are many who take on various positions, status, or titles only to have others exhibit obeisance and reverence unto to them, because they feel they cannot attain honor or respect any other way. They have not approved themselves to God let alone to man due to their arrogance, haughtiness, and self-pride. Their super egos have put them upon a superficial pedestal as they sit with their spectators, called Bibles, and dictate and judge God's people for self-gratification and satisfaction. Haman was very aware that he received that position under false pretense, but because he was full of pride, did not tell the king that he was not the man who saved his life.

So when Mordecai refused to give Haman respect because of his profound title by not bowing down him, for he would bow to no man except his living God, Jehovah, Haman became infuriated with rage and decided to get even by asking the king to annihilate all the Jews. Haman is of those individuals who daily attempt to deprive or misuse others' joy by plotting to destroy their established character or standing in the community, as well as inflict the damage to promote their cause. They may tell others you are disgruntled and impossible to work with, that you are not a team player; or they may even go as far as stating that you are a troublemaker. When they cannot get the reaction they expected from others, they go to someone else in a prominent position to force or persuade him or her to go along with their malevolence agendas or schemes. That is what Haman did; he went to the king and told him that there were Jewish people in his city that did not obey the laws that he declared, like everyone else. Since Haman was in charge, the king had no reason to question his intention or aim for wanting the Jews to be killed for disobeying his laws.

You have people on the job, in your community, and in your churches that will behave the same way. Even though you are doing everything within your power to stay on the straight and narrow pathway and worshiping the Lord in the spirit of truth and holiness, they will not be pleased until everything and everyone is under their control or influence.

The world today believes if it can get rid of you, it will have more enjoyment in doing calling good evil, evil good: "Woe to those who call evil good, and good evil; Who put darkness for light, and light for darkness; Who put bitter for sweet, and sweet for bitter!" (Isa. 5:20, NKJV). This warning was given to those in Judah who relentlessly committed offenses against the law of God to pervert the ethical sensitivity of the law abiding citizens who were making effort to remain virtuous, so that the people would confirm sin as being good and good being unappealing and immoral, calling it morally objectionable. God's judgment will fall on the most serious charge to the ungodly and wicked: they love evil; they call that which is moral perverse (Ps. 52:3). You must not become overly consumed with the deeds of the wicked, for evil leads to punishment by God eventually, if not immediately.

As the righteous, be precautious and perceptive of the deeds and their profit as immoral examples. Those who boast in evil will always give a clear indication of their stand with righteousness, based on their value system and unwilling commitment to abide by the instructions of God's word. It is foolish to boast in something as short-lived as taking pleasure in evil deeds and intentions when God's goodness will endure forever. To some doing to evil is like a spectator sport or fun-filled game; these fools get enjoyment from unlawful activity, but the wise have divine wisdom and understanding, showing reverential esteem for the Lord and His people (Prov. 10:23). The foolish lack sense, judgment, and discretion, speaking before they grasp any reasonableness of the divine truth. Evildoers take God's mercy for granted, their joy comes from callous inventions (Amos 5:10–14).

Only the enjoyment in heavenly things can keep you from yielding to corrupt and dishonest role models that incorporate self-centered and self-seeking ambitions. The Scriptures clearly state: "A good man out of the good treasure of his heart bring forth good things, and an evil man out the evil treasure brings forth evil things" (Matt. 12:35, NKJV). Iniquitous proceedings and sinful activities are measured as the overflowing manufacture of a heart that is filled with the spirit of wickedness; on the other hand, delightful proceedings and righteous activities are a byproduct of an abundant heart that is filled with the Holy Spirit and running over with the adoration of God and man. In addition, God gives peace to His elect people, a predestination based entirely on His sovereign will. This predestination came to rescue humanity from the ruin of sin through salvation, which is offered to all through faith in Jesus Christ. Those who are elected to be saved are those who accept God's offer and have become His chosen ones: "For I know the thoughts that I think toward you, says the LORD, thoughts of peace and not of evil, to give you a future and a hope" (Jer. 29:11, NKJV). This peace does not come with preliminary qualifications.

There are individuals who desire to see you destroyed because you will not submit to their authority, even though it has been attained by illicit or improper means. The issue will remain between you and the individual until they receive a breakthrough or deliverance. Until then, they will draw others into their inner circle of hostility and dejection. Once Haman obtained approval from the king after deceiving him, he sent letters out into all the land that decreed that all Jews—young and old, men and women—would be killed or destroyed on a set day and time. Haman was like many people in authoritative positions who obsess over attaining the power to impose their commands upon someone. There are "Hamans" on your job that get together with bosses and strategically plot how to terminate your present position. They are very thorough, mapping out the time, day, and place for your dismissal. They have no care about how you will support or take care of your family and children. They are only concerned about how you did not meet the guidelines of their program or go along with their schemes—how you would not go out to happy hour with your coworkers, socialize with the office busybodies, or spread rumors. Haman wanted all the Jews, including Mordecai, to know that he was a big man in the eyesight of the king. At the same he was an enemy in the sight of the Lord for trying to cause harm to God's sheep.

Mordecai began to call upon the presence of God, for he was distraught when he heard about what was going to become of the Jews. He did not allow the enemy to keep him down; he picked himself up and regained his joy. He was steadfast in the Lord, and the spirit of the Lord spoke and told him what to do. About this time, Esther heard a rumor about what was going to become of her people, the Jews, and she called her steward to confer a message to Mordecai.

Esther wanted to know if what she heard was true, so she waited with composure for the steward's return to give her the report. Mordecai told Esther's steward about what was going to occur to the Jews on the thirteenth day of the twelfth month, which was when the written decree promise was to be carried out. He also reminded her that her own life was in danger, since she was a Jew. He told her that she needed to speak to the king, even though it would cause her to risk losing her life. Anyone who came into the king's chamber without being summoned would be put to death unless the king extended his scepter and gave him or her pardon. Esther had not been summoned by the king for more than thirty days.

Many receive a great reward, furthering their lives, only to have a Haman acquire authority and try to bulldoze over their successful contributions to the company or demolish their advancement within the corporation. Maybe the Haman at your job or church is mad because you do not flatter them in front of others or give them positive reinforcement for their selfish achievements. They are self-seekers who want to further their own position. Alternatively, your foe wishes to see everyone who is not the same way of life, nationality, creed, or religion wiped off the face of this earth; they institute discriminating profiles or prejudice to further their schema to destroy those they detest. These ill-willed individuals do not behave in the way God wants His children to act, even though some represent themselves as members of the body of Christ.

The world today deems it can cancel out your resource of

peace. If it can pull you back into bars, night clubs and non-religious organizations, it will have more control over your will once you have turned your back on the ministry work and church service. The hideous principality operating behind this ruthlessly destructive and persuasive power trip does not respect or give any regard to one's concerns or the feelings of their participants. Being bothered and worried will fill your spirit with fluttering anxiety while you are in contact with others. Do not permit the archenemy to make you neurotic, causing you to experience a combination of anxiety, compulsion, obsession, phobias, and depression.

Fear will clog up the flashlight or spotlight of God's glory that reveals the secluded skeletons in the closet and expose all ugly secrets. Fear is the natural response to a perceived threat to one's security or general welfare; it can be a hindrance to the enjoyment of life and is induced by delusion; it will linger and overpower positive emotions such as love and joy. It can possibly lead to an inability to engage in the normal activities of life. Fear is frequently found in popular customs and regarded not as pure emotion but as wise behavior, such as the fear of God. The appropriate attitude of believers toward God is commonly said to be more in the form of esteem, astonishment, or admiration rather than terror. When you confine your attitude toward God as reverence or awe rather than fear, you may lose sight of those features of the divine character that induces obedience through His sanctity and righteousness for there is unlimited knowledge and power.

The issue will remain between you and the individual until they receive a breakthrough or deliverance. Until then, they will draw others into their inner circle of pity, hostility, and dejection. Since the beginning of mankind's existence, the a desire to impose one's will upon another person or beings has led to active conflict using many forms of control or manipulation by crafty, deceitful, or insidious means especially for one's own advantage (Gen. 3:1–7).

This marks the first chronological event in the history of the Bible—that humanity's mind and will fell under the deception of satanic influence. Today Satan continues to misinform through the uncontrolled craving from the intellectual and perceptual faculty. He counterattacks God' trustworthiness in minds and hearts of the believers and asserts without proof that God's commands are self-serving. Satan's invasion symbolizes three specified areas of human life: (1) *good for food*, dealing with the physical senses of man, (2) *pleasant to the eyes*, dealing with the emotional senses of man, and (3) *desirable to make one wise*, dealing with the spiritual sense of man. You have innate authority within you to detect good and evil because of the disobedience of Adam and Eve, who were at first innocent and pure in the eyes of the Lord. After their disobedience they knew that they were naked and made themselves coverings, clearly indicating their state of shame and embarrassment. Prior to their disobedience Adam and Eve had no direct experience with these issues, even in their correlation with each other or with God. (See Genesis 2:25; 3:7–11).

> It is joy to the just to do judgment: but destruction shall be to the workers of iniquity.
>
> —PROVERBS 21:15

## UNDEFEATED JOY

In spite of opposition, Esther believed that God brought her into that unique setting with a distinct purpose—to help save the Jews' lives. Mordecai reminded Esther that she might be the one that God would use to bring deliverance and peace for the

Jews. She knew that she could not hold her peace at this time, for all the Jews would be destroyed, including her. Esther was consciously aware that God put her in this unique position to save the Jews. This was her responsibility, or the Jews would no longer exist in Persia. Esther was aware that she had to intervene and speak up on behalf of the Jews, to go to the king pleading for amnesty and the removal of the enactment for destruction of the Jewish nation. It was her singular responsibility to fight and be accountable for her people's survival.

Joy comes through triumph, the joyfulness or exultation of victory. Christ's victory on the cross allows you to have the same power today to conquer any supernatural element or foes that will come your way (Col. 2:15). Through Him you also can claim the victory over the devil and his angelic forces; the worst thing that can be done was done to Christ when He suffered, bled, and died on the cross. But He rose again to provide an open demonstration for the enemy and to show his inability to conqueror Him, even in His most trying hour. Christ endured the cross with joy and dismissed it as contemptible or unworthy of its dishonor or ill repute.

> Looking unto Jesus, the author and finisher of our faith, who for the joy that was set before Him endured the cross, despising the shame, and has sat down at the right hand of the throne of God. For consider Him who endured such hostility from sinners against Himself, lest you become weary and discouraged in your souls.
>
> —Hebrews 12:2–3, nkjv

Even though it brought Him much pain from sinners who tried His courageousness, self-determination, and longsuffering, you can maintain mental or moral strength to persevere and withstand danger, fear, or difficulty by following in His footsteps. While for the believer, secular joys are not to be viewed as proverbial trait from dishonorable evidences, they must be easily distinguished from the spiritual ones—the two must remain separated—since they can create perplexity. Oftentimes spiritual joys are expressed by the metaphors of unusual pleasure or delight, intimate or close union, victory in endeavors, and thriving economics, all to advance or edify the kingdom of God. In turn, spiritual joys should elevate you above the secular happiness seeing as material attainments are regarded as unexpected benefits from God. The believer's critical examination or observation is a time for joy. Peter and John found their pruning and purging an occasion for rejoicing because they had been counted worthy of suffering humiliation for the name (Acts 5:41). Suffering transfers joy to believers who are united with Christ in His suffering: "Beloved, do not think it strange concerning the fiery trial which is to try you, as though some strange thing happened to you; but rejoice to the extent that you partake of Christ's sufferings, that when His glory is revealed, you may also be glad with exceeding joy" (1 Pet. 4:12–13, NKJV).

Joy should bring you into a greater relationship with others, as the disciples and the apostles had with the people in the early church; it gives you an opportunity to express gratitude and thanksgiving to God and others in ministry. Believers should proclaim their stand against those who find themselves righteous in their own eyes, people who are conservative in dealing with the enemy's claim on life. You will never take authority or dominion unless something takes place within an essential or enduring component; so if you hold onto this false sense of peace, the enemy will masterfully take control and victoriously win against your unknowing family members or unsuspected church members. It is your responsibility to give them the unadulterated truth, the gospel message of Jesus Christ to them and this perverse generation of unbelievers.

There comes a time in all our lives when we will truly desire the things of the Lord and do His work. God has given you all individual assignments, and what we read in the Scriptures prepares us for the quest by providing lessons from other men and women of God who were on this pathway before you and were overcomers by the Spirit of God. We are put on this earth for such a time as this, to carry out God's divine purpose and goal for our lives: "yet who knows whether you have come to the kingdom for such a time as this" (Esther 4:14, NKJV). You are not put here by luck or chance; you are here to complete what Jesus began, reconciling lost souls back to the Father in love. This is true whether you serve God in ministry part-time as a Sunday school teacher, you minister full-time as an evangelist who spreads the gospel to lost souls, you are a prophet who brings divine clarification from God to the body of Christ, or you are a preacher who ministers from behind a pulpit. You cannot save yourself in the closing stages, but failure to act may delay or prolong the purpose for which you have been predestined to carry out. You must have faith in God's promises, although crisis and tragedies might befall in your family generation to generation. God will not allow you to be destroyed; now is the time to take the risk and walk out of faith. God is able to use common or ordinary people to perform extraordinary goals and fulfill extreme dreams.

Esther called her handmaids and declared a three day fast. When your adversary is working against you, begin to fast while yielding yourself over to the Lord. God will give clear and accurate guidance. You may come under attack by spiritual wickedness many times, wherein the enemy will try to distract or hinder you from going higher in the Lord. You may feel days, weeks, or months behind what the Lord has commissioned you to do, but if you receive the new word you hear from the Holy Ghost, it will be for your good. Esther knew she needed to beg and fast before the presence of God, since this attack was far greater than she was ready to handle and she had no answer. The only One who could give her an answer was Elohim. During the time of fasting, Esther believed in her heart and had great joy that God would deliver His people. You must remain steadfast as you wait on the Lord to give you the resolution or revelation of the situation, for all things work together for the good of those who love the Lord.

The next day, Esther was standing in the outer court and King Xerxes saw her royal apparel from where he sat on his throne. The king was very fond of looking at his beautiful queen and summoned her to come into the inner court. When she approached the king, he held out his golden scepter, giving Esther permission to come before him. The king was pleased to have a queen who was respectful and humble. He did not withhold anything from Esther. Esther, unlike Vashti, did not use her preeminent position to be defiant in front of the guests, which gave her favor in the king's sight.

The king asked Esther what he could give her, offering up to half of his kingdom. Esther was not hasty in responding to the king's question. Esther was very careful not to do anything before God had commanded her to do so, realizing that her family and friends lives were in her hands. She did not reply to the king immediately, but instead she invited the king and his right-hand man, Haman, to a banquet that she had prepared for them.

Then the king said he would tell Haman about the queen's

request and the two would be at her banquet the next evening. God had given Esther favor with the king such that there was nothing he would not do for her. The king was moved by Esther's plea and granted her request that he and Haman come to her regal banquet. At the banquet, King Ahasuerus even repeated to her in front of Haman that he would give her whatever she desired. Esther declined to answer the king at that time.

When Haman passed the gates that night on the way back from Esther's banquet, he saw Mordecai once again refusing to show any respect or reverence by bowing before him, and again he became full of rage and anger. Yet he quickly recalled that all the Jews would be murdered soon and that he would not have much longer to look at Mordecai sitting outside the gates of the city. Haman restrained himself, went home, and shared the wonderful news with everyone in his house and neighborhood that the king had given him a great promotion in which he was to preside over all the princes and servants of the king. All the same, his joy was overwhelmed because he of one person that would not submit to his rules and ways—Mordecai. Haman looked on outer things to give him contentment and happiness. He was the second man in command, but he was discontent because of Mordecai. He went to the extreme, requesting that the Jews be wiped out, just because one man would not stroke his ego by bowing down to him. Haman refused to understand or take into respect Mordecai's religious beliefs. Instead, he became like many people who make their own assumptions or conclusions about other people without asking them why they are a certain way. He was like many people today who are not satisfied with their title or position until everyone puts them on a pedestal.

Haman had been overjoyed with the news of being invited to the banquet with the king and queen. Then he began complaining to his family and friends and stated that he had no joy as long as Mordecai was sitting at the king's gate every day. Many people will lose their peace when we walk into a room, come into a board meeting, or start a conversation with other people. Many have to deal with reality of not be compatible with everyone, even people at work and in his or her social network. If you are obeying God, the problem is not you; it is those who are not in total control of everyone or everything will lose focus on the assignment. They are people-pleasers craving to be affirmed or confirmed by others to feel accepted, whether it's on a job, in their homes, or even in the body of Christ. Unfortunately, if they have to hurt someone to get the attention they need, they will do just that.

Haman had the same problem with Mordecai. Every day he walked by the gates everyone gave him the same response, except Mordecai, who would not acknowledge that Haman was king of the playground. His uncontrolled anger led to emotional vindictiveness and the desire for revenge against all the Jews. Individuals like Haman are not ready for leadership positions; they are inexperienced and ill-advised decision makers. There are personal decisions made daily that are the basis for business failures, family disagreements, and disunity within the house of God, which create great loss. Those who fall prey to this, too often follow their delusional feelings, imagery, or emotions while in a state of disorientation, distress, or panic, and see this as an investment to a new or more strongly innovative goal or desired purpose that leads them farther away from the guidance and instruction of the Holy Spirit. As free moral agents, you do have the freedom to make you own choices that are not determined by prior causes or by divine intervention, but never confuse that with a spirit of insubordination or waywardness.

It is vital before you go forth in any business endeavor or

personal ministry vocation or before you attempt to tell others how to come in line with the decreed and sound declaration from God, that you have your own affairs in order, seeing as in the end it can bring vast disgrace and damage. Many times the Lord will reveal to you what will become of your foes. When that happens, we must also be like Esther and do things decently and in order, for when judgment does come, they will need a lot of prayer, a sympathetic ear, and a compassionate heart.

> Deceit is in the heart of them that imagine evil: but
> to the counsellors of peace is joy.
>
> —Proverbs 12:20

## Time for Joy

Between the time of the two feasts, Haman was ablaze with great anticipation over killing the Jews. He ordered gallows to be specially made, and Haman planned to request at the banquet that the king allow him to hang Mordecai there. Meanwhile, the king was restless and ordered some of the palace record books be read to him to help him sleep. He discovered that though Mordecai had once saved his life by uncovering an assassination plot, the king had not honored him. The king wanted to give him acknowledgment for his bravery.

In the middle of great times of anticipation, your foes will be shocked to see how God will reveal their plans and schemes that were to be use to sabotage your purpose. If someone does not respond to the saboteur according his or her needs and wants, like Haman, he or she will become very impatient and cruel in their actions. He or she will enlist others to stand against you for taking a stand for the sake of righteousness. Although the words of the wicked hurt and injure like a sword piercing the body, the tongue of the wise promotes healing by speaking soothing and confronting words. In times of danger, make sure that you have an overabundant supply of the fruits that come from the Spirit of God, joy and peace. You can tell who truly belongs to the Lord by their actions and deeds, "Then they said, 'Come and let us devise plans against Jeremiah; for the law shall not perish from the priest, nor counsel from the wise, nor the word from the prophet. Come and let us attack him with the tongue, and let us not give heed to any of his words'" (Jer. 18:18, NKJV). Just like Jeremiah, there will be many who will turn on you, and request counsel from depraved and iniquitous leaders who elect to defame God's word spoken. God does understand that you can become frightened and frustrated, especially when you feel that you are traveling this journey alone. Even when you seek to express favorable character or tendencies by leading others to repentance, keeping them on the straight and narrow pathway, or being an ethical example of set apart for God's use, there are those who will resent you for not tolerating morally wrong behavior. Sometimes they will resort to physical assaults after verbal attacks no longer work. Scripture says, if that happens you are to turn the other cheek (Matt. 5:39). I can witness to the fact that my oldest daughter had someone throw a drink on her at a football game just because she decided that she wanted to be set apart for God's use and not hang around troublemakers. Also, another daughter at the age of five had another child spit in her face and dump dirt in her hair because of her outward appearance. Moreover, in both cases these individuals missed having two remarkable individuals as friends, I told my daughters to pray for the individuals and to let them know that God loves them, and so should you. On the other hand, you are to make intercession on behalf of your enemies; I do believe that people spend so much time plotting and scheming that they fall to put any or no time in changing themselves for the better.

Now, after being reminded of Mordecai's faithfulness, the king immediately called Haman and asked him what he should do to honor a person worthy of some recognition. The Lord was keeping Mordecai's identity hidden from Haman so that he could bless him. Haman thought that the king wished to recognize him, so he told the king to dress this person in royal garments and let him ride down the streets of the city for all to see. When King Ahasuerus told Haman that he was referring to Mordecai, Haman felt humiliated. The king told Haman to take the royal garments and other fine things and give them to Mordecai to wear on his ride through the city. Due to the fact that Haman wanted Mordecai dead, Haman was filled with deep despair. Your foes will be shocked to see how God will reveal their plans and schemes to sabotage your purpose and special duty. If someone does not respond to the saboteur according his or her needs and wants, like Haman, he or she will become very impatient and cruel in their actions. He or she will enlist others to stand against you for taking a stand for the sake of righteousness. Christ urges followers to forfeit revenge rather than claim permissible privileges, and to forgive rather than to seek retaliation or even demand stern impartiality, for He has set the pattern that you should implement as a part of your Christian lifestyle or way of living.

Lying lips are abomination to the LORD: but they that deal truly are his delight.

—Proverbs 12:22

## The Joy Feast

The Lord will not allow the enemy of this world to execute his will over your family or you; He will preserve you. Keep your prayers faithful and sincere with a humble heart, and the Lord will defeat your opponent. He will grant you everything that your heart desires, "Delight yourself also in the LORD, And He shall give you the desires of your heart" (Ps. 37:4, NKJV). Position yourself and the consequences of your life exclusively in God's hand, and discontinue your own effortless labors, awkward schemes, and challenging manipulations; remain confident in His faithfulness by constantly relying on Him for spiritual sustenance; then there will a joy feast. He will vindicate you in the presence of your enemy. God will do all this when they least expect their present position to come tumbling down. The day of their judgment for all their rotten doings will come. In order to ask the king to rescind his edict against the Jews, Esther prepared a second banquet and asked both the king and Haman to attend.

On the day of the feast, Esther could not contain her joy, for she knew the God of the Jews was going to bring justice to her people on that night. She arrived promptly with her king and the banquet began accordingly. She knew that God would give her another opportunity to reveal her enemy, Haman, before the King. Your life basic theme should be to acclaim trust in God for everyday livelihood even in the presence and sight of wickedness and temptation, because regardless of their momentary prosperity, the wicked will eventually fall into ruins.

Once again, King Ahasuerus stated to Esther in front of Haman that he would give her whatever she desired. Esther told the king her request was for the deliverance of the Jews and explained that Haman tried to bribe the king into killing the Jews. When Haman reacted by lunging at Esther on the bed where she was reclining, the king demanded that Haman be put to death—and approved the queen's request that the Jews be spared. This story teaches how God protects His people from their foes. The Jews remember their deliverance from Haman at the Feast of Purim, which is still celebrated in the present day. There will be many followers wanting this gift of joy, when they see that we are not going to be conquered or defeated by our enemies. Queen Esther was a true example of someone who never let the enemy see her give up. Even when Haman was against the Jews and wanted to take away their joy and their lives because of his independent conflict with Mordecai, Esther abided in the Lord and fasted while awaiting the breakthrough for her and her people. God gave her favor with the king, and this was how her people were saved. Esther knew that she had to humble herself so that the Jews would not be killed.

The Lord will not allow the enemy of this world to execute his will over your family or you; He will preserve you. Keep your prayers faithful and sincere with a humble heart, and the Lord will defeat your opponent. He will vindicate you in the presence of your enemy. God will do all this when they least expect their present position to come tumbling down. The day of their judgment for all their rotten doings will come. Never forget, after you have been cleared of all immoral and unlawful actions, God will honor you openly in the present of your enemies.

You will feel joyful to see happiness on the face of others, even your foes, because you denied yourself of certain wants or desires. The spirit of Esther exhibits spiritual attractiveness that grants her exceptional merit. She learned how and when to exert her influence, gaining favor from the king. Most likely God's definitive fate for you is far greater than your tribulations, suffering, and anguish. The Bible imparts inspirational fundamentals and spiritual realities relating to the tribulations of believers. First, the tribulations of Christians are patterned after the suffering of other believers; as tribulations were inevitable and expected in the Messianic ministry of Jesus, so tribulation will be required among His followers, "These things I have spoken to you, that in Me you may have peace. In the world you will have tribulation; but be of good cheer, I have overcome the world" (John 16:33, NKJV). Second, tribulations of the believer are articulated in the logic of participation in the sufferings of Christ (Phil. 3:8–10). Esther reached this pivotal moment, no longer concerned about royal position but wanting deliverance for her people. She could see all the things that she gained would become worthless and repulsive rubbish in comparison with life—both hers and the Jews; once the day of execution arrived she would be murdered along with the Jews, for she was a Jew by biological lineage. Her position in the Persian kingdom could not override the King's decree. Third, the tribulations of believers contribute to spiritual growth, prosperity transformation into the likeness of Christ, "And not only that, but we also glory in tribulations, knowing that tribulation produces perseverance; and perseverance, character; and character, hope" (Rom. 5:3–4, NKJV). Finally, tribulation teaches Christians to how console and encourage others in comparable situations, by enabling those who are openly or silently suffering from a persistent state of counterinfluences, opposition, or discouragement (Col. 1:24).

True joy is giving of oneself for others to be content, happy, and pleased. You will feel joyful to see happiness on the face of others, even your foes, because you denied yourself of certain wants or desires. The spirit of Esther exhibits spiritual attractiveness that grants her exceptional merit. She learned how and when to exert her influence, gaining favor from the king. Most likely, God's ultimate fate for Esther was to use her in His perfect plan to rescue an entire nation from destruction. As Esther had prepared physically to become queen, God had prepared her spiritually so He could trust her to ensure the liberation of His beloved people. When Esther learned of Haman's scheme against her people, she maintained her contact with Mordecai. She repeatedly demonstrated humility and honor. God is calling and choosing Esthers to His work. By the interception of Esther, this horrific massacre was prevented and Haman was hanged on the same gallows he had intended for Mordecai. Soon after, the Jews established an annual feast name the feast of Purim, as a memorial event of their marvelous and extraordinary deliverance. This story, which never mentions the name of God, in the concluding stage revealed supernatural evidence of His presence.

Today many scholars maintain that there were a number of moral and ethical practices on Esther's part that can be viewed as debatable concerning her eagerness to intervene on behalf of the Jewish people. First, she did not identify herself as a Jew to the king until she went to him for requested favor, to spare her people's lives. Second, she was agreeable to marry a pagan, in spite the customary belief of her people. Third, she did not feel out of place in a harem, secluded house, or part of a house allotted to women in a Muslim household. Fourth, she did not have mercy on another human being life, Haman. Fifth, she did not observe the Jewish custom dietary laws. Sixth, she was not at first willing to help her own people, because she would need to disclose her identity to the king. Seventh, she did not concern herself with the plundering of her enemies. Although not clarified, the author never condemns her shortcomings, but seems to be more concerned about describing her triumphs with approval.[6] You must remember, even though God chooses you for a certain cause or purpose, it does not necessarily mean that you are mentally equipped to carry out the assignment, for the scripture states, "Watch and pray, lest you enter into temptation, the spirit indeed is willing, but the flesh is weak" (Mark 14:38, NKJV). I can truly identify with Esther; it does take much time to comprehend that you can make a different in other people lives. Jesus committed Himself to the will of the Father even though He knew it meant crucifixion. As His a chosen disciple, you must ready to submit your will to God's will, but that can only be done after praying and fasting, so the spirit can overpower the flesh. I believe that true and undefeated joy generates a supernatural passion and affection for others without any stipulations or ultimatums; bearing injustice, disrespect, and irritations; and standing with solid bravery. A person with this potential does not operate or react based on natural instinct, but rather by the guidance of the Holy Spirit. Everyone and everything is called to praise the Lord with gladness and joy in peace. In your comings and goings, have joy led forth with peace (1sa. 55:12). All the heavens and the earth are called to be witnesses of goodness, therefore everything that has breath will sing praises to the Lord in the spirit of joy and peace.

## Joy Is...

### by Kimley Dunlap-Slaughter

Showing *love* when others *hate.*
Having peace when others have uncertainty.
Giving life when others cause death.
Being a leader when others are followers.
Showing happiness when others are despondent.
Having humility when others are prideful.
Giving forgiveness when others are indignant.
Being truthful when others are liars.
Showing gentleness when others are inconsiderate.
Having freedom when others are in oppression.
Giving encouragement when others cause discord.
Being moral when others are immoral.

These are the true characteristics of joy in Jesus Christ. Are you still asking, what is exceeding joy? To sum it up, joy is being freed from the powers of oppression and the prison of self-afflicting circumstances. Joy is waking up every morning with new joy and peace. The joy of the Lord causes the following:

1. Reclaimed peace
2. Renewed faith
3. A recommitted life
4. A repentant heart
5. Rectified personality
6. Reprieved anger
7. A peaceful mind
8. Resistance to evil
9. Rekindled endurance
10. Restored hope
11. Released power
12. Revived joy

When a man's ways please the LORD, He maketh even his enemies to be at peace with him.

—Proverbs 16:7

## 2
## HOW DO I GET THIS
## THING CALLED JOY?

*Make a joyful noise unto God, all ye lands: Sing forth
the honour of his name: make his praise glorious.*

—Psalm 66:1–2

YOU GET JOY FROM serving God, the same joy that Jesus
had when walking on this earth encountering various
trials and persecution, which were sent by the enemy
to thwart His purpose. The true sons and daughters of God
believe that as we ask God for His protection and guidance,
He will do so. God wants all His children to enjoy the things
that He provided or supplied for them on earth, but we must
be capable making wise decision on what is of God and what
is not of God. You can boost your health and feed your soul by
nurturing your inner man with spiritual food so you can have
wholesome life. You must be prepared to make a list of unwanted
desires that can hinder your physical, mental, emotional, and
spiritual walk. There are four ways to enrich your life on earth
and improve our way of living. First, the physical side: you have
to eat healthy foods, which will help you stay in good physical
shape and give you positive energy as well as exercise daily.

Second, the mental side: stimulate your mind with intellectual thoughts that will challenge and enhance your artistic gifts and talents. Third, the emotional side: keep a private journal so you can record your feelings and thoughts. Fourth, the spiritual side: you must meditate daily and reflect on what you are grateful for, incorporating devotion and praise to increase your prayer and faith life.

If you put all your trust and faith in Jesus, then the Holy Spirit can bring back to your remembrance what joy is. The Book of Psalms is a compilation of writings about joy. The word *psalm* is defined as "a holy song or poem." Joy is cheerfulness, contentment, and amusement with songs that are refreshing and stimulating. Only the Spirit of God can come in to help you cope and deal with days of sadness or when you lose interest in things that used to excite you, you found to be interesting, or gave you enjoyment. The cares of this life can bring aches and pains that will leave you emotionally fatigued, physically tired, and mentally drained. Experts would define this as signs or symptoms of someone suffering from depression, but, on the other hand, these can be foreign agents of the devil put in place to extinguish your happiness and peace of mind. As believers you have a direct path that always leads you back to a divine resource that can prescribe an antidote or treatment to every mental illness or physical sickness, if it is God's will. Anything that comes in to cease spiritual development, growth, or maturity may not necessarily be of the enemy, but could be to measure your faith, if you feel there is no need for change in diet, use of regular exercise, daily scripture reading and devotion. Do not be misinformed; such conditions can present themselves as life-threatening situations because the evil one can invent unseen side effects, but can prevailed by having an open communication line with God. Remember, joy and peace are fruits that cultivate and reproduce vigorous, nutritious, and nourishing attributes, which are needed to transform the old man.

> I beseech you therefore, brethren, by the mercies of God, that you present your bodies a living sacrifice, holy, acceptable to God, which is your reasonable service. And do not be conformed to this world, but be transformed by the renewing of your mind, that you may prove what is that is good and acceptable and perfect will of God.
>
> —ROMANS 12:1–2, NKJV

Christians must demonstrate an optimistic attitude toward God, and there must be a complete surrender of the whole person to God—including body, mind, and spirit. You must consider yourselves no more your own, but the entire possession of the Creator of heaven and earth. Your lives are scrutinized as morally pure and pleasing to God according to sacred teachings. As a new convert, you have a new attitude of resistance from old values, goals, and activities of the world, which would pressure you to their shape. You are constantly being molded into the image of Christ-likeness living productively within the community of believers, for your transformation made by God in the spirit must be shown in your daily life. If you trust God in every situation and have confidence, He will provide the answer to any problem, for there is nothing too hard for God (Jer. 32:17–19).

You must always be ready to make a public confession of faith to the Lord's promises and serve God in the spirit of obedience, which usually precedes enlightened comprehension. Like Jeremiah, your conviction in the Lord can be the buffeter against evil forces that have come to transfer overpowering fright, acute extreme anxiety, and unreasonable terror. There are many in the body of faith who suffer from panic disorder, an anxiety disorder characterized by recurrent unexpected attacks of panic accompanied by bodily or cognitive symptoms, such as shaking, shortness of breath, or feelings of being overwhelmed. There is no fear in God, but fear of man brings a snare (Prov. 29:35). Scripture states we are to reverence God and keep his commands (Eccles. 12:13). The fear of God is shown by keeping His biblical principles.

All humans are religious and moral beings who find their fulfillment in God's teachings that lead to a loving relationship with Him. Knowing that God's final verdict is soon to come should offer motivation to comply with His established order now. In view of the fact that He has not given His children a spirit of fear, "for God has not given us a spirit of fear, but of power and of love and of a sound mind" (2 Tim. 1:7, NKJV), you must be reminded that God has given you unchanging power to overcome obscurities, love for the unbearable, and good judgment over self-control that is necessary in carrying out your assignment. There will be come a time you may be tempted to be embarrassed to witness for Christ or associate with true messengers, for you do not want to experience the insensitive and ruthless mistreatment as the disciples had suffered for righteous sake. The Word teaches that those who suffer for the gospel will find God's power. This power is so great that He has done away with death and assured us of never-ending life. As the child is heir of the parents, you are heirs of God, now that you have been united with Christ, and share the speculator blessing of eternal life with Him (Rom. 8:17).

Your suffering as an ethical disciple in corrupt world system that does not recognize Christ is one of the conditions for eternal inheritance and salvation. The world does not understand that the beginning of fear expresses factual understanding of God's promises, for His love casts out all presence of fear: "There is no fear in love; but perfect love casts out fear, because fear involves torment. But he who fears has not been made perfect in love. We love Him because He first loved us" (1 John 4:18–19, NKJV). This perfect love in God is transforming the evil heart and reestablishing an intimate relationship to Him. While you are living in love and have the presence of His love, you have abiding faith in Christ Jesus. One of God's promises made to His people is that He will answer prayers. There is a Negotiator who is partial to us and sits on the right hand of God petitioning forgiveness on humankind's behalf (Rom. 8:34). Christ Jesus has been appointed to judge and bring condemnation upon sin, therefore there are no new trials or tribulations for believers to face that Christ or the disciples have not endured with longsuffering. Furthermore, unless your righteousness exceeds the righteousness of the religious leaders of present day, you will in no case enter into the kingdom of heaven.

Your personal sense of impartiality and morality as it relates to God and each other is stated by your level of integrity and honesty, which correlates to the way you conduct yourself, your actions or behavior based on the wisdom endowed from the love of God, or lack thereof in your life. True righteousness comes about by the life of God in the believer, and God is love. The love of God is not unlike the love that Christ has for you. It is only in Jesus that God's love shines and fully exposes the emotional or moral nature of man capable of separating it from the intellectual nature; for in the eyesight of God, any other act of outward righteousness is simply viewed as unclean and unfit for the Master's use (Isa. 64:6). Not only is all creation helpless to save itself, we do not even have the ability to take hold of God in faith unless He somehow gives us this ability. The gift of anticipative grace offers us deliverance from the power and effects of sin. Now Christ sits on the right hand throne of grace to uphold the promise, daily imploring for humanity's spiritual benefit. One can say that "God's right hand" refers to the Messiah, the Lord Jesus Christ, and He is of equal position, honor, power, and authority with God. (See John 1:1–5.) The fact that Christ is "sitting" refers to the fact that His work of redemption is done and when the fullness of the Gentiles is brought in (Rom. 11:25), Christ's enemies will be made His footstool as the end of the age comes, all prophecy is completed, and time is no more (Ps. 110:1). The people of God make their request known unto the Most High, who will hear their prayers and attend to them. It may not be today, tomorrow, or next week; but He will come and see about them. We have hope and joy as we wait for His response or answer to our call. From this point on, exhibit joy in the middle of your trails and give God all praise and honor for your triumphant victory in Christ Jesus.

John gives a great testimony concerning His allegiance or duty in ministry. Oftentimes he had to reassure his confession of belief and trust in and loyalty to God, his reason for following the message concerning Christ, the kingdom of God, and salvation precepts, and his response to followers' lack of fidelity to the declaration of Christ. He had to affirm that the ministry of Jesus was given to Him by God from heaven, and reaffirms in his personal testimony that he was a forerunner of the gospel message (John 3:22–36). There will be much agony, pain, and suffering as the Lord wages war against the antagonist of this world, but believers must be steadfast and unmovable to their vocation of faith. While you are busy rejoicing over what others have done, stay focused on what is really a priority in your confusing environment—the work of the ministry. Through Jesus, you are a new creation with access to permanent joy that cannot be tarnished by assaults or criticism.

## JOY COMES THROUGH SPIRITUAL GROWTH

Many people think that God is the great killjoy, one who spoils the pleasure of others; nothing is farther from the truth. God Himself knows joy and He wants His people to have full knowledge and experience the components of spiritual joy. Steadfast joy can be manifested to you because of your relationship with God and your obedience to Him. You become one in thought and action, for He will begin to disclose His mysteries and reveal His revelations. There is a broad distinction between mere gladness and spiritual joy. Spiritual joy rises from within the soul and does not depend on the outward circumstances of life. On the other hand, false joy is merely a sensation or a spurt of emotions (conscious mental reaction); yet absolute joy lasts forever. Those who apply serious effort or energy for wisdom and knowledge will also find joy, a gift coming from God when you attach yourself to Him and His work.

The book of Psalm reflects almost every range of religious emotions and spiritual state of mind that anyone on earth could experience, starting from the lowest depths of despair to the highest expressions of praise and worship. This book can speak directly to you, as does all of its contents, yet also conveys written answers to your every mood and status of emotional and spiritual development. In this vast treasury box of spiritual truth, there is encouragement and motivation to inspire God's people down through centuries. The universal appeal of the psalms results partly because they are poetic in form and were originally intended to be accompanied by music.

The Book of Psalms, more than any other book of the Bible,

could be called the inspired record of experiential religion. The emphasis is where God will dwell and receive His praise offering, which refers to His activity in both creation and natural history. He will obtain praise from apparatus used to produce music as well as the fruit of the lips through songs; therefore, all life is to praise Him—human beings and animals. This joy extends outside of current events and goes beyond set limitations, which are the probability or improbability of those events being produced from the Spirit to move you beyond the here and now, so that you can redeem the qualities of the Supreme Ruler. This is dissimilar from mere status of comfort, happiness, and safety that comes from man based on emotional well-being or mental stability; it is psychologically intoxicating, physically powerful, and spiritually influential in the midst of any disturbance at can engineer serious disorder due to nature or unnatural reasons.

In the Old Testament there are many kinds of spiritual ecstasy reported in the Bible, which makes it very difficult to give a basic definition; in general one should view joy as this positive attitude or pleasant emotion. The Bible reveals many levels of joy that can be described as "gladness," "contentment," or "cheerfulness." (See Psalm 16:11.) The more excellent joy that people of God should have is considered consecrated and wholesome, which helps you rise far above any rundown of environmental condition to focus on the glorious Creator. The path of life is one in which you live in ongoing union with God; not even death can bring an end to that affable companionship. You can have a cheerful or happy disposition by nature in the Lord in spite of your secular position, status, or title. (See Psalm 21:1.)

God's strong displeasure parallels with expressions of grief and sorrow briefly, as His acts of kindness parallels with delight and elation for a lifetime; these harmonious relationships are typical of His characteristics that are revealed throughout the Bible, both Old and New Testaments. Believers must be aware of God's fundamental attribute of mercy:

> For His anger is but for a moment, His favor is for life; weeping may endure for a night, but joy comes in the morning.
>
> —PSALM 30:5, NKJV

A celebration of the reality of divine pardon, God does not impute iniquity since the man has confessed sin and been forgiven. A reflection of God's work regenerates the inner man, which transforms you inwardly. You must continue to have a teachable spirit, so that you can defeat the internal struggle of sense of right and wrong along with the conviction of your transgressions will drain away cheerful and happy disposition (Psalm 32:1–2, 11). As the Almighty Creator deserves your best creativity in praise, it should never come out of corrupt or deceitful intentions, but truth, righteousness, justice, and goodness, which form a reason for offering our praise to God in the spirit of excellence.

There are numerous expressions of grief that can help you when the weighted down with depression or oppression coming from a depraved, heartless, and insensitive world system. There are several psalms that contain cries for vengeance and have been called imprecatory or cursing psalms (see Psalms 35; 59; 69; 70; 109; 137; 139; 104), in these the author prays that God may afflict the evildoer with just punishment. You must be apparent in your understanding and be watchful while evaluating the imprecatory psalms; while they have some degree of tactless outbursts of vindictiveness against relentless enemies.

They are primarily pleas for the moral judgment of God upon those who defy and oppose Him. As in conventional poetry, which initiates from cogent responses and emotions that are articulated by proficient verbal communication in order to bring an intense message to the forethought of the listener, the psalmists expressed the pain of unjust suffering and called upon God to hasten His conscientious sentencing upon the evildoers of the era. Even if the theme of the audible, articulate, meaningful sound is produced by the action theme seems harsh to the alert audience, in that time and culture the theme of God's righteous judgment is altogether proper echoed from the Old Testament traditions.[1]

David was one of the first writers in the Book of Psalm, who on several incidents wanted to be vindicated by God for the cruel chastisement and malicious mistreatment coming from his enemies. Later He begins to take a moral inventory, taking personal account of self, and sees that he had not always lived a noble life before God, so he wrote a psalm that deals with the need for holy heart for a regenerated soul. When God cleanses the heart through the Holy Spirit—His Spirit—the instantaneous response should be praise and witness. Outward worship is a pleasing sacrifice to God only if it expresses the inward spiritual conditions coming from a broken spirit and contrite heart. Ceremonial and traditional worship on Sunday is absent of these provisions for they accomplish nothing that can change the composition or structure of the inner man; however, it if is offered as an immediate result of praise and witness, God is pleased.

> Restore to me the joy of Your salvation, And uphold
> me by Your generous Spirit.
>
> —PSALM 51:12, NKJV

Afterward, David makes a petition that goes beyond his known and unknown enemies that includes all wicked transgressors, which is another common plea in the psalms aiming to motivate God's hand to action. Even if your persecutors behave like a group of undomesticated, undisciplined, or uncultivated vicious animals seeking to destroy everything that is liberated from wrongdoings, erroneous beliefs, or misapprehension of prophesies of God, you are obligated to sustain confident expectation in the Lord, who will provide you a way of escape. If instant death comes and removes the wicked out of your life too quickly, you may lose an opportunity to witness forgiveness and unrestricted affection. The unlikeness between the trouble of the oppression and the beauty of deliverance is highlighted in the contrast of good and evil, light and darkness. Life in the Old Testament represents the bodily existence in this world in fellowship with the true and living God. The conviction grows that if God's people had truly enjoyed fellowship with God, even death could not disrupt that relationship. God's unique qualities and superior providence are an integral part which gives off positive integers, as well as His acts are the foundation of rejoicing upon the earth and in the heavens. Psalm 67:3 demonstrates the praise that God deserve because of spiritual salvation granted to His people; however, it will convey cohesive happiness throughout nations, which is the basis of one's faith.

David was an eyewitness to the betrayal from a close companion with whom he visited the house of God in communal fellowship and worship, a friend turned foe. He became emotionally distressed and hysterical over the betrayal (Ps. 55:12–14), as doe many who have been emotionally wounded in the house of God by selfish leaders and laities. This is the time to reminiscence on the comforting promise of the Lord. He has complete dominion over the entire universe (Ps. 55:22). Furthermore, the glory of the Lord is God's creative majesty that calls forth homage from His creation through songs of praise that impart emphasis on His incomparable power, His righteousness, and His faithfulness (Ps. 89:5).

There are many who request that God deal with their oppressors or tormentor only to forget that they have caused harm to others along the way; so before you ask the Lord to deal with the evildoers, make sure that there is no familiar ways or secretive thoughts hidden within in you. Unlock your heart and release all thoughts or actions contrary to God's will to the Lord so that He can clean all material defilement:

> Search me, O God, and know my heart; try me, and know my anxieties, And see if there is any wicked way in me, And lead me in the way of everlasting.
>
> —PSALM 139:23–24, NKJV

This kind of favorable admiration, exaltation, and celebration is required of the righteousness person, and manifested from the true and living Spirit of God. This book of doxology covers inspiration for more hymns and spiritual songs than any other book of the Bible, even today, concluding that God is to be praised both in His earthly and heavenly temples (Ps. 150).[2]

The book of Psalms is a literary work, which deals with spiritual growth through noteworthy concepts and expressions of joy from a forgiving viewpoint. Without forgiveness no one will be uncontaminated or unpolluted enough to stand in God's presence. He is to be revered and worshiped in the beauty of holiness, which ultimately determines one's attachment with God which comes from being forgiven. One can see God Himself rejoicing in His creative and innovative workmanship. As the Creator, He spoke the universe into existence as an expression of His divine will. (See Genesis 1.) The Old Testament view of man is that he is an animated body rather than an incarnated being or living soul, for God's wondrous works are to both proclaim and mediate on His goodness. The foundation for declaring His greatness and goodness should come from everything that has breath (See Genesis 2:7.) This is a marked by excessive treatment of details, as the potter shapes a vessel from clay; the physical body was lifeless, both man's physical life and spiritual nature were deprived of life, but after God ejected supernatural oxygen into an individual recipient, he jumped directly into activation from God. You are required by the Lord to respond to His promises with joy because He is King of kings, Lord of lords, and the Prince of Peace.

> Make a joyful shout to the LORD, all ye lands!
> Serve the Lord with gladness;
> Come before His presence with singing.
> Knowing that the LORD, He is God;
> It is He who has made us, and not we ourselves;
> We are His people and the sheep of His pasture.
>
> Enter into His gates with thanksgiving,
> And into His courts with praise.
> Be thankful to Him, and bless His name.
> For the LORD is good;
> His mercy is everlasting,
> And His truth endures to all generations.

—PSALM 100, NKJV

In the New Testament, Matthew 13:1–23 deals with the parables of four believers. The sower, Jesus, scattered seed (the Word of God) and it fall on diverse kinds of soil (hearers or believers). Thus, the results were different for those who applied the Word differently based on their interpretation. It also tells how one can have continued delight as followed Christ. That joy came in the parable of the four believers, but when examined closely the first three kinds of unfruitful believers appear to be interested only in having a fire escape from hell, while they profit as much as possible from this present age with ease and undisturbed problems.

*The first soil*, the wayside ground believer (v. 4, 19), represents the neglectful or disobedient believer. *The second soil*, the stony ground believer (v. 5, 20–21), represents the hard hearted believer. The seed of the word of the kingdom falls on shallow ground. *The third soil*, the thorny ground believer (v. 7, 22), represents the difficulty or contentious believers who rejected the seed (the Word of God) and took no joy in it. *The fourth soil*, the good ground believer (v. 8, 23), represents the faithful believers who, after receiving the seed (the Word of God), bring forth spiritual fruit. They walk by faith and not by sight. Perhaps the amount of fruit that each produces is indicative to how much truth regarding the kingdom each sees and commits to their way of life. The seed sown on the hardened path produced no fruit, whereas the seed sown on rocky and thorny ground produced some temporary fruit However, the seed sown on the good soil produced from thirty to a hundredfold.

In every case, the seed sown was the same, but the condition of the soil determined the end result, and such is the kingdom of heaven. In Matthew 13:10–17 Jesus explains why He spoke in parables, to give emphasis to the "unhearing ears," the condition of the soil of one's heart which reflects the eagerness and readiness to hear what the Holy Spirit attempting to convey for your purpose for living. The extraordinary impact of God's independent kingdom supremacy is determined by human response. God's kingdom can be rejected, temporarily accepted, or fully and fruitfully accepted; the decision is yours.

This pointed parable vividly pictures the varied response to Jesus' proclamation of the word of the kingdom from (1) that of the hardened heart of believers, (2) to that of the temporarily responsive heart of believers, (3) to that of the disobedient heart of believers, (4) to that of the receptive heart. The reward for responsible stewardship holds servants liable and ready to give account to primary causes and motives by which there is great accountability. With God, the basis of reward is not how much you have, but how faithfully you serve. Joy will come through spiritual growth when temperance can be planted within the inner man, producing strong character.

Many believers are still very childish and underdeveloped, needing adequate charity and benevolence toward the brethren. Yet, they childishly foster and hold grudges, giving offense by discriminating against others and showing cruelty. Refusal to grow spiritually will sabotage and cheapen all moral reasoning and intellectual apprehension, making it painstaking to be receptive to the genuine Word of God. Christians must trust and walk in a deep, abiding sense of joy that is only understood by someone with childlike faith and innocence. Meanwhile, learn how to coexist and live together without turmoil or struggle in spite of differing opinions and you will no longer be barren as a result of egotistical decisions, thoughtless opinions, and overbearing efforts. Sin promises something for nothing, but in the end you will finish by taking what you cannot afford to pay back. On the other side, virtue is like an investment and its fruits multiply. The Lord guarantees it according to His spoken and written Word, since the journey is made possible for those who truly want to surrender their union elements unto Him, "for with God nothing will be impossible" (Luke 1:37, NKJV). These components are body, emotions, thoughts, and sensations that compose the uniqueness and distinctiveness of a person.

The Bible gives two examples of believers that were wrestling with spiritual development issues throughout their spiritual journey, yet they never wavered in their faith. Paul gives one illustration and Peter gives another. Paul tells the Corinthians how he could not come to them with tough love, for they were too immature and impertinent to understand his intentions (1 Cor. 3:1–3). He told them, since they refused grow, they would remain spiritual and emotional babes, new converts. They still desired to be fed milk and not meat. The believers at Corinth remained in or of the flesh, walking under the subjection of strife and divisions. They were behaving as men in the world, showing dissatisfaction and ill will because of another's advantage, success, or possessions. They were unable to work together without competing and contending for the spotlight and being divided by personal agendas. This becomes drastically venomous to the body of Christ, causing internal decay and deterioration. Peter gives a word of admonition to his followers, just as Paul gave to the Corinthians, to lay aside all malice, guile, and hypocrisies. It was time for them to put down their milk bottle or pacifier and seek solid spiritual food (1 Pet. 2:1–2).

It is time for you, too, to grow up and become an example to a dying world, showing them how to walk circumspectly. The hour has come for you to move along at a modified pace and placing trust along with total dependence on the true Savior with childlike faith and hope. Is there a sufficient amount of joy in your life? Are you faithful to the Lord? If you answer yes to these questions, then no weapon formed against you shall be able to stop your from fulfilling your destiny or reaching your desired objective. Nonetheless, if you are not faithful, then you cannot have true joy. You might think that you are happy and full of joy, but you can be deceived into believing a lie. Examine yourself very circumspectly; the days when you could do what ever pleased the flesh, you would do because it brought pleasure and joy to the carnal man. This type of childish characteristic will keep you from retaining your inheritance in the Lord, for you are walking in the spirit of disobedience, misled by craftiness that has spread throughout many congregations like a virus or cancer. Remember, the devil seeks to uproot and cause destruction to the new man. His ways are extremely poisonous and noisome within the body of Christ. God's will and His Word bring in an antidote to halt the teaching of false doctrine and the distortion of the true gospel.

The evil one's mission is to hinder the hearer from understanding and comprehending the message of God and being saved. As a result, the devil is able to remove the message from their hearts, leaving the hearer absent of the truth. Jesus also warned them about being people who hear the Word but allow it to be overcome by the pleasures and temptations of the world. Like thorn bushes, they must be pruned so as not to overtake the garden, you should not to allow the seed, God's Word to be choked by evil influences. It is the only defensive and offensive weapon that you can use against the enemy of your body, mind, and spirit. The strongest antidote for the broken heart is God's truth, which is powerful and sharper than any two-edged sword. It is able to separate the soul and spirit, the joint from the marrow, and to discern the intellect and intents of the heart (Heb. 4:12). It is the answer to all emotional, mental, physical and spiritual complications.

As heirs, you have been given freedom from all offensive material produced by this world's debased system. As children of God, you need supplemental vitamins and minerals from the Lord of host. The Word of God has all the spiritual protein one needs. In addition, it offers the fruit of the Spirit, the bread of heaven, and meat for the weary. This love and compassion is supplement spiritual growth with endowing joy. First, you must realize that as a child of God, you are not mature enough to make sound decisions or rational choices; which means you must rely on the instruction of Father God for spiritual growth and improvement. You will need a foundation built from the voice of God. It is time to move from childish functioning to the childlike attributes of Christ (Gal. 4:3). This process involves significant, radical changes in behavior, thought process, emotions, and attitudes. These psychological changes largely determine the kind of adult that a child will become.

There have been many psychologists who have made great contributions to the study of mental illness, understanding of personality, clinical psychology, human development, and abnormal psychology. In addition, social learning theory stressed the importance of observational learning, imitation, and modeling. Children's intellectual development, developmental psychology, cognitive psychology, genetic epistemology, and education reform as well as psychoanalytic theory explore development throughout the life, including events of childhood, adulthood, and old age. In spite of these remarkable assets to humanity growth and progression to exist, there has only been one man who was a true psychologist, Dr. Jesus Christ, who came down to earth thirty-two flights (generations) to make a spiritual diagnosis for humanity—to God's chosen people to identify the disease that was put here to destroy humankind's joy and peace, as well as help us to see more clearly the signs and symptoms impending from a sinful nature. He provided thorough investigation or analysis of the root cause or nature of this preexisting condition. He diagnosed the woman at the well and told her about her problem (John 4:7–30). The Samaritan woman at the well was mixed up with a wrong crowd, she had reputation throughout the village of been married five times and living with a man who was not her husband, as well as committing adultery and fornication. Her story comes as a lesson to people, they that should not live by carnal pleasure, because it can bring you much distress, embarrassment, and emotional pain. The story shows that a well of grace is ready to refresh the soul parched by sin and suffering, and that Jesus came to save the lost and sick and serve those who still need both physical and spiritual healing, not just the converted. The Samaritan woman's spirit is enlightened with the prophetic truth that Jesus revealed to her based on her present condition. She went on to lead many townspeople to conversion in her area through her zeal and love for God (John 4:39–42). She is a direct illustration of spiritual thirst that the human heart has for goodness, mercy, and truth—a thirst that cannot be quenched until individuals recognize that they have a spiritual need, eternal salvation. As believers we are fully aware that Christ is the true clinician and psychologist who came to earth after thirty-two generations to show mankind how to function in a volatile environment surrounding and depraved upbringing and to deliver them from anything ranging from acute mental health issues to physical deformities.

The childlike faith of innocence and trust in the parent's counsel is much needed in childhood, adolescence, and well into adulthood. This type of innocence allows freedom from sin or shame, exhibiting a firm belief and certainty of hope through our greater Confidant, Christ Jesus. God has given all Christian parents a measure of temperance and the structural pattern for how to train up a child in moderation. Jesus followed His Father's instructions all the way to the cross. The parent's vital role of developing and training a child is to pass on the spiritual traits and skills learned from the Word of God, with the assistance of other spiritual counterparts. There are three stages in the move from childish to childlike behavior.

God breathed life into man before any influential psychological theory came into existence or had the chance to birth the diversities of thought behavior or patterns. The fact that the brain has the mobility to process growth and development for a considerable period even after one's physical birth, should remove all doubt that early experiences do indeed influence and modify one's nature to reality and can continue to affect all preexisting behaviors, which will enable us to institute a fresh spirit outlook on life. In spiritual terms, this is the phase where some believers remain childlike in personality and individuality due to their innate inability to develop and mature because they continue to remain in unproductive in unfruitful environments and connected to unreliable resources. When they have become exposed to the appropriate experiences that would help them become more effective and productive the Kingdom of heaven, instead they are stagnating the progression of self and others. They have premature thoughts, immature ways, and reflect lack of maturity in their deeds. It has been noted that psychological growth is also affected by emotional, mental, and physical factors. It is very important to keep outside forces from causing the decay of the mind, body, and soul. Contrary to popular belief, you must protect your spiritual storehouse from outside disturbance. As the physical and mental growth begin to collide with the spiritual, this is where you begin to be influenced by peer groups, social cliques, and church schisms seeking acceptance and approval, rather than spiritual pastors, leaders, or laymen who can provide you with spiritual inspiration or and insight based on sound scriptures. This way you are measuring your spiritual growth according to dysfunctional peer standards and predetermined feelings of close friends or immature adults who do not have all the adequate answers for their own life.

Mature individuals are expected to learn to solve problems and begin to form a self- image. As a mature Christian at this stage, if those around you are not supplying you with data that advances the work of the kingdom, you must disconnect with dysfunctional and unhealthy social ties early on, before any real harm can take place within the inner man. This is even true of information coming from teachers, evangelists, and ministers of the gospel of Jesus. As children of the light, you are no longer children of darkness, and you walk in the occupation of your calling (1 Thess. 5:5–6). Those who have leadership authority must understand that it comes with leadership accountability, so you are no longer servants of sinfulness but servants of godliness. True believers are servants with spiritual clarification, the inner light of enlightenment or truth that prevents you from foreshadowing wickedness since you have been made a new creation by His Spirit. At this stage of maturity, you are to be spiritually pure and loving to everyone with mercy, kindness, humbleness of mind, meekness, and longsuffering and are more responsible for carrying out the organized missionary work of Jesus Christ (Col. 3:12–13).

Lastly, do not become weary in well doing, for everyone develops and matures at various speeds, because an ability has to be a trained before it can become a capacity; hereafter, learning is increased from repetitive coaching and positive reinforcement through spiritual coaching. In this life and the life after, there are no two individuals who are the same; hence, individual growth will bring different results and outcomes. The Holy Spirit will assist you in reaching God's purpose or destiny for your life. Stay in there and pass the test of faith to go on to the next level of blessings. Spiritually, Christians at this level of maturity should be capable and strong enough to revise or reject standards and values that go against the principles of God's commands. It is important you find out if you are suffering from just spiritual issues or having problems relating to social issues, for you might be in need of psychological counseling.

O ye seed of Abraham his servant, ye children of Jacob his chosen (Ps. 105:6). Sibling rivalry in the body of Christ is normal between the immature or babes, but the mature saint should no longer have any ill will toward others. In God's sanctuary there can be no room for any hateful behavior or malicious speaking against leaders or co-laborers of the Lord, running others down to make oneself look good in the eyesight of men, the above sins are a contradiction to God's command to love one another fervently and from a pure heart with clean motives. Just as babes desire the milk, you should feed on the Word of God so that you can grow spiritually (1 Pet. 2:2). You must be prepared to become teachers of beatific things, so avoid foolish disputes, debates over long-established standards, confrontational unresolved personal issues, and bitter contention over traditional operation in the church since they are unprofitable and useless to the establishment of the heavenly kingdom on earth. You must be able to separate yourself from those who suffer from perverse individuals who persistently continue to sin without any godly sorrow, refusing to heed counsel and closing their heart and mind to the door of correction (Titus 3:9–11). In human beings, the rules governing material possession or property are culturally determined and learned by direct and indirect influence of positive and negative role models. As the child blossoms with toughness and durability to weather the storm, God is testing their individual stamina against failure, hard conditions, and illness. The Father desires for His children to be raised and molded with a spirit free from defect, disease, or infirmity and filled with His grace and mercy. There is no room in the house of God, for territorial behavior regardless of the environmental conditions, since everyone should be seeking the same spiritual relationship. It is healthy for you to be interested in understanding your own immature behavioral patterns and shortcomings, and that only comes through testing one's faith level. God does not want His children to oversimplify and to settle for easy explanations, make excuses for the evildoing, or lack of spiritual judgment. This testing will reroute the presence of evil. The question is: can you withstand the test?

## PASSING THE TEST

Do you recognize that your trials will help you thrive and go to the next assignment in God? Your spiritual growth will come when you do not avoid praising God and instead rejoice in your tribulation and persecution, since this is how character development will come. This process will bring growth in the midst of crisis. Your spiritual promotion will proceed when the character development tests are passed, signifying that you are ready and able to receive God's endowment.

Just as a natural father teaches his children how to prepare for society, God instructs us how to resist temptation and the traps of the deceiver. Your earthly parents train and teach you while you are young and impressionable. Then, when you come of age, your supreme parent, God, takes over. He holds authority over your life as you are molded into the character of Christ and become like Him. Therefore, we must submit and yield to our superior ruler, God, to have the higher call in Christ Jesus. The scriptures tell us that all things are possible in Christ Jesus and that you can do nothing without Him: "With men this is impossible but with God all things are possible" (Matt. 19:26,

NKJV). An illustration earlier on in the Scripture talks about hard it is to enter into the kingdom of heaven, which states that it is easier for a camel to pass through the eye of the needle, than for a righteous man to enter into heaven (Matt. 19:23–24). This young man found the offer to be too costly, and he turned away with grief and sorrow. All who turn away from Christ's call will live to regret that decision; yet there will be some who will give up earthly possessions and material gain to follow after Christ. So Jesus tells His disciples that there is nothing impossible for God; if that man accepts God's complete lord-ship over one's riches, he will find salvation in the Lord and a wonderful reward.

> The fear of the LORD is the beginning of wisdom: a good understanding have all they that do his commandments: his praise endureth for ever.
>
> —PSALM 111:10

> Great peace have they which love thy law: and nothing shall offend them.
>
> —PSALM 119:165

> Happy is he that hath the God of Jacob for his help, whose hope is in the LORD his God.
>
> —PSALM 146:5

God will hold everyone answerable for his or her actions, whether he or she planted good seeds or spread vicious seed; we are to walk in the spirit of peace. There is no time to pay attention to the foolish and harmful things of this life. As co-laborers desiring boundless joy for the brethren and planting seeds that are unshakeable to do the work of the ministry, you are required to do everything under your control to maintain those seeds to take root and produce fruit. You are not to be like a fruit fly, which is annoying and inciting arguments among the brethren, which will prevent the spread of joy within the body of Christ.

Furthermore, if there is no self-control about your easily aroused weaknesses, you are going to continue riding this spiritual roller coaster, which through my reading and studying, I have found many psychologists who say with much confidence that the origin, development, and nature of human nature is a complex and extremely controversial subject. There are many present various psychological views on discipline, genetically determined, or learned behavior. Your political prejudices, private theories, and ideological obligations do play a vital role in influencing the views that individuals will take to persuade their nature and the differences between each human being.

If you continue to have contradictory or antagonistic qualities or attitudes with a major mental abnormality, it will give the adversary and your enemies access to your ability to determine right from wrong, to make logical and rational decisions that are needed in order to survive this adventure. The ambiguously minded man is volatile, someone that moves arbitrarily from one idea, interest or thought to another (James 1:6–8). James says, he or she is disturbed and can be easily agitated in all his or her reciprocal deeds. Not having the stability to overcome the irrational behavior is very costly and a detriment to your mind, it is very vital that you maintain full awareness and control, for what is received into your spirit will reach a plane of maturity. The perversion or distortion of the gospel with dishonest beliefs and opinions that undermine God's ordinances and commandments will bring great calamity. God is requiring you to clean your hands from forms sin and evil and to rid your mind of impurities or pollution from corrupt influences (James 4:8).

## The Joy of David

As we can all see, some of the songs David wrote to help him deal with the day-to-day attacks that he was going through are listed in the Book of Psalms. Few people have had or have as many enemies as King David. Some of his enemies died trying to kill him. The same may be true for some of you; perhaps you have seen some of your enemies fall ill. That is why it is important for us to remember what David told Saul when he cornered Saul in a cave with no one around except the two of them. Even though God delivered David's enemy, Saul, into his hands, David declared that he could not harm Saul because he had been chosen as an officer of God (1 Sam. 24:10). David respected the call that God had put on Saul's life, even though Saul was not obeying God.

There will come a time when you must examine the matters of your heart, whether you will choose to demonstrate the same type of love that Jesus showed on the cross. In order to reach your destiny in God, you must operate in the spirit, not the flesh. Saul acknowledged that by not harming him, David gave him just respect and honor as the King of Israel, notwithstanding his numerous attempts to kill David. That display of love is what God expects regardless of how a friend, family member, boss, or foe may treat you. Respect must be given. In the meantime, trust that, as the Scriptures promise, God has prepared a bountiful table in your presence with you as the honored guest. Since He has made complete provisions all for your physical appetite and spiritual need, there is fullness joy in knowing that God considers you a privileged friend, a respectable guest.

He has applied His confidential heavenly scent especially used at favorable and formal celebrations upon our heads (Ps. 23:5).

No matter what individuals scheme to put an end to your task, the Lord will make them be at peace with you. David felt on numerous occasions that he was alone and he had no one on his side but the Lord. He was grateful that God returned His favor to the children of Israel by granting them the ark of God. After returning with the ark of God, he led the Levites into a praise dance of worship. David became so elated that he began dancing, leaping, and spinning around in the street; but from Micah's response it appears that David had little else on but his linen ephod or apron. He was not afraid to dance before the Lord in front of all the people with exuberant and joyous praise as the house of Israel brought up the ark of the Lord with shouting and with the sound of the trumpet (2 Sam. 6:14–15).

Michal, Saul's daughter, watched him from a bedroom window with hate in her heart, for David's display embarrassed her and left her disconcerted (2 Sam. 6:16). She could not understand David's reason for praising God, for she was not a worshiper. It is very important that you connect with individuals who have the same kindred spirit and can be in agreement with your spiritual relationship and public fellowship with God. These individuals imply complete accord usually attained by discussion and adjustment of differences; they will give their valued opinion even when it does not comply with your personal stand. David did not try to justify himself to his wife, as you do not have to justify yourself, for there is no need to defend your confession of faith or spiritual walk before doubters.

There will come times when you do not have any inkling why you are praising God; you praise for who He is, for laying His life down for your sins, for showing you how to love, and for giving the greatest gift of love. When you love someone, you often do things that man thinks are silly. Take for example a wife who stays home and leaves her career to take care of her family because she wants the best for her children and family. She chooses God and her family, regardless of the odds. She wants to be there to help and assist them with their homework and be there for her husband when he comes home from work and from business trips to ease and encourage him when he is having a rough day. To many it may not seem rewarding, but to her and her family, it is a blessing. The children enjoy seeing their mother at home when they come home from school, and her husband appreciates having a listening ear while he sits and has his dinner. It is good to be engaged in fresh conversation with someone who has a positive and encouraging attitude about his or her day.

That was what David wanted when he got home, a fresh conversation about this, but instead he encountered his angry and contentious wife who felt that she had been disgraced in front of her family, friends, and all the servants. She was probably frustrated and embarrassed that his dance would have given his and even her enemies some scandalous rumor to spread. Michal missed was her opportunity to have joy with her husband. The Scriptures tell us that Jesus received the same response when He returned to Jerusalem to preach and teach the gospel. Matthew 13:57–58 tells us, "A prophet is not without honor except in his own country and in his own house. Now He did not do many mighty works there because of their unbelief" (NKJV). Michal refused to comprehend or desire to understand David's joyful worship to his God who had delivered and protected him from dangerous animals while he herded sheep, fighting Goliath with a rock and a hand made sling shot, and running from Saul's javelin or other attempts on his life. David had always been a praiser, even in times of mourning and grief.

Even you must continue to praise God in spite of bereavement and unhappiness, for there some folks who are determined to hinder your goal. Therefore, you need to disassociate yourself from them because they can become hazardous to your predetermined course of events.

Meanwhile, you must find humor in others' ways of expressing admiration and exaltation unto the Lord. Your negative reactions could jeopardize your expected or potential reward. That is why it is important to be steadfast when God is blessings others and moving miraculously in someone else's life. There will come a time when we will want others to feel the same joy for us when God is blessing our family, friends, and loved ones. It is vitally important to identify with your brother or sister in their times of joy as well as in their sorrows. This is a Christian's advantage and obligation (1 Cor. 12:26).

David knew regardless of how things looked around him that he was always going to give God praise and honor. It was his way of keeping his joy when his enemies were trying to get rid of him, when he felt deserted and betrayed, or even when he felt like he was in harm's way. Many of the songs recorded in the Book of Psalms were King David's way of meditating and reflecting on what God was doing in his life by keeping his enemies at bay.

You were created to worship the Lord in song and dance. Dancing before the Lord is simply an outward or physical expression of your inner relationship or experience with the Lord. You dance, leap, and run for there is exceeding joy in knowing the Lord is your Redeemer, not because of circumstantial or emotional stimulus, but because of who He is. The afterimage of the King of glory continues after the external and internal stimulus is withdrawn from the service, showing God to be mighty and strong. There should be no set time;

you should always be able to have open and private worship, go in your secret closet express your love and adoration for your Lord with dances, shouts of joy, and with the singing of songs. Dance, dance, dance before the Lord with all your heart! This outpouring can only bring you closer to His destination for your life. God will reestablish what He has in store for His people. He is holy, He inhabits the heavens and Earth, and He applauds the praise of the people (Ps. 22:1–5). King David had a heart of worship and spent many of his days writing psalms, sacred songs of praise, worship, and adoration to his Lord.

When my youngest daughter was between the ages of two and five years old and no one was home but her and me, we would put gospel radio on or a gospel CD in and worship for hours until I noticed that I had not gotten any housework done. My daughter learned something great from that process at a very early age, how to offer praise and worship to God in spirit and truth from the fruit of her lips. When she would go to church, she would stand up during the praise and worship service, only to find many adults staring at her with disapproval. It was very confusing to her that she could be free to worship at home but could not worship Him among others Christians, especially in church. Adults would give her a look like she was too young to praise God. She shared with me in the car in small quiet voice, "Mommy, I'm not going to stand up and praise God in church any more." I replied, "Why baby?" She responded, "Because people look at me funny, and I don't like people to look at me like something is wrong with because I want praise God like we do at home. They make me feel as if I'm doing something wrong." I replied, "Baby, people look at Mommy funny too." "But you are a grown-up, and they don't laugh at you," she said. I told her that no one knew her heart but God, so she did not have to feel embarrassed or ashamed when she wanted to praise Him. How disturbing that people in the house of God, still today cannot grasp the concept of praise and worship in spirit and in truth for Jesus is the One that gives joy, but you can permit adverse situations, rivalry opponents, or forces of darkness to subdue your praise. For, it brings glory and honor unto God.

> Most assuredly, I say to you that you will weep and lament, but the world will rejoice; and you will be sorrowful, but your sorrow will be turned into joy.
>
> —JOHN 16:20, NKJV

## DAILY INTERCESSION OF CONTINUOUS JOY

Your daily prayer and supplication should make intercession on behalf of others to the Father. Peace and joy will keep you, considering they are gifts from the Father and that all the Father's gifts are unlimited. The scripture teaches in the Book of James that every good and perfect gift comes from above, coming down from the Creator who does not change (James 1:17). So, if all of God's gifts bring joy, ask God for the power to overcome and vanquish the forces of evil. God will keep you in a perfect state of tranquility when your senses, opinions, thoughts, strength of character, and reasoning remain on Him. Trust in Jehovah forever and recognize His strong power has never ending duration (Isa. 26:3–4).

As heirs of God, guard your heart and do not give consent or authorization to the enemy to delete and obstruct this possession. Joy is the pearl given to you by the Father for your laboring in the vineyard, and the book of Ecclesiastes states that you should be gleeful and joyful in the fruit of your labor (3:13).

Again, you see in Scripture that God is giving His children

another good and unrestricted gift for their laboring. You have a perpetual gift of joy, so go take back what the enemy has stolen. Joy is yours today. Remember that Satan is a thief and robber who will put up a fight to keep your precious possessions. Therefore, realize that joy and peace are the things in life that are worth fighting for, and never give them up without a fight. However, you do not have to fight alone. Rather, you do not have to fight at all, because once you become joint heirs into the family of Christ, God will fight all present and future battles for you (2 Chron. 20:14–17).

Even today, God is not daunted in defending His children. He will not allow anyone or anything to cause hurt or harm to His children. Peter wrote that if you suffer for Christ's sake and seek to do the will of the Lord, allow God to handle all the details. Do not return or render evil for evil, but instead always pursue peace (1 Pet. 3:11). Your job is to do well, regardless of how anyone else treats you, talks about you, or if they cause bodily harm to you. The Lord will not allow any harm to come upon you (v. 13–14).

When the judgment or vindication day comes to your antagonistic contender, do not rejoice or boast, for boasting is morally reprehensible (James 4:16). Do not glory in someone else's suffering. To brag about your skills or talents with pride and satisfaction is sinful. Anyone rejoicing about any of these things is full of sin in the eyes of the Lord. This is the characteristic of a wounded person, who is functioning out of foolish heart and has not permitted the Spirit of God to take ownership and residence, so the supernatural powers of God can come in destroy all evidence of carnality. The flesh cannot go behind the veil, which is in the presence of God; only that which is spiritual can. When a child wants something from his or her father, they will not yell their request from another room because they know that the father is going to request their presence. The same is true in the spiritual realm; God summons your presence when you come to Him with earnest petitions. In addition, before you can get in His presence you must be purified and sanctified since no man can come to the Father except in spirit and truth, in the name of Jesus.

You will be able to praise Him, but you will never get what He truly has for you until you go behind the veil, into His presence. Behind the veil is where God deals with you one on one. There is no line as you wait for an intercessor; it is God and you. You cannot pick up the phone and call your prayer partner to help you access God; it is time for you to enter into His presence yourself. This is a gift that we have because of what Jesus did on the cross. Why are you not using it? Entering into God's presence is the key to the door to God's heart, along with keeping His Word and acknowledging Him. Display endurance and perseverance in the days of adversity, and like Job, count everything that you go through with happiness (James 5:11).

Well, my brother or sister, by now you should have some concept of how to receive this miraculous gift of joy accompanied by peace that comes exclusively from heavens itself, from Jesus Christ. Moreover, like David who learned to encourage himself, you can do the same. I do not know about you, but if David wrote songs that gave him so much joy back then, I think you can do the same today.

Jesus told the disciples that the joy that would follow His resurrection would be so strong that "no one can take [it] from you" (John 16:22, NKJV). As believers, you must not become overpowered by the cares of this world or travail and toil in days of sorrow or distress. The closer you come to reaching your destiny, the more the enemy will try to send disaster your way to take your delight sneakily or without permission. This is why in times of testing, confine or carefully guard your joy closely.

Remember that whatever we ask in the name of Jesus, the Father will give it to us (v. 23), so ask for the joy that is beyond expression or imagination of man's weakness. The Father is willing and able to make or provide whatever is at hand when you ask in the name of Jesus. The present of joy is ready for the taking, if you will only ask. Jesus is willing to give you this for no cover price or charge because He has paid the full debt on Calvary. Many of you have asked of God, but not in the name of Jesus; this is the time to ask in the name of Jesus for marvelous joy (v. 24).

The undeveloped saints must keep in mind that in the Christian life there is unconventional joy to help you stay in the faith. There will come many days when all you have to keep you going is the joy of the Lord in your time of distress. I am a living witness that the joy of the Lord will keep you when enemies are great and friends are few. The Lord will defend you. All the way to the cross, Christ never said an argumentative word; He endured to the end and faithfully finished His task—to offer Himself as payment for our sins. The blessing that comes out of Christ's joy is yours for the asking.

## THE BLESSINGS OF JOY

In the Sermon on the Mount, there were many blessing offered to the joyful; during that Jesus was giving His followers commands on spiritual behavior. The Sermon on the Mount called for the believer to uphold moral and ethical ways of living. Jesus knew before His departure that all believers would be unable to do this in their own power. Therefore, He also explained that He would help believers by providing for them and giving them joy, even in the midst of difficulty (Matt. 5:7),

The Beatitudes are a liberating and fabulous example of how

to express one's love through joy, even when other resources are limited. Jesus was aware that man could not live by physical extravagance alone but required spiritual stability to protect him from the wiles of the depraved one. The gates of hell cannot prevail against the revelation of God, for the blessings of the Lord will make your heart rich.

> To hunger and thirst after righteousness is when nothing in the world can fascinate us so much as being near to God.
>
> —SMITH WIGGLESWORTH[3]

## THE BEATITUDES

Blessed are the poor in spirit: for theirs is the kingdom of heaven.
Blessed are they that mourn: for they shall be comforted.
Blessed are the meek: for they shall inherit the earth.
Blessed are they which do hunger and thirst after righteousness: for they shall be filled.
Blessed are the merciful: for they shall obtain mercy.
Blessed are the pure in heart: for they shall see God.
Blessed are the peacemakers: for they shall be called the children of God.
Blessed are they which are persecuted for righteousness' sake: for theirs is the kingdom of heaven.
Blessed are ye, when men shall revile you, and shall persecute you, and shall say all manner of evil against you falsely, for my sake.
Rejoice, and be exceedingly glad: for great is your reward in heaven: for so persecuted they the prophets which were before you.

—MATTHEW 5:3–12, NKJV

The Beatitudes demonstrate that Jesus wanted all of His followers to have joy in the middle of all their affairs. The believers should remain precautious of their attitude, behavior, conduct, and habits, and there would be an everlasting reward of blessings in their daily interactions with others, where they should witness profusely, drawing others into the kingdom of God. Everything that the believer has to go through is counted as a blessing when he or she has the joy of the Lord as his or her strong power and tower. The word *blessed* in the Beatitudes refers to the believer's ultimate well-being and spiritual joy. It is available to followers that have firm courage and endurance during ridicule and who persevere when disaster comes down their pathway, recognizing that there is a spiritual reward of the kingdom of God if we show joy when trials and tribulations come. God wants us to be humble, promoting peace, repentant, virtuous, charitable, and filled with the joy of the Lord.

Still asking how do you become a recipient of this joy? From the Spirit of God, inherited to humanity after Christ ascension? No, it was here all along, but many could not understand the concept as they still cannot today, since they are so captivated by selfish ambitions, worldly affairs, and immoral habits. The Scriptures say if ungodly and unmoral fathers can supply gifts to their children, how much more shall the heavenly Father give suitable presents to them that ask Him (Matt. 7:11). Jesus wants us to understand that if we receive gifts from our earthy father or parents, why would we not believe that our heavenly Father could not reward us in the same manner? If we ask anything in our prayers in the name of Jesus, God will hear our petition and answer, if it is His will. Everything that comes from the Father is in ample supply in all respects.

In laymen's term, life is an open stage and God is the great producer, Christ is the director, and the Holy Spirit is the co-director, the script has been written over millenniums for your life, and all the cast in the movie have been screened for the role. There will be many scenes that will be enjoyable for some, unpleasant for others, so you can take the role in *Pleasantville*, a place where life is has some ups and downs because the confusion of several citizens, but things work out for the good in the end. You do not have to take on a role in a *Friday the 13th* or *Jason* horror movie that will leave you frightened to go to sleep or frightened to deal with life, because all around you are bloodcurdling creatures or satanic murders. However, God cast you in the role you were chosen to portray. In God's movie, called the *Kingdom of Heaven*, some are cast for leading roles and others are behind the scene working, responsible for making things come to life as well; but always remember that favor is not unbiased, it is just.

# 3
## WHO HAS TAKEN MY JOY?

*Knowest thou not this...That the triumphing of the wicked*
*is short, and the joy of the hypocrite but for a moment?*

—Job 20:4–5

O ONE CAN TAKE away your joy, you choose to give
it away, whether it is to neighbor who offended you,
the person who cut you off on the highway, or the
emotional crisis that comes upon your family and loved ones.
The challenges that you go through in this life can cause you
to forfeit your joy to another. There are many times when life's
demands can bombard your mind with oppressive artillery of
defeating thoughts and explosive words. Your survival tool for
the fight against the enemy of your soul is the Bible, the Word
of God. If you are frightened by Satan's tactics, you will not be
able to call the enemy into a dual to take back what has been
stolen from you. Joy is the intensive, exhaustive, and freely given
gift that is presented to the followers of Christ; it is what keeps
you close to God's heart. Failure to guard your mind, body, and
soul will cause a loss of joy. Many individuals lose their joy due
to thoughtlessness of the Lord's covenant. Joy is an abundant
and valuable supernatural resource. Though it was expensive

to obtain—the debt could only be paid with Christ's blood—it comes freely to us.

## LOST JOY

This lost joy can be seen throughout Saul's rule as king (1 Sam. 8–31). Saul was the first king of Israel and one of the most tragic figures in history. God reluctantly appointed him to lead His people after the Israelites cried out for a ruler because all the others nations had a ruler (8:4–22). Nevertheless, God granted their petition and made Saul captain over Israel to bring them out of bondage at the hands of the Philistines (9:16). The anointing placed on Saul's life signified consecration unto the Lord for a particular calling and divine equipping for the task. Israel's existence as a nation was threatened by the Philistines, who had mastered the technique of forging iron and had an arsenal of iron weapons. Israel's old system of government under judges, who failed too adequately unify the Hebrew people, was not equal to that of their opposition. Israel was not content doing things the way God wanted them to be done. Instead of changing their ways and seeking after God, the people clamored for a king. God appointed the prophet Samuel to anoint Saul for the task of leading His people. At the time he was chosen, he was only a young member of an insignificant clan (9:21).

Since He is a loving and generous God, He gave the people the desire of their heart, a king. In the beginning, Saul surprised everyone with his aptitude. He was brave, generous, and modest, and he would not take orders blindly from the old guards. In the end, however, Saul became not just a monarch but also a dictator over Israel, domineering, manipulative, and power-hungry. God knew Saul's heart condition from the beginning. He knew that power would eventually turn his heart cold and that the mounting pressures and responsibility of ruling would slowly undermine Saul's personality and character. He became moody and suspicious, and grew jealous of young David's growing popularity and notoriety—so jealous that he even tried to kill David. Saul won many victories over the Moabites, Ammonites, Edomites, Philistines, and Amalekites (14:47–48). He was victorious in battle and defeated every enemy from all around Israel. Saul became a famous warrior, but he allowed his fame and position to go to his head.

Saul gave God only partial obedience by not stopping the people from taking the spoil from a sinful nation they conquered (15:2–9). God did not want the children of Israel to take anything from the Amalekites, for they were an evil nation. Rather, He wanted all the possessions and land to be destroyed by fire. Saul violated his oath and the covenant he made with God when he was appointed king. The act of resisting and refusing to carry out the order of God is a vicious iniquity. For Saul, it was a type of idolatry because his failure to listen to the Lord's instructions showed that he feared the people more than he feared God. It cost him his position. After his act of disobedience and rejection of God's commandments, the Lord began looking for another captain to oversee His people (15:23–28).

Saul's first sign of lost joy was when the town's women were complimenting him and David on their accomplishments. Saul took the comments as negative feedback about his leadership. He felt that they were comparing him to David and allowed rejection to rise up in him. His insecurity allowed resentment to take root in his heart, causing him to lose his joy and peace. He was displeased and very angry with the women and began to feel indignation toward David (18:7–9).

Many times, Saul tried to kill David, though David had done nothing more than perform his obligation and duty as a servant of Saul. God sent David to the kingdom to be Saul's understudy, but Saul grew to increasingly paranoid and delusional. Saul became exasperated and irritated by David's daily presence around the palace, and he yearned and sought to kill David at any given opportunity (18:10–11; 19:9–10).

Saul was driven by despair and sought to consult the prophet Samuel, but it was too late. Samuel was dead. Now, Saul had put away those that had familiar spirits and wizards from the land. When he saw the host of the Philistines, he was afraid and his heart was greatly troubled, so he inquired of the Lord. But the Lord would not answer him by dreams, revelations, or prophets because he had been disobedient to God's word. Once again, Saul wanted to get his own way instead of going humbly into the presence of God. When he did not hear from the Lord, he summoned his servants to find a medium, or psychic, to consult the spirit of Samuel (28:3–6).

Earlier, Saul had banned all fortunetellers, soothsayers, magicians, witches, charmers, and other mediums from the land because they were an abomination to God. However, even though he knew it was against God's Law, he sought out a witch from Endor to ask her to bring back the spirit of Samuel so that he could know the will of God. Samuel's spirit rose from the ground, and he began to tell Saul that his defiance would bring destruction upon Israel and his family. In fact, he said, the Philistines would take them into captivity the next day (28:18–19). Since Saul did not heed to the voice of the Lord and execute the Amalekites when given an order to do so, it cost him and his heirs the throne.

The prophesy manifested itself the next day at the battle of Mount Gilboa, the Philistines, who he previously capsized in battle, defeated his outnumbered and poorly equipped army. He committed suicide by launching his body onto this sword (31:1–19). There is a great expense to pay for open and bold resistance against the Lord. It could very well cost your life, possessions, authority, and welfare. On the other hand, David's steadfast obedience showed that serving God does pay off, no matter how things around you may appear; remember his testimony as a reminder to stand upright.

In conclusion, Saul was a man who never had any joy, for he rejected his new heart from the beginning of his reign that was placed upon him at the time of his ordination from Samuel the prophet. Because he did not trust and put his faith in the Lord, and because he turned to the medium to give him the answer to his problems instead of seeking God diligently, his mission ended in defeat and the disastrous death of him and his family.

Another example in the Bible of someone who allowed another person to deprive her of her joy was Queen Vashti. Queen Vashti was the wife of King Ahasuerus, a ruler of great wealth and fame whose kingdom, Persia, included 127 provinces, which spread from India to Ethiopia. In the third year of his reign, King Ahasuerus held a great celebration that lasted for 180 days. The king requested Vashti's presence before their guests, but she refused to come. It is believed that she failed to answer her husband's summons because he was drunk with wine at the festival. Her decision to revolt against the king displayed open disrespect and a refusal to submit to his authority. In the end, it caused her to forfeit her place in the palace as queen.

The same is true for a child of God; you want to go ahead and obey the Word of God even if you feel that someone will make a spectacle of you. If you refuse to yield to those who have authority over you and always are having a fractious continence and attitude, when promotion time comes around, you are once again excused due to your inflexible refusal to submit to authority and failure to outride longsuffering for the betterment of the kingdom. Once you try to analyze others problems and issues, it will steal your glee. Whether it is for a moment, a day, or a month, it can cause a loss in the end. Determining the extent, dimension, capacity, or measurement of how much joy is in your life due to other events or clamor concerned with and understanding only the easily apparent and obvious things of life.

The state of wretchedness, poverty, trouble, misfortune, and calamity will try to bring an eclipse into your pathway. This eclipse will come like a thief in the night to elude your enjoyment and pleasure of praise, worship, and fellowship. Basic eclipse experiences, the darkening of a felicitous body and heavenly beauty, can cause lost joy. An eclipse occurs when the vague sign of one object in space falls on another object or when an object moves in front of another to block its light. A *solar eclipse* takes place when the sun appears to become dark, as the moon passes between the sun and the earth. A *lunar eclipse* occurs when the moon becomes dark, as it passes through the shadow of the earth. The earth and the moon always cast shadows into space and the moon orbits the earth about once every month. Likewise, the moon most often escapes being eclipsed by passing over or below the shadow of the earth. Therefore, a solar or a lunar eclipse can occur only when the earth, sun, and moon are in nearly a straight line.

A solar eclipse occurs when the moon's shadow sweeps across the face of the earth. Visually, there are three kinds of eclipses: *total, annular* and *partial*. A total eclipse occurs if the moon completely blots out the sun. An annular eclipse occurs if the moon darkens only the middle of the sun, leaving a bright ring around the edge. A partial eclipse occurs if the moon covers only part of the sun.

In the supernatural, an eclipse occurs in the life of the

believer when you put something else before God, such as become an idol worshiper or try to serve two masters. The inferior object or subject will attempt to distract or sabotage all spiritual evidence of improvement or development in order to win over to an unspiritual or unmoral lifestyle. However, a solar or lunar attack comes when your life begins to line up horizontally with the will of God, just as you begin to walk into your purpose. They will dispense severe forces of bleak and dreary dark shapes casting upon faith and hope with doubt by definite but unspecific cutting off light from you. In addition, it sends a widespread growing darkness bringing in dimness, doubt, and sadness that exudes vague indication, faint suggestion or unrealistic appearance to natural vision of the believer.

God is ready and willing to give you a breakthrough against the resistance of the oppressor who is trying to give you a breakdown and take your composure and composition. By, putting someone else's emotions and feelings before self, one refuses to become narcissist. The spirit of narcissism is someone thinking only of himself or herself causing many to lose values of morality and forfeit self-footing or grips with all reality. One who begins to think there is no problem do or committing evil. *Webster's Dictionary* defines *narcissism* as self-love. We feel liberal in the bond of peace, by loving and serving each in the spirit of meekness and lowliness.

Brothers and sisters you must be patient and tolerable when it comes to associating with other believers; God creations are all peculiar and remarkable in His eyesight. Meanwhile, do not become jade in well doing, for in due season, you will reap what you sowed. Henceforth, many of us need a refresher course on how to sow love, peace, joy and happiness into the lives of others, which brings forth a much better harvest in advancing the kingdom of God or building the body of believers. As free-will agents make sound and sapient choices, which deliberate things in your mind. In retrospect, no one can take anything that God has given to you unless you freely turn it over. It can be a counter command allowable or with admission; you open your spiritual house and allow a seizure. The Lord Jesus knows that man cannot complete this race alone; therefore, He left a manual to the race, the Word of God, to redirect and lead you to the finish line on a straight and narrow path.

## Champions of Joy—Finish Your Race

Before one becomes a champion of joy, you must finish the race for Jesus. Jesus is the forerunner who won souls for the kingdom of heaven by paying the highest cost. He never got faint or weary since He relied on living water to quench His thirst.

A race is a competition or test of speed, usually while doing some kind of physical activity like in running, rowing, swimming, riding, driving, or flying. Various kinds of recreational racing were popular with the people of ancient Greece. The successful runner in the early Greek games was crowned with a wreath of laurel leaves and was honored by all the people. The Bay Laurel tree is an evergreen shrub with large, glossy, and aromatic leaves. The foliage of the tree was woven into wreaths to represent fame, honor, and victory. In ancient Greece, the citizens would play sports to see who would come out the conqueror; who would overmaster his or her opponent and would emerge the victor, the winner of the battle or race. This Christian expedition is not held on an entertainment field; it is a spiritual battle fought in the spirit realm over your mortal soul. The winner will be either Satan or the Lord. *Webster's Dictionary* defines *game* as "activity engaged in for diversion or amusement, a procedure or strategy for gaining an end."

In the New Testament, there are direct references to sports

competition, predominantly in Paul's letters. For those living in Corinth in the first century, representation from competitive games would be simply spoken not only from everyday life but also because it was the location of the Isthmian games, A.D. 51, an event second only to the Olympics in status.[1] Paul used the footrace as a diagram of Christian endurance, reminding them that even though all contestants run in the race, only the winner receives the prize (1 Cor. 9:24). He used the stern and relentless training of the athletes contending in the games as a correlation to the obedience required for the Christian life, affirming that all dedicated athletes must tolerate some physical training in order to win a perishable wreath. If athletes do all this to win a perishable crown, how much more should Christians endure and undergo discipline to receive an imperishable crown (v. 25). Paul uses himself as a model of someone who did not run the race pointlessly or without cause. The runners in the games ran toward a fixed mark, possibly a concrete or unanimated object; today there are lines marking the end of a racecourse. The runner did not run carelessly but for one purpose, and that was to finish the race (Phil. 3:12–14). Likewise, you must have sound mental and physical restraint so that the spirit man can bring itself under strict control (1 Cor 9:26–27). Just like Paul, all believers must battle and struggle with sinful desires with the merciless zeal of competitors in any given arena or field. Paul used athletic games as an analogy for his entire life, concluding that he had "finished the race" and was therefore ready to receive the "crown of righteousness" (2 Tim. 4:7–8, NKJV). To sum it all up, the finishing line is Jesus who is the source and perfecter of your faith.

Listed below are various speeds of walking, sprinting, hiking, or running. Read over the list and determine at what speed you are moving through life.

1. Vigorous runner

2. Hurtling sprinter

3. Aimless stroller

4. Power walker

5. Steady pacer

6. Dutiful jogger

7. Steadfast sprinter

8. Committed marathon runner

Are you moving too slowly in your spiritual life? Too quickly? If you are doing either, it is probably time to change your speed. The best runners start and end by sprinting, but pace themselves between the start and finish lines. The choice is yours: would you like to finish exhausted and weary or invigorated and rejuvenated?

Christians who go through the race of life like vigorous runners busy about kingdom business. They are not busybodies, but are diligently about establishing the vineyard. They do not move slowly or aimlessly. They are ready and willing to answer the Father's next call. This individual has eagerness and enthusiasm accompanied by a natural discernment.

Christians who move along the track like a hurtling sprinter react very quickly, not praying or pondering before making decisions or jumping into new projects. They do not wait to hear the voice of the Lord for direction or insight. They leap with aimless sprints, lacking follow-up, and are always in a hurry. Everything is done in a rush and without any, or very little, caution or efficiency. They become very exhausted, fatigued, and even jaded in the race, which causes them to lose effectiveness.

When Christians begin to move like an aimless stroller, who strolls along taking inattentive, slow strides, they are lukewarm in their commitments and lack enthusiasm. Their walk is inconsistent, and they waver in all their decisions, making life more complicated than it has to be. They will never reach a normal level of efficiency due to indecision and failure to surrender their lives totally in the care of the omnipotent One.

The power walker strides with overwhelming confidence and with a positive attitude, coming from optimistic view on life. They are very influential in witnessing to others and spreading the good news. They are leaders, who have divine grace and radiant anointing upon them and their personal endeavors. They are not complainers, nor do they show pretentious or hypocritical behavior, when things do not turn out for their good. They race with vibrant joy.

The Christian who keeps a steady pace, either walking or running, must have extraordinary stamina and a high resistance to fatigue, hardship, or distress. They race with much endurance and strength if they have been trained and guided under the authority and unction of the Holy Ghost. Pacers run the race with a set speed, delivering the gospel message to the lost. They are prepared to be steadfast and unmovable in the test that is before them, and their perseverance makes them successful in overcoming evil.

The dutiful joggers are unvarying and faithful in their performance. With a focus on the goal, they neither slow down nor speed up too much. They are not easily moved, but instead have positive foundation in Christ Jesus.

The steadfast sprinter runs the race full speed, but can last for only a short distance. These Christians participate in the ministry for a brief period, fervently working on a number of projects and ministering with passion, but they soon become tired or overcome with worry. They are quick to withdraw when things are not going smoothly. They are very easily distracted from the goals by challenges or setbacks that require more attention or energy.

The committed marathon runner is an enduring messenger of the gospel of Jesus Christ. They do not become weary in well-doing. They have learned how to pace themselves through tribulation and persecution. They are in the race for the long haul.

Although there are many contestants in this race and many ways of proceeding, only God can tell you how to complete your course. There are numerous passages in the Bible about running the Christian race, and these all are wonderful illustrations from biblical passage of a Christian runner.

> The race is not to the swift, Nor the battle to the strong. Nor bread to the wise, Nor riches to men of understanding, Nor favor to men of skill; But time and chance happen to them all.
>
> —Ecclesiastes 9:11, NKJV

> Do you know that those who run in a race all run, but one receives the prize? Run in such a way that you may obtain it. And everyone who competes for the prize is temperate in all things. Now they do it to obtain a perishable crown, but we for an imperishable crown. Therefore I run thus: not with uncertainty. Thus I fight, not as one who beats the air.
>
> —1 Corinthians 9:24–27, NKJV

> And I went up by revelation, and communicated to them that gospel which I preach among the Gentiles,

but privately to those who were of reputations, lest my means I might run, or had run, in vain.

—GALATIANS 2:2, NKJV

You ran well. Who hindered you from obeying the truth? This persuasion does not come from Him who calls you.

—GALATIANS 5:7, NKJV

Let us lay aside every weight, and the sin which so easily ensnares us, and let us run with endurance the race that is set before us.

—HEBREWS 12:1, NKJV

Paul explains that for believers, the race of life is a contest with many contestants. It is not a physical competition between the runners; rather it is a spiritual race that needs to be completed by all candidates. There should be no competition since everyone is on the same team and have the same objective, to win souls for Jesus, while we finish our commissioned course. As various dangerous barricades, hazardous obstructions, and treacherous defenders come your way, keep your focus on Jesus Christ, who is the Supreme Runner; everyone has been commissioned to complete or finish the spiritual path in life with a steady pace, not a sprint, thereby having potential to stand against the wiles of the enemy. When the believer sets his or her eyes on the cross and presses through all the stress and tension in his or her life, he or she will find a prize at the end of the race, in the name of Jesus. Keep reaching for the ultimate goal in Christ Jesus, so that you and everyone one the

Lord's team can finishes the race a winner and receive the heavenly prize—eternal salvation.

Jesus Christ, the high ambassador of God, ran His course of life and completed His race with overwhelming joy. Paul tells the believers not to look at life as sprint but as a marathon. Paul's goal in completing his race was the same goal that Christ had. He did not want to leave this earth without finishing divine assignment. The believer must never forget that life is a race, and your goal is to strive for the character of Christ. In addition to taking away the memory of your sinful past, Christ died for and rose on the third day to give you a new beginning. In the meantime, honor the memory of your salvation and celebrate the day of your deliverance as a memorial of the old man dying and the new man coming into existence.

You must leave behind your sinful lifestyle and the old habitual ways that will keep you in religious bondage. We should not want to leave planet Earth without finishing our assignment, so do not think that there is nothing more that can be accomplished for the work of the ministry. Reach for those things that pertain to the knowledge of Jesus Christ. To win this race, we must continue to have the work of the ministry in the forefront of our mind and keep all perspective goals and aspirations in line with the Word of God. In the Olympics or other races, the winner often receives a medal and sometimes a cash prize; therefore, in this spiritual race, the champion will receive an interminable crown of glory and will be with God and Jesus. The believer who wants to become a true conqueror and winner must try to attain heavenly perfection by following after Christ. I count not myself to have apprehended, but I leave those things in my past behind as I reach forth in life and move towards God's glory. I press toward the mark for the prize of the high calling of God in Christ Jesus (Phil. 3:12–14).

What Paul meant when he wrote Philippians 3:12–14 was that he chose to be free from all cares and would finish the spiritual course with exceeding joy through the aid of the Holy Spirit. Paul knew that he would be able to finish his mission with the aid of the Holy Spirit because he knew that he had no power of his own. You must identify with Paul's point of view. The best way for you to have joy in this life is to do the work of the ministry so that when you win your race, there will be a prize waiting for you—an unchangeable life with Jesus. What an awesome prize!

Paul was focused on finishing his race, just as his predecessor, Jesus, was. The words that mark success in the race for spiritual redemption come from the parable of the talents (Matt. 25:14–30). It describes the reward that will be given to the propitious steward. In that passage, Jesus explained that the reward for the good and faithful servant would be that he would be greeted with the following when he gets to heaven:

> Well done, thou good and faithful servant: thou hast been faithful over a few things, I will make thee ruler over many things: enter thou into the joy of thy lord.
>
> —MATTHEW 25:21, NKJV

In this passage, Jesus was giving the disciples a parable about wise and foolish servants. Servants that obey the instruction of the Master will be rewarded in the end. All obedience and surrender will bring in a great profit to the servant of Christ.

There is no better time to live for Jesus in the spirit of peace, love, and joy, and to finish this race, handing off the baton of unity. God does not care what color, nationality, or creed we are. When we stand before Him on Judgment Day, He is going to judge based on our work, endurance, and perseverance in the ministry of Jesus Christ. Just as it's easier to win a race when someone is right there handing you water in the time of thirst, it is better to run this Christian marathon when we have other brothers and sisters who are endorsing, nurturing, and encouraging us in the Word of God.

In conclusion, there are no runners-up in the race of life. There is an earthly and a heavenly reward waiting for each person who fights the good fight, defends the feeble minded, and supports the weak. A true champion is one who puts others above himself, bearing and carrying their burdens, taking on the challenge of the call of God, and maintaining a steady stride in the race. You should not put your trust in your own ability to be victorious in this life, for there is no prize if you seek only recognition from man and not from God. Men are not the key to your future and cannot offer you much once the race is over.

These things are irrelevant to one's purpose and destiny that God has mapped out. If someone thinks the only way to have timeless joy is by gaining material possessions on this earth, he had better take a closer look at history to see all the famous people who died from AIDS, alcoholism, and drug overdose. They all thought that the more they obtained in their life, the more peace, happiness, and joy they would have. People who seek status and approval from the world, running for material rewards, will find that their pursuit was in vain. Unrestricted joy can't be bought; joy has no price tag, and it only comes through the Holy Spirit who delivers it from Jesus, your mediator, for receiving all gifts from the Father. He is waiting for you to ask for it. His Word tells you in the Book of James, "Ye ask, and receive not, because ye ask amiss, that ye may consume it upon your lusts" (James 4:3). Ask the Lord to pace your steps, strengthen your stride, and give you good stamina so that you may complete the marathon of life.

Paul was expressing to the New Testament church how to earnestly encourage other brothers and sisters in Christ, how to have hope and joy while rejoicing in salvation and redemption during times of affliction. To learn how to admit faults to one another is not necessarily to be taken as a command to admit every sin to another believer, but, to identify when one has done wrong. Christians are to be prepared and ready to offer prayers for each other to reinforce each other's spiritual life (James 5:16). The believer who holds fast to self-control is able to possess the inner strength to control his or her desires, actions, and thoughts. The sound doctrine of Jesus Christ builds up in faith and protects against corrupting influences and manipulation by false teachers. As ambassadors of Christ, we must operate under faith. The believer's salvation cannot be achieved by human effort or merit, but it is instead granted by way of God's mercy and grace. His grace protected man from banishment, but through Christ's sacrifice to save humankind. The cleansing and washing by His blood provided regeneration and renewing by the aid of the Holy Ghost.

## HAVE JOY REGARDLESS

Paul utters another example of having joy regardless of circumstances or situations. All followers of the gospel of Jesus should have fulfilling joy and be like-minded, having the same love and commending spirit. Jesus had joy. Philippians 2:6–7 says that He thought it not robbery to be equal with God, and He made Himself of no esteem status or honorable position, by taking upon Himself as a servant to human life, who came to Earth not in the image of God but in the body of man.

In the above scripture, anyone can see that Christ even gave up His place in heaven to come to Earth and become equal to the believer to make evident how possible it is to have eternal joy and peace even in a worldly domain. Jesus tells the believer that if he or she wants to help with building the kingdom, let him or her follow after Christ. He said, "If anyone serves Me, let him follow Me; and where I am, there My servant will be also. If anyone serves Me, him My Father will honor" (John 12:26, NKJV). Paul prompts the church at Philippi to have joy in the midst of struggles that they face for the sake of the gospel of Jesus Christ, for when Christ returns they will receive a heavenly crown. He says that if they have any questions, they should pursue his example of joy, which follows after the example of Jesus.

There will be some days when you feel despondent or unhappy; this is a trap of the enemy to bait you back into old habits and ways. Wait on the Lord and He shall renew your strength.

> But those who wait on the LORD Shall renew their strength; They shall mount up with wings like eagles, They shall run and not be weary, They shall walk and not faint.

> —ISAIAH 40:31, NKJV

The faithfulness of God is steadfast and unfailing in keeping His promises to deliver you from the enemy, who is trying to make you give up when you feel weighed down and overwhelmed with attacks that have become unbearable. However, never give up because God is able to bring you through any encounter with victory in Christ Jesus (1 John 5:4–5). As soon as you declare that you have been born of God through conviction in Jesus Christ, God has put His own Spirit in you.

Deeming God's public affirmation of Jesus is the only way to have undying existence, when you accept as true that God's salvation is free and you have privileges to answered prayer and forgiveness of past, present, and future failures. Thus you are able to overcome the temptations, false teachings, and persecutions of the sinful world system. A lifestyle of sinful living will subtly remove joy from its dwelling within your heart, making a way for evil. Even when you desire to do right, the mind will overcrowd the heart if you are not anchored and fixed in Jesus. That is why Jesus instructs the believer to watch as well as pray, for the devil is like a roaring lion seeking and lurking to find whom he may devour. Guard your joy and peace in the Lord.

## THE ADVERSARY WISHES TO TAKE YOUR JOY

In Romans 7:17–25, Paul is saying that even though he knows to do well, evil is always trying to tell him that what he has done is not good enough. No matter how dutiful you are in resisting the enemy, temptation is lurking around on every corner. Temptation is there through the flesh to sabotage all of your godly intentions and character. The devil is constantly bringing allies together to fight against the sons of God to steal your joy. Fight for joy and peace; they will give you the upper hand in your spiritual fight with the adversary, because when you have joy and peace you can see clearly with your spiritual eyes, helping you know how to anticipate the traps and snares that are ahead. You can hear God's still, calm voice as He speaks and gives you direction and instruction with your spiritual ears. You must stay in the Word and keep the Word hidden in your heart for the days when you feel defeated.

Sons and daughters of God must not become victims of the devil by letting him crowd your mind with thoughts of defeat and failure. The heart of Jesus Christ makes you feel that there is enough joy in your life and you can take on all hurdles that come your way. Esther was so overcome with great joy that she gave a feast in honor of God's victory and many people of the land converted to Judaism (Esther 8:17).

On the day of the Last Supper, Jesus sent Peter and John into the city to reserve the room for them to eat in that night. He told them to find a man carrying a pitcher with water and to ask him if he had an extra room in which Jesus and His disciples could eat the Passover meal (Luke 22:7–12). That night Jesus began to tell his disciples that it would be the last meal that they would have together. Then he turned to Peter and told him that the enemy wanted to try or test him. Jesus knew he would be targeted as prey, so He gave Peter words of encouragement by promising him that He would pray that Peter's faith would not fail and that he would not succumb to the enemy. Jesus was fully aware that Peter would later renounce Him as his acquaintance or associate, his Lord, his teacher, and, most importantly, his Savior. Still, he told Peter the desire of the evil one so that he would pay attention and not fall into Satan's hands. Jesus said, "Simon, Simon! Indeed, Satan has asked for you, that he may sift you as wheat" (Luke 22:31, NKJV). Jesus was making reference of how Satan wanted to sidetrack Peter as he had Judas, in the area of physical temptation Jesus prayed for Peter as He prays for all who follow Him (v. 32). Peter was unaware of his capability to sin, so he quickly replied that he would go with the Lord anywhere, including prison and death. The Lord prophesied that Peter faith would be tested, and that he would deny knowing Jesus three times before the dawn of the next morning (Luke 22:34).

So are you still wondering who has taken your joy? No one has the power to take it if you do not give it away. Do not permit the enemy to deceive you into thinking that it cannot be recovered. All throughout God's Word, believers are exhorted about the deception and control the enemy has under the heavens. The enemy will never let you have joy, so never believe that things in his territory can bring you joy and happiness. They are all temporal; none of them will last forever. Even so, everything that God gives is long term. That means it will retain its value and benefit to your life over a long period of time. Allowing God to come into your heart and mind brings great dividends and transforms your life with the newness of joy and admiration.

The Book of Ecclesiastes says it will do man no good to profit in his material gain and possession, then die and leave it all behind (1:3–4). Ecclesiastes also tells us that there is a time for everything, even a time to rejoice in the Lord (3:22). If you could see a video of how your wealth, house, land, money, jewelry, and other material riches would be spent by your children after you died, what kind of stewards would you teach them to be today? The response and actions of them receiving their inheritance would possibly be different from what you expected. Imagine if you witnessed your son using the money to do illegal things, one daughter giving it all away to a boyfriend, and another spending it all on shopping sprees such that within five or ten years' time they had spent and crushed all of your possessions and wealth. There would be nothing for them to leave for their children. How would you feel?

Maybe you would feel like Solomon, who learned that it is better to have heavenly wealth than earthly wealth alone, because temporal wealth accomplishes nothing; it all becomes worthless without the help of God's divine knowledge or perception. In other words, during his lifetime, through godly insight, he learned that nothing has real value if you lack absolute joy and peace. Without that, he was unprofitable to the kingdom of God. Having material possessions without the love of God makes individuals conceited and boastful. Nothing seems to have spiritual value or worth, which is why so many people spend their lives trying to obtain earthly possessions while never finding joy in living or reason and purpose for their existence.

You can have joy in your laboring for the Lord, and He will give the increase, according to His riches in glory. Therefore, if you want to have joy, have compassion for others—visiting the sick, feeding the poor, clothing the less fortunate, and housing the homeless. Those things will give you true joy. Remember that Jesus had no house or means of transportation, but he had unvarying joy.

Many things may be going amiss in your life thus far, yet you can still have steadfast happiness. Yes, the enemy will come to sift your joy and peace, but Jesus has left His joy, which is your strength (Neh. 8:10). That is why you must ask earnestly and meditate on the things of the Lord to keep you from falling into the snares and traps of your adversary. In the garden of Gethsemane, Jesus told the disciples the importance of not falling into the temptation to the chief fiend, by praying daily without pause or vacillation. One of Jesus' last commands for the disciples was to pray so that they would not to fall into temptation (Luke 22:40). Daily prayer will enhance one's relationship and fellowship with God, which provides substantial encouragement to the heart. This causes the heart to be complete and filled with joy.

## Lost Joy Through Persecution and Torment

In the Book of Job, Job endured persecution and torment through longsuffering, but in the midst of his trials, he still had exceeding joy (Job 1–42).

As I began to research the Scriptures to find the answer, and I could envision how Job had to have joy in the midst of his problems, because he never doubted God. Yes, he did query and interrogate God's intent, but I do not believe it can be viewed in the same content as doubt. After God permitted Satan to strike Job the second time, Job was shocked when he heard about his children being taken away in a whirlwind and that nothing or no one was left standing in the house except the servants who gave him the report. He realized, however, that all things were in the hands of his Lord, who established all creation. Even when Job went into mourning over the loss of his children and his earthly possessions, he fell into a humbled posture and began to call out to El Shaddai (1:6–21). Then his wife became very angry and told Job that he should curse his God and die for what God had done to his body and in taking their children away (2:9–10). Later, when his friends heard about the evil that had come upon his household, they came to express deep sorrow with Job. However, he went into solitude and did not desire any contact from visitors (3:7). He wanted to be left alone with God to find out why this great disaster had come in his life. During his brief hour of seclusion, he did not want to worship or praise God. When he finally asked his friends for their counsel, all they gave him was judgment.

In the course of Job's days of persecution, he began to wonder whether or not he had the ability to withstand his present trials. The wisdom of God that made him successful in the past was not with him. Job was in grave need of spiritual support, but his friends proved to be undependable and unreliable advisors. Finally, Job pleaded with his friends to stop accusing him of any wrongdoing in the way he lived his life. He told them that God would show him to be innocent of any act of behavior that was askew (6:29). Job told his friend Bildad in Job 9:15–28 that he will make a petition unto God to stand before him as an innocent man, not sinless, but innocent of any sin that could account for his sufferings and loss.

Job's response to his friend Zophar, recorded in Job 13:15, was that in the midst of his trials, He would trust and believe in God, while defending himself before Him. Job did not understand why God was not responding to his plea for help, but he had absolute confidence when the Lord showed up, He would declare him not guilty (23:10). Furthermore, he acknowledged that God was the only One that could blot out his transgressions and iniquity. In order to truly and successfully recognize who stolen one's joy, there must a trust in other believers as a support system, so that you can be encouraged and strengthened along life's dangerous highways and byways (Prov. 27:17).

In Job 14:1, 2 and 4, Job tells us that man who is conceived by a woman is of not many days and excessive of trouble. He sprouts up like a flower and is cut down like a weed because life is brief and incompetent, man will disappear like a shadow and cease at will. Jehovah God is the only one who can bring a clean thing out of an unclean anything. In the beginning, God created man like a tree that revives even after it has been cut down; but sin separated mankind for immorality. Now man is seen as a flower that lives its short life and returns to the dust and ashes from which he was formed. Jesus is the one who can give to man the distinction to ageless life through His resurrected blood.

Job still trying to fight to keep his joy, tells his friends, in Job 16:19–20 that God will be his advocate and He will resume him to foregone joy, for He sees his tears and knows they are sincere. In addition, he points out to his friend that God has hidden the truth from their hearts of understanding; therefore, He will exalt Job for their condemnation and conviction. It was a test for not only Job, but for his friends to extend love and compassion during his time of lugubrious disapproval and lamentation (17:4).

Later, he became sarcastic because he felt his friends did not know what they were talking about, accusing him of bringing this upon himself. The upright men shall be astonished and amazed while the innocent and pure shall shake himself in opposition to the hypocrite. The righteous shall interdict his way and outride with decent direction of strength (17:8–9).

The enemy presented himself again in Job's friend Eliphaz, who would not submit Job to have any peace over this situation. Eliphaz's peculiar reasoning to Job's current issue was all things have their origin in God; man's giving back what God has given him does not enhance God in anyway. Indeed, God is indifferent to man's goodness consisting of kindness and generosity to all mankind.

Job defends himself once more, as he tries to encourage and resupply himself with joy. Job is thwarted over his apparent inability to receive a clear word from God. He answers Eliphaz's reply, saying that he treasures God's stature more than his daily food and that he is fully aware that God is testing him. He realizes that the testing is not for purging away his sinful rubbish, but to bring him out as a spotless and precious creation (23:10).

Then, his friend Eliphaz tells him that God is permitting this, because he must have been defiant or opposing to God's law. Likewise, God's light will lay open, will allow everything to be seen or left unprotected, that is not like Him. Many know not the direction of the nature nor abide in the paths of obedience. The murderer rises with the just, seeking to eradicate the poor and needy. The thief comes out a night to commit his crimes. The adulterer watches and waits for sunset surmise to commit the act of infidelity, even going about hiding the real nature of the immoral character. The world uses darkness as their element or the medium in which they thrive. By contrast, God's law is the light against which they rebel (24:13–15).

Job's friends began to speak crazy things to try to justify their defense against Job, but Job remained sober until it was his time to speak. He told his friends that he would not speak any evil to God about what was taking place in his body and mind. Job gave his friends a parable, telling them that if they continued to compare him as an unrighteous man, God will prove and vindicate him as an innocent and righteous man. God would deal with them for providing injudicious, ill-advised, and unjustified counsel. Job tells his friends that he will continue believing and trusting in God despite his denied justice. He is aware that God permitted his body to be afflicted with pain and sorrow. Job states that as long as there is breath in his body, he will be steadfast and not speak any evil against God nor let his tongue utter deceit. Job refused to receive the counsel of his three friends and comments that his integrity will be with him until his death.

He held fast to acting justly and would not charge or blame himself for a fault. Job told his friends who falsely accused him, that a day would come when they would be treated as perverse men. As long as they felt that they are more virtuous or pious, God would figure their heart (27:1–11).

In Job 32 it tells of another friend standing around listening to the comments and dialogue between Job and his friends. Elihu decided to give his opinion to Job and his friends by telling them they are liable to erroneous or inaccurate circumstances. He told Job that he was being fallible and not seeing precise and clear, for what he was being confronted. Job should accept God's reprimand for his graceless manner. Elihu insisted on speaking up because Job was being prideful and his friends, becoming furious, were no longer giving logical or rational opinions. Elihu reminded them that not all great men are invariably judicious, neither does the mature expound on the supposed thoughts from God (32:9).

And, in Job 33:2–4, he turned to Job and addressed him with his heartfelt words of love and not conviction; through the knowledge of God.

Elihu shared with Job that it is utterly important to give judicious counsel, while coming from a just and honest heart. He wanted his words to be for truth and knowledge with clarity, as he allowed the Spirit of God to use him. Yet, he wouldn't be in Job's presence on that day if it were not for the Almighty.

Elihu warned Job to take heed to God's warnings, he did not come as the others to discourage or condemn of any impropriety or sinful intentions. God speaks to men in order to deter them from the sinful desires, for it is the one thing that can withdraw man from his purpose or destiny, while hiding his pride from himself. Listening to God's monitions will protect against perishing or early death (33:17–18).

Elihu was illiterate and artless minded in trying to undermine Job's relationship with God, still insisting that Job needed to repent with a sincere heart for some misdeed. He told Job that when he repented to God, everything that was occurring in his life would desist and he would return to the old life. Job's prayers would be answered, favor would come back, and his joy would be returned (33:25–26).

Job's problem was justifying himself to others throughout his entire physical persecution and mental anticipation. God was trying to move Job to the next level of blessing right before his accuser, the devil. He allowed the enemy to come in to take his joy through his trials and tests, but God sent a true friend that gave him wise counsel and encouragement. And his friend, Elihu, told Job's friends that Job was not an unreasonably or disobedient man but God was preserving him for a specific reason, henceforth, he did need to turn to God for understanding, for He has all power in every situation.

In the story of Job, I received two messages that God was projecting and leaping out to catch my attention. The first was of Satan, ratifying him to come before the presence of God and incriminate a brother of faith, Job, who was innocent of any unlawfulness. Second, God knew Job's heart, and he would go through these light afflictions while maintaining his joy regardless how hopeless and impossible everything appeared around him. Job was still going to give God the highest laudation. You must do the same, no matter how the enemy comes to attack your health or wealth, keep serving and living for the Lord. God knows all things regarding His children and the universe, Satan does not. He has no way of knowing how much you love God, because he does not know the nature of your new heart. On the other hand, he does know the nature of your old heart, since he had the same heart condition and state, expounded in Jeremiah 17:9–10. And the Lord would remove Job's deep spite cup of suffering and excruciation, because God has all power in his hands on heaven and earth. Only God can amputate the evil from your heart.

## RESTORED JOY

Job had godly sorrow being full of pride and his own rectitude, because every man is unrighteous in the eyesight of God. The blood of Jesus covers the deathless soul and gives clear perception for the Father to see chastity or virtue. God restored Job's wealth and family. The Lord God blessed Job's latter days greater than his beginning, and replenished him with a great compensation (Job 42:12).

Job's joy was reformed and restored, and he lived a full life. In the story of Job, you can see an example of someone being persecuted and tormented for righteous sake, because God wants to get the glory out of Job's undeniable proceedings to present to Satan that he doesn't know His child's heart. But I think the most important lesson for me was to see someone temporary lose their joy, because they did not have the answer to why they were going through trials. And the same is true with the child of God today. You must without delay commence and hold on to all hope and peace—without those two you cannot have joy.

The child of God must understand how important it is to keep your hope and everything, regardless of the opposition. We should be intrigued by the testimony of Job's suffering and persecution; he went through it and came out victorious. The number of animals he had were twice as many, God replaced his sons and daughters that he lost in the whirlwind, and he received longevity of life—he lived to be a 140 years old. What a great example! What a better outcome when you keep your joy: healthier days on earth, longer life span, wealth to share with the kingdom of God, and more earthly possessions to share with others in the family of God.

Let us take this moment to give God sober, fervent love

and admiration for all the wonderful things He has invested in our recuperation from the trials and tests of the adversary. Praise Him for all that He has done in your life and all that He has brought you through. Thank Him for keeping you on the mountain and strengthening you when you were in the valley. Thank Him for keeping you on the ship Zion during the storm. Thank Him for strengthening your mind in condition of rarity of peace when the enemy was trying to terminate and kill you. Thank Him for His grace and mercy that allowed goodness to be with you all the days thus far. Thank Him for His promise of eternal life. Thank Him for love and hope in Jesus Christ.

After, seeing what God can do and bring you through, determine to fight the fight and not allow the enemy or anyone of take your joy.

Below is a questionnaire to see if you still have your joy:

1. Are you temperamental?
2. Do you find yourself easily agitated with others?
3. Do you feel that you are on an emotional rollercoaster?
4. Do you maintain or sustain peace when others have disharmony or disarrayed lifestyles?
5. Do you want to take revenge on those who hurt or harm you?
6. Do you find yourself having power struggles at work, at home, or at church?
7. Do you feel no matter what others do to try to make you happy, you are feeling miserable?
8. Do you not give God praise when you are going through trials?
9. Do you have peace?

10. Are you a peacemaker?

11. Do you easily lose your temper?

12. Do you wake up in the morning giving God praise?

13. Do you easily lose your peace?

14. Do you easily give in so as to fit in with the crowd?

15. Do you find yourself not praying as often as you feel you should?

16. Do you feel yourself unworthy before God?

17. Do you feel miserable all the time?

18. Are you content in who you are in Christ Jesus?

19. Do you find it hard to have peace in the midst of your circumstances?

20. Do you feel that you are more than a conqueror in Christ Jesus?

21. Are you full of delight?

22. Are you happy in Jesus?

23. Do you need material things and possessions to make you feel happy?

24. Do you need to be validated or accepted by others?

25. Do you feel that you have salvation?

26. Do you have hope?

27. Do you feel miserable for no reason?

28. Do you bring joy to a room?

29. When you come into a room do people desist talking?

30. Are you a worshiper?

31. Do you associate yourself with people who are like you?

32. Do you find yourself always witnessing to others?

33. Do you have joy in your testimonies?

34. Are you full of joy?

35. Do you delight yourself in the things of the Lord?

36. Do you feel as if someone has taken your joy?

37. Are you trusting in the Lord?

38. Is God first in your life?

39. Do you feel as if you have left your first love?

40. Do you believe that God is on your side?

41. Do you have the fruit of the Spirit?

42. Are you producing good fruit?

43. Is joy one of your attributes of fruit?

44. Do you know what joy is?

45. Do think that you should keep your joy in the time of tribulation?

46. Do you encourage others to express their joy?

47. Do you believe in having peace regardless?

48. Are you sometimes or constantly unhappy?

49. Do need to have many friends to be happy?

50. Are your friends the only people that bring joy into your life?

## 4

## WILL MY JOY SUSTAIN ITSELF?

*And the ransomed of the LORD shall return, and
come to Zion with songs and everlasting joy upon
their heads: They shall obtain joy and gladness.*

—ISAIAH 35:10

I N THIS CHAPTER YOU'LL see how God paid the ransom
for your sustaining joy. The price tag was marked paid in
full to cover the ransom for total and immutable joy and
gladness, freed mankind from all penalties, making amends
or atoning for all unrighteousness and restoring us to favor by
establishing revision and improvement.

You are now a worthwhile and valuable asset to the advancement of the dominion of God. Tested by others and outside
informality, you must have no fear and be unmovable. One of
the most outstanding testimonies you can use from the Bible
regarding someone's joy being kept during a test, was David.
David permitted God to disarm his enemies and remove equiv-
ocal fear or hostility from their inward parts. On numerous
occasions the adversary tested him, as Saul continued to attack
David's life due to jealousy and envy that was brought on by
a spirit from the Lord. Because Saul's heart was not right; he

could be used to test or persecute David. But David's heart was like God's, therefore he did what someone with the heart of God does, he prayed for his enemies and did good to them that persecuted him.

You will see in the scriptures how often Saul sought after David, however, He refused Saul's authorization to excoriate his joy. Yes, he did flee him many times for his own safety and withstood taking vengeance into his own hands. I believe it was so easy for Saul to fall unto the mendacious management of the adversary, because Saul was chosen by the people and not by God; therefore he was going to do the things that pleased the people. When the people gave David more accolades than him, Saul became resentful, jealous, suspicious, and wanted to kill David. David was dealing with the same attitude in his house that happen in early scriptures regarding Cain murdering his brother Abel. Abel gave a more pleasing offering to God than Cain. The same is true with the believer today. If someone else appears to be more blessed, you may become jealous and try to extinct their reputation and calumniate their name because you are not receiving the same attention or blessings from God as others. Saul's character was that of an inexperienced and childish leader, full of malice and strife; he continued to operate out of his flesh.

## God Kept David

The first attempt on David's life is in 1 Samuel 18:9–11. Saul became watchful of David's actions from that day forth. The next day an evil spirit from God came upon Saul and he prophesied in the midst of the house as David played the harp with skill as he did everyday. Then, Saul took his javelin and threw it at David, meantime stating he would kill or punish him. Fortunately he hit the wall instead.

The second attempt is recorded in 1 Samuel 19:9–11. The evil spirit from the Lord was upon Saul while he sat in his house with his spear in his hand as David played his harp. Saul sought to kill or exterminate David while aiming a spear at David, trying to pin him against the wall with it. But, David dashed out of Saul's sight and the spear went into the wall. That night David fled for his life and returned home to his wife. Saul sent messengers to David's house watching and waiting from him to return there in the morning. David's wife Michal told him to leave the town that night because tomorrow her father was going to slay him.

The third attempt on David's life is in 1 Samuel 21:10, when Saul was after him again while he was with his friend, King Achish of Gath. Even though David intended to flee from Saul, he never lost his joy because he continued to confer with the Lord to direct his path. If he had lost his joy, then human nature would have told him to discontinue running, stand up for himself, and be a man. If he killed Goliath, he could truly uproot Saul. (See 1 Samuel 17.) The lesson to learn from David as his enemy was seeking daily to decompose him is that he never permitted his enemy to take his joy or peace away.

In reality today, you have opportunities to take vengeance into your own hands or else trust God to fight your clashes. One day David was alone with Saul in a cave and he had him cornered, yet David abnegated to cause him any physical harm. David fell prey to the temptation of his self-will by cutting off Saul's skirt to try to opprobrium Saul for what he was doing to him. David told Saul that the Lord would rule against him if he caused any bodily harm toward God's anointed, so his action toward Saul was due to Saul being under God's grace (1 Sam. 24:6).

When Saul was leaving the cave, David followed making a

compendious statement to him, "You are my lord," and bowed before Saul. He told Saul that on this day his eyes had seen how the Lord had transferred Saul to him in the cave. Some had asked David to kill Saul, yet he spared his life. David was not going forward with destroying Saul, his lord, due to him being chosen as God's consecrated. David did cut a piece of hem from Saul's robe, yet didn't select to kill the king. Now there is no breach of law or duty made before God or Saul. Yet Saul hunted David from sunrise to sunset to dissolve his soul. So David told Saul that from this day forth the Lord will be the arbitrator between you and me. And when all things pertinent to the matter come to light, the Lord will avenge me (1 Sam. 24:8, 10–12).

This is an incredible insight of how God desires his children to react when they are being talked about, lied about, derided, despised, and berated for righteous sake. I know there are many of us who right now do not know why God has us in the body of fellowship where we are located right now. You cannot seem to understand your purpose there; God has need of you to be the beacon light in a tunnel of ambiguity. If the true children of God were to live and commence in fellowship within the same assemblage, then how would we all come into the unity of the faith? The house of the Lord is to be a safe haven for the lost and wandering children of God to come in and receive rest for their weary and wavy souls; not a place for condemnation and persecution. If that was the case, there is no need for the unbeliever or sinner to come into the faith since the world is already scurrilous and abusive. Since it caused them to remember the place they left, they might as well return to the prince of this world. For those who are in need of deliverance, would never see the error of their ways. Due to the veil or scales covering their face and eyes we need to allow the Holy Spirit to come in, purge out the undesirable things from their vessel of dishonor, and make it a vessel of honor. The hypocrite will remain in repudiation, stating that this is who I am, take it or leave, unwilling to be dedicated to religious use in mannerism and all conversation (1 Pet. 1:15).

David was never seduced by the enemy to talk to Saul loudly and blaringly; he addressed Saul in a proper manner and with a blithe disposition. I believe David knew somewhere deep inside his heart that God had a greater purpose for him and all he had to do was retain trust in His withstanding power. As believers, we must believe or know our purpose in the Lord or we will become as lost as the agnostic because you have chosen to operate in your own ludicrous will and mind without the joy of the Lord (1 Pet. 1:22–23).

## David Knew His Purpose

Before Saul left David's presence, God gave him a word of wisdom. God was truly with David, and Saul would never be portioned any opportunity to take his life or cause him bodily harm. He told Saul with sonorous respect, God is all knowing (omniscience) and all seeing (omnipresence). God was pleading David's case and mandated Saul to spare his life in that he was without any offense. Saul turned to David and told him even though he was trying to kill him, he was aware of God's hand being on David. Many times he sought after David to subvert and kill, but David never returned evil toward him and compensated Saul with beneficence words. At that moment, Saul knew that God was going to reward David as the King of Israel for his obedience and endurance during his time of persecution, and he asked David not to terminate or kill his family for his wickedness (1 Sam. 24:13–20).

This is an amazing story of how God will sustain your joy,

even when your enemy is speaks flattery and flatulent words to win you over or throw you off guard with a defense. You do not have to be concerned or worry how to overturn your enemies; God will do that for you. They will execute forged love and affection to defeat you from regaining strength while under attack and keep you in a state of frailty and debilitation. Saul did exactly that; he tried to amuse and conciliate David into sparing his life, meanwhile failing to realize that God was in control of the outcome. Later, he turned around and sought after David's life again. Saul was plagued with maliciousness and spiteful contempt and aversion toward David, because of his gifted calling. And the Lord permitted David another opportunity to uproot his enemy, and he didn't. God analyzed the condition of David's heart again by giving him an opportunity to extirpate Saul. The Lord put an impressive sleep on the men, and no one was aware that David had came into their camp while they were sleeping. He took Saul's spear and a cruse of water from his bolster. David had a combination of circumstances favorable for his purpose of taking Saul's weapons while he was slumbering (1 Sam. 26:12).

When Saul was convinced he was not able to kill David, he knew it was time for him to give up his rival, for he was never going to win. Saul admitted to David that he sinned by trying to abolish him. He gave his word that he would no longer try to harm him. God made it clear or evident to Saul that David did spare his life for he was much loved and cherished by David. Saul deduced that he behaved as a fool who was full of transgression and sin (1 Sam. 26:21).

From that day, forth Saul made peace with David and returned to his place of residency. Saul blessed David as he departed. He told David that he would be prosperous and be victorious doing wondrous things for the Lord. This is a beautified analogy of how God will make your enemy to come to be your footstool (1 Sam. 26:25).

God will give opportunity for you to see the enemy when he is frightened and tortured by the demonic defenses from his distorted unreasonable mind and heart. The same was true with Saul; he had become so inhumanely and obstinately disobedient that he was no longer hearing the voice of the Lord. Seeking wretched counsel from familiar spirits brought destruction upon his household and put an end to his family's lineage. When Saul, his men, and sons went to battle with the Philistines, they utterly devoured them all but Saul, who was wounded, and his armor-bearer. The evil one had Saul's mind full of hesitation and vacillating with fright that he plunged himself onto his sword, rather than face the town as uncourageous and spineless (1 Sam. 31:4).

You must not release your joy into the hands of any man. Keep in mind, when David's enemy was fast approaching, he resided in the arms of God. God's love was manifested within David's desire and pleasure to express inviolable inspiration and admiration to give God glory; henceforth God named him a man after His own heart. David was a man who was stout-hearted, courageous, and brave, and had not subjected his mind under the sanction of the evil one during his testing of faith. David was known in history as the man gaining the distinctive trait and quality of God's inclination and tendency. As conjunctive heirs of the kingdom of God, we should take ownership of two things in this life: joy and peace, rejoicing in all things pleasing and satisfying to the Almighty.

The contradiction between David and Saul was one man resentfully envious of another's gift or relationship with God. David would not be distracted from his purpose and vision, not allowing any man to would not abrogate his journey. Saul would not suspend from trying to steal David's destiny, going as far as murdering another man for warning and helping to escape David's capture. Saul did receive a new heart from the Lord, but he chooses to exuviate the operation or function of that renewed heart, refusing to yield, surrender, and submit to the power and authority of God. Saul was more concern about people pleasing rather than God pleasing; therefore his entire life as a king was in constant state of desolation and unhappiness. Saul was the driving force used by God to try David with enduring pain, aggravation, and distress, which he did with composure and without complaint. These trials would purify and sanctify him to operate successfully in God's consecrated position. God would have a leader who was in concord with His laws and commandments. His people would have a competent leader who could withstand and congest trials, tribulation, and temptation—David was living proof.

There are many people that will come into your life by way of a job, social involvement, or in fellowship with the body of believers who are *dream killers, vision stealers* and *joy robbers*. You must remain focused on your task at hand, as David did. David earnestly prayed day and night, asking the God to keep his enemies at bay. Regardless of David's sins, he was faithful in serving and obeying God and his household was richly blessed. His son Solomon, growing up in a godly and sanctified home under a purified leader and role model Father, had great admiration and respect for the Lord. Therefore, when Solomon took over the kingdom after his father, he desired no wealth or riches but God's divine and profound wisdom and knowledge to lead and judge God's people with dignity and courtesy. They are many who will tell you that you are too serious about God's work; tell them you are not only concerned with grave or important matters but also committed. Many people are serious, careful, or sober about everything they do but not committed, consigned, or entrusted by God. In the terminal hour, there is a need for superfluous committed disciples to bring edification and honor in the name of Jesus to a dying world. No matter what the world or people may bring your way, keep up your sustaining and prolonging joy.

Let us clarify or make clearer and free from impurities how to understand dream killers, visions stealers, and joy robbers:

First, *dream killers* try to prevent the vital or active qualities of fond hope and aspiration of the images and thoughts of your purpose and destiny. They have a killjoy spirit that will spoil completely or lessen other's enjoyment and gratification. They will try to tell you that the fanciful vision or sequential thoughts are all in your mind and you will never flourish. They make you feel as though you cannot accomplish anything without a certain title or have gone to a certain seminary school. They cannot help the new convert grow without making them feel pointless and worthless. They cannot reassure the backslider of their hope in Jesus without making them feel condemned or incriminated. When they truly receive the healing of the Holy Ghost, their eyes will open and scales will fall off and they will have to extend love to reach the lost, babes in Christ, and backsliders. Until pride and ego no longer overbear the decision-making or firmness of the mind we will never become a new creation or creature. The behavior will remain habitual and conventional to the old nature or man, unable to have a brand new beginning.

Warning: Be careful of the dream killer: they will distract you with mundane matters and indulge you in indolent talk while pervading rumors or secrets about others. They lack sensation and conscious concerns or feelings of others. Their advice is insentient, without life, conscious or perceptive to the will and purpose of God for your destination.

Second, *vision stealers* attempt to gain slyly or artfully innermost combining ideas and intellects inasmuch use them as revelatory insight from God. They have nothing new under the sun going on in their lives; the same thing that was happening over five years ago or last year is still co-existing this year. They take slyly or surreptitiously your mental images of kingdom building, taking away your forethought and using them dishonesty in a secret manner by presenting your ideas as theirs. They befriend individuals to steal their ingenuity and originality and use others' testimonies and public avowal. Never lose sight of them being thieves—one who steals secretly or mysteriously while their victims are not alert and are unarmed. They have the distinguishing traits of a cat burglar who breaks in at night to commit a theft, crime, or other felony through an opening in the dwelling. Remember, this type of thief can only come into your dwelling if there is an opening, gap, or opportunity given to them by way of disclosing your intentions or expectations from the Lord.

Warning: Be cautious of visions stealers, they come into your life to kill, steal, and destroy everything that God has breathed and spoken upon you. They are unable to be happy or joyful of another's success, accomplishments, or achievements in life. Even the people who are close to them are baffled by their underhanded sense of humor and always trying to annihilate an individual's reputation, distinction, or personage.

Third, the *joy robber* feels inferior and is very unhappy, never having anything good to say, even about the mercy and grace of God. They are joy predators, which will cause you to miscarry by prematurely depriving the necessity and resolution for your existence. Unable to carry the vision of the Lord in a healthy vessel, you cannot survive under insufficient and undeveloped surrounding. They will evoke impoliteness and rudeness in your spirit, infecting you with a disconsolate or cheerless temperament and lack of energy to be comforted. Some are like home invaders who come to you with a pretentious spirit of meekness and lowliness to retrieve personal and confidential information regarding the affairs of your household, which they later use to bring nuisance danger within the confines of your home. Others are trespassers who squander away time trying to retrieve valid and useful information about family, private, or personal affairs with hopes of bringing sabotage into individual's lives, homes, jobs, church, or friendly association. In any case, they are repulsive, tending to present strong disservice or aversion against the brethren, while motivating a lot of chaos and tumult in the body of Christ. God is not pleased or satisfied with any of these individual frailties, nervousness, compulsion, or coercion driving against unresolved details, fault, mars, or blemishes.

Warning: Be careful to avoid the joy robbers; they are unwholesome to your morals, values, and standards of righteousness and joyfulness. They do not stop until they cause physical, mental, or spiritual pain on you, your family, and loved ones. Their aim is to overtake you; and if others happen to get in the way, then these innocence by-standers will become victims of unfriendly fire. They come to rob your joy by force, coercion, or persuasion; no matter who gets hurt, they must receive self-satisfaction and self-gain. Regardless of the form, shape, or size the enemy may present himself as a wanderer in this extraneous land, do not give way to his sly and insidious method.

Peter was another example of someone who was sought out by the adversary to exterminate; he repudiated his master, the

Savior, at an enervating moment. He told the town's people that he was not a disciple nor was he a follower of Jesus Christ. Peter was very disconcerted like some many others on this pilgrimage that are in need of acceptance and approval by man.

In Luke 22:31, Jesus tells Peter that Satan longs to sift or try him in hopes of bringing him into spiritual ravage or destruction. Jesus was giving Peter forewarning of the evil one coming after his true joy and peace. But, like so many others, Peter was insensitive and unconscious of how the enemy was going to try him. The Lord assured him that He was praying for him to remain courageous and strong. After the death and resurrection of the Lord, before His ascension, Peter and the other disciples received the endlessly gift of joy—the Holy Spirit. After He received the impartation of the Holy Spirit, he would now be able to carry his ministry with fervor and boldness. Afterward Peter became an intrepid and unafraid messenger of the truth as he warns the church about the devices, traps, and deployment of the enemy. Although they have not seen Jesus Christ, believers rejoice with unspeakable joy and are full of glory (1 Pet. 1:8).

As fellow co-laborers of the good news, we must never let the enemy see us sweat; we must remain unyielding and unmovable toward the advancements of his conniving, resist his temptation, and not take vengeance in our own hands—let God fight our battles. In 1 Peter 2:16–17, Peter tells the church not to use their salvation as a weapon to do what every their flesh desires for them to, especially when it comes to hurting another brother. Christians are to put a muzzle on the ignorance and error of foolish and unlearned men and women, teaching and preaching liberty as servants of God showing an example of not being fractious against those who have authority over you, as long as such surrendering does not interfere with the law of

God. You must operate under genuine freedom in serving God and living as one who pleases outside of the perimeter of holiness. Exhibit love to brethren with fear and reverence toward God, giving honor to those in leadership.

Saul was one who believed he had power as the King of Israel to annul and abolish anyone that got in his way. The people chose him, but He did not know that David was chosen by God—a great difference since there is no favor or blessing granted from man, only God. God is exalted higher than any counsel, elder, or leader anywhere.

Saul thought because he was the king that he did not have to love David, or give homage to God if he chose not to. Saul went to soothsayers and fortunetellers to reveal his outcome, yet was scornful to hear the words and voice of God. But David kept God's law, and he ponder it in his heart with great servitude, daily reminding himself that the servant is subject to his master with fear, not just to the good and gentle employer. Although Saul was engaging to kill him, he never forgot his place in the kingdom and that was a servant until God put him into his rightful position. David endured with patience and longsuffering.

## A HEART WITH JESUS' JOY

The condition of your heart will determine the quantum of joy which you are capable of handling without malfunctioning. The prophet Jeremiah tells us that the heart is deceitful, rascally lies and cheats, gives a false witness and defrauds others, and is fallacious of others for self-improvement and self profit. And no one can know the heart but God. So, if God knows your heart, then He also knows what is best for you. That means the only way you will have joy is to divest the old heart filled with degraded and delusive judgment.

129

Jeremiah was speaking of hearts that were repulsive, unhappy, vicious, and malicious against the desires and wishes of the Lord for ministering and serving the lost. Jeremiah had first hand knowledge of how important it was to receive the heart of the Lord, for the people in his day were overcrowded with baleful and vile hearts. They prayed asking God for deliverance and He would not answer for He knew their hearts were unpurified and unsanctified. Then the Lord told Jeremiah that the people had forsaken His law, which He set before them, and had not obeyed His voice, neither walked after His laws. They were walking after the imagination of their hearts and another god, Baalim, which ways were taught to them by the forefathers (Jer. 9:13–14).

There is no force on heaven or earth that can elude or evade from the wrath of God, the Supreme Ruler. God sits high and looks low; He knows every man's heart condition. God informed Jeremiah of the condition of His people's heart: it was deceitful above all things and desperately inhumanely perverted and cruel. Who can know it, but the Creator? He alone can search man's heart and handle the reins of his heart. He will reward every man according to his ways and to the fruit of his doings (Jer. 17:9–10). Before receiving the heart of Jesus, the stony and fleshy hearts must be expunged and rid of impurities coming from being black hearted, broken-hearted, chicken hearted, coldhearted, disheartened, down hearted, fainthearted, false-hearted, half-hearted, or hard-hearted. The Holy Spirit will come in and begin to circumcise, cut off all or part of the foreskin, the loathsome, troublesome, and burdensome unwanted and undesired things from the old heart and substitute with a transplanted heart of Christ.

Someone who is *black hearted* is shamefully satanic, evil, vile, and scandalous; in complete darkness with a very sullen and angry countenance. They see things humorous or satirical in a morbid and cynical way. The *brokenhearted* are crushed by misfortune, deep sadness or disappointment and inconsolable. The *chicken hearted* are easily frightened or startled, showing an embarrassed timidity—complete with doubt and suspicion, on guard by exhibiting ignominious and despicable exorbitant with fear, unable to stand boldly against their adversaries. The *coldhearted* lack the temperament of steady composure of mind or natural habitude, and are reluctant to forgive, apologize, or be kind to others. The conventional contrivance of *disheartened* or daunted personality is bereaved of courage, with low spirits and easily humiliated or embarrassed. The *downhearted* feel disparagement, low esteem, and discredited or debased by others. They are never given any real or trustworthy responsibility or accountability due to past commitments that fell through on their behalf. The *fainthearted* are indistinct, their courage is pretentious showing defiant certainty. They do not see, hear, or perceive things clearly; they are very obfuscate and not detailed or defined with personal boundaries. They show the deficiency of self-doubt and are unable to determine the extent or nature of missionary focus, becoming weary and giving up in doing well. The *false-hearted* are betrayers of trust, faith, or allegiance, while deceiving and manipulating others to meet agendas and programs of faithless and treacherous promises or commitments. They feel neither bound to obligation nor responsibility to kingdom building, rather kingdom pestilent. The *half-hearted* have belittled enthusiasm, intense or eager interest, zeal or fervor with little or no firmness of purpose, determining, or adamant intention. They have little interest or concern regarding things that do not affect them personally. The *hard-hearted* is ruthless, merciless, relentless, and pitiless. They will bring a lot of sorrow and grief into a gathering of people while blocking the transmission of spiritual impulses during praise and worship that release deliverance, salvation, and healing within the sanctuary.

In Romans 12:1–2, it tells us to lay our bodies on the altar as living sacrifices, holy and satisfactory unto God. Our minds must become transformed from the cosmos' way to God's way, which is every man's reasonable service. So in relation to everything we do in this walk, we are to take vesture of this new or renewed mind. There will not be available joy when sinful and shallow habits or character traits of selfishness, pride, jealousy, and antipathy exist. In order for the believer to become ample with the spirit of joy, he must become a new creature. The epitome of joy comes when you can behold the Lamb of God and envision His beauty and marvelous sacrifice.

The Lord desires strongly to give all a heart modification or transplant with the fullness of joy that comes from the Spirit of God. This modification or restructure will bring redeeming qualification or revelation of meaning to the sons and daughters of God. He will take out bitterness, and put in restored joy. Once, you have received the heart of God, all joy is at your fingertips. You are capable of putting the spirit of misery to death and burying it. Conditional feelings of unhappiness are unsuccessful that come with physical, mental, and spiritual suffering, desiring the effect of pain, sorrow, poverty or distress. This condition or state will limit the planting, cultivating and harvesting of God's vineyard.

Many times people lose joy due to self-inflicting or inciting conditions, events, or incidents due to having depreciating and demeaning behavior, actions, or conduct, causing you to fall lower to chastisement and punishment. As ambassadors of Christ, do not fail to put off, receive, or submit to the will of God or obsequiously follow His spiritually immaculate word.

There are few believers being persecuted for righteous sake; in fact, there are more being chastened for disobedience or insubordination by not submitting to the authority of God.

If the opposite were true, why are there so many different church denominations, so many different beliefs in what is holy and sacred, and so many ways to come into God's holy temple? Jesus acknowledges there was only one way to come into the house of the Lord and that was in spirit and truth. Everyone must come to the Father by or through Jesus. In order to come to the Father, you must receive a new heart, which gives a spiritual pass to enter into His gates with thanksgiving and come behind the veil and commune with Him. In order for the Lord to get us back into holiness, we must receive the heart of Jesus.

We long to be big hearted, goodhearted, kindhearted, lighthearted, single-hearted, softhearted, tenderhearted, truehearted, warm-hearted and wholehearted—characteristics of the heart of Christ Jesus. *The big hearted* are generous or magnanimous, those who overlook injury or insult and rise above pettiness or meanness. The *goodhearted* are beneficial and generous, those who has favor, advantage and great benefits from the Lord. The *kindhearted* are sympathetic, cordial, and gentle, those who share or understand the feelings, emotions, or ideas of others, yet able to express pity and compassion or commiserate when necessary. The *light-hearted* are free from worry or concern, those who excitement and vigorous attitude toward life. The *single-hearted* are honest and sincere, whose motives and intentions are truthful and genuine, without deceit or pretense. The *tenderhearted* are compassionate, caring, and sympathetic, those who show sorrow for the sufferings or trouble of others with the urge or desire to help. The *truehearted* are faithful patriots to the body of Christ, loyally defending and supporting the ideals of leadership under loving obligation. The *warmhearted* are kind and sympathetic, having a mutual liking or understanding arising from sameness of others' feelings. They share or have the ability to share, another person's mental or emotional state with or in love. The *wholehearted* release all their energy and enthusiasm with sincerity to aid and help the ministry and spread the good news.

But there are types of hearts no one takes joy in exemplifying today, the bleeding heart and servant heart. The *bleeding heart* is a heart of a person frequently regarded as too sentiment or too liberal in his approach to social problems. The *servant's heart* is the meek and humble heart of Jesus. Both represent the heart of Jesus, having and showing the tender and delicate feelings for mankind, for whom He laid down his flesh—for ultimate salvation, deliverance, reconciliation, and restoration. His heart is free from guise or guile and radiates everlasting, empowering, enabling, and everlasting joy, by which can defeat all attacks from our opponent. His heart is a complex conjunction of feelings and opinions regarding sanctification and holiness to the unbeliever; but all men must go through Him in order to get to the Heavenly Father. There is no key susceptible to emotional appeal to the heart of God, except by way of receiving Jesus Christ as our personal Lord and Savior.

Our new heart will leave us reunited and intact with zest; rejoicing in the midst of a storm, appreciating the life which is given from God, delighting in the Lord, and having happiness and gladness all earthly days and then throughout all eternity. This heart has a recondite spirit of excellence while dealing with abstruse or difficult subjects. We can now walk into a season of absolute, complete, and full substantial joy. Remember that there is stability in Jesus' tranquility in spite of persecution and torment. We are safe and obscure or concealed under the mighty hands of the Lord.

There are those who do not gently exercise authority over others, and what their harshness is deliberate and intentionally willful (1 Pet. 2:18). Peter emphasizes that we cannot be good to the furtherance of Christ, if we never suffer or struggle against the trials of this world. When we suffer brusque and curt powerful blows which shake us and bring disturbances into our lives, we are to stand still and see the salvation of the Lord. There is no glory given to the Lord if we are protected from antagonistic forces from our shortcoming and have no patience to endure. But if you are enduring suffering as well as calmly tolerating impertinence, surcease, and tumult this is counted acceptable servitude unto God (1 Pet. 2:20).

Peter relates to the believer that there is nothing unfamiliar about undergoing sore and ill nature hardship for Christ's sake, it is your duty. You must bring about gladness inasmuch as partaking or participating in His sufferance. When his glory becomes transparent, you shall rejoice with exuberant joy (1 Pet. 4:12–13). Now that you know that it is not necessary to lose or forfeit your joy into the hands of any man or thing; remain etched into the cornerstone of Jesus. Believe that you will receive your just reward, if you do not lack moral strength or will power. When the Master, the primal Shepherd, comes for His bride, He will reward her with a crown of glory that will never fade or perish (1 Pet. 5:4).

The church must remain on notice of how the enemy will come in like a flood and bring diversions. These diversions will distract the believer from their assignment and responsibility to the gospel of Jesus Christ. Peter knew this since he was a hot head. You must not become big headed, rebuking the devil and demons and forgetting that all power in heaven and earth comes from God. The power Jesus has converting and giving a new heart is not for self-glory but God's glory. For the creature shall never deem that he is higher or greater than the Creator. This was Lucifer's problem when he was in heaven. The mystifying and perplexing matter cost him a position and place in the heavenlies. Even Jesus never put himself above the Father. He was constantly asking the Father's permission before he did anything, counterchecking to see if His actions were in God's Will. Jesus never took any glory or praise away from the Father, acknowledging Him as the supreme Creator at all times.

## SUSTAINING JOY IN THE LIONS DEN

In the book of Daniel, there is a story being told about Daniel, a well-known Biblical character who was a slave held captive in a magnificent palace. Nebuchadnezzar, king of Babylon, captured a group of people from Jerusalem. Among them were several young men of royal descent, and Daniel was one of them. Daniel lived during the period when Judah was expatriated to Babylon for their insurgence toward the law of God's word regarding idolatry and His covenant keeping.

Daniel's name means, "God is my judge." Daniel, Hananiah, Mishael, and Azariah were classical literature teachers of the Sumerian and Akkadian writings. Daniel was like Joseph, who was able to have joy in the middle of deep misfortune and never renounced what was purposed in his heart—to worship God wherever you go. God granted and endowed favor with delicate and impressionable love toward Daniel from the prince of the eunuchs (Dan. 1:9). Meanwhile, God brought bias partiality on Daniel as He did Joseph. The prince of the eunuchs told Daniel that he feared the king, who had subjected all to consume and absorb the same food and drink. He asked Daniel why he should be permitted special privileges over his kindred or the other children of Israel. The eunuch was afraid for his life, which would be in jeopardy if Daniel did not comply with the king's authoritative command (1:10).

Daniel abjured to eat the food, which by Jewish law was forbidden. The Israelites considered the food from Nebuchadnezzar contaminated since the first portion of it was offered to idols. Likewise, a portion of the wine was poured onto a pagan altar. Instead, Daniel stuck to eating a simple diet instructed by Jewish law. Melzar, the eunuch, told Daniel that his contrary action would eventually cost him his life, since the others were eating the meals prepared from the king's table without mumbling or complaining. Daniel presented a solution to Melzar: to allow him and his three companions ten days to eat pulse—made of peas, beans, and lentils—and to drink transparent mineral liquid. Daniel promised and assured Melzar that if they were permitted to eat according to their religious belief and customs, their appearance would not deteriorate while abstaining from the daily nourishment of meats, and that this would not impede their knowledge and expertise to perform their jobs in the kingdom (1:11–14).

Melzar conceded and took away their portion of meat for only ten days. When Melzar evaluated them after ten days, their wisdom was sharper than ever or far better than the others. He found their countenance to be fairer and fatter in flesh than all the children which did eat the portion of the king's meat. After seeing the outcome, Melzar took away their portion of meat and wine permanently. From that day on they only ate pulse and drank water, and God extended their acquiring skills and good judgment. Daniel had comprehension and understanding in all visions and dreams (1:15–17).

After this the king wanted to see them and requested they be brought before him. The king fellowshipped with them and found none within his palace to be as intellectually acute as

Daniel, Hananiah, Mishael, and Azariah. The king examined their wisdom and understanding and found them ten times better than all the magicians and astrologers that were in his entire realm (1:18–20).

You may feel overwhelmed and allow a fallible decision or choice to forfeit your joy to others' subjugation. You are not to submit to being disparaging and belittling of conductors who don't give approval to mobilizing and attributing to your destiny. Bosses and co-workers are out of your control and power, but God has all power and control that can give you the peace and joy. The Lord will allow your enemies to make peace with you for their fear of whom you serve and who is looking out for your well being. If you are in a job that does not permit you to have serenity in your mind, that may not be the place for you. If you lose your mind, how will you be able to cope and function productively and effectively on any job? You must pray and ask the Lord to show or give you a way of escape, for peace of mind is far better than any salary or career.

Later Daniel's favor persisted when he interpreted a dream that had the wise men puzzled; then the king made Daniel ruler of Babylon. Daniel was once again sitting at the table of favor with presidents and princes because of an excellent spirit in him. The king thought to set him over the whole realm (6:3).

Only God can sit you at the table with dignitaries and famous people even when you come from a humble and meek beginning. God has control over all future happenings and occurrences. The joy of Jesus, left here through airwaves of the Holy Spirit, can withstand the counterattack of the forces of pessimism.

## JOY CAN WITHSTAND COUNTERATTACK OF THE ENEMY

God requires that you give Him all the laud in excellent as well as poor health. God's favor on Daniel drove the presidents and princes to jealousy, as they sought to find error in his testimony. But they couldn't find any fault with his faithfulness. Daniel was eased of all transgressions or sins. They conjured up a plot to find fault with David concerning the law of his God (6:4–5).

These men were talebearers looking for a rumor or a lie to make or create a story to discredit Daniel, yet make them look incorrupt or honest. The talebearers converged together to manipulate the king to believe that Daniel was nefarious, dissipated, irregular, rascally, and impure. The presidents, governors, princes, counselors, and captains all came together to artfully encourage the king to make a decree that no one be allowed to pray or make petition to any god or man except him for thirty days. If anyone was caught doing so, they would be cast into the den of lions (6:6–7).

This sounds like church folks that are angry at another member or leader in the congregation who is not doing things the way they want or cannot be subsumed by their perpetrate ways. They are Pharisees, Sadducees, and hypocrites—those that only accepted the written law and tradition and passed over the living or oral law. They withered the kingdom of God through their self-ambition actions and deeds. Jesus states how precarious it is to remain as whitened sepulchers, which are beautiful in outward appearance but inwardly full of dead men's bones and uncleanness. He says you may be able to fool man with your righteous indignation and just outer appearance, but your soul is filled of hypocrisy and iniquity.

There are unbalanced men and women who have nothing

better to do than bring unresolved inner child issues into the body of Christ. This type of dysfunctional state is preternatural and does not prepare personages bountifully in serving the Lord. Every family in the world has a member or members that cause mental arguments and quarrels within the family circle because they are in need of help. That help can come only by way of prayer and supplication. Why not pray more and complain less for those who are in the body of Christ causing great destruction and devastation? I know some are concerned that they will tell all abstruse and hidden secrets; others are afraid since they are so close with certain leaders and elders of the congregation, nothing good will come of it. If you allow individuals that are overpowered with demonic infiltration of this atmosphere to dominate, it will cause internal perdition or contamination to the entire body of Christ.

They need a spiritual therapist who can treat their debasing and contagious disease of physical or mental derangement by healing through restoration and deliverance for the good of the entire church family. In the natural, a family suffering from a dysfunctional foundation will cover up immoral or inglorious things that acquire within the family walls; but the malice, guile, hypocrisies, giving offense, and acrimonious speech will uproot the fiber foundation, the Word of God. The true psychoanalyst, Jesus, specializes in treating mental entanglements from rivalries along with repression of unforgiveness and bitterness. Jesus will prescribe the Word of God as a remedy to bring compound psyche back to self-possession and stability.

Many of you can confirm that there have been times when others have tried to bring you down before the pastor, ministers, and others leaders within the church because you did not tolerate or compromise with wrongdoing. Man will tend to fight with you in this principle, but this was predestined to be apart of your test and trial; standing the test of time, with duration and stability. They will go as far as manipulating and being mendacious by stating to others that you are a peevish and discontented covenant breaker. Others will feel that they are more worthy or anointed to be in charge than you, but this was in the will of God. You may have felt as if you were going to lose your mind and no one understood what you were going through. While some brothers and sisters in your local assemblage may reject you from being inside the ministry of God, have reliance on God and trust that He will give you another assignment. He will open a door or window of opportunity into the wilderness and desert surroundings to help extinguish the thirst and hungry of the unsaved and lost.

Although Daniel was fully aware that the proclamation was signed and the possible consequences he faced, he went into his house and kneeled on his knees and began praying and admonishing God, as he did three times each day before the decree was written (Dan. 6:10). God will protect you when others conspire together and make up lies about what you due to jealousy and envy. The wicked men were watching outside Daniel's window and, as expected, saw him praying and making supplication before God. There are some tares in the body of Christ, which will follow or watch comings and goings just to get enough information on others to wipe out their reputation and good merit before the brethren.

That's why it is very important for us to have a productive prayer and fasting life, which keeps us humble and meek before our Lord, who will intervene for the purpose of producing rapport and understanding on our behalf. So when foes rise up, we shall not be overtaken or surprised by what they say or do. All the leaders went to the king and reminded him of his edict stating no prayer time for thirty days. And that if anyone were caught doing so, they would be put in the den of lions. The king said this was true, and according to the law of the Medes and Persians, it could not be modified. The talebearers feigned that they were performing their civic duty to inform the king of disobeying individuals. They told the king that the individual was Daniel, one of the children of the captivity of Judah, a slave. The men said that Daniel was aware of the king's decree, yet still petitioned his God three times a day. Those wicked leaders did not like the fact that Daniel was favored, peculiar, and had joy serving his God (6:11–13). How can you trust in the Lord, or better yet beseech Him, when you know the enemy is on your heels?

After the trap had been laid, King Darius became very displeased with himself for having written the decree and set his heart to deliver Daniel. The king became weary with mental and physical exertion trying to make a rational decision. Later, the men came back to confront the king about his official order or calculation. The king told Daniel that he had no choice but to throw him into the den of lions, but he had confidence that Daniel's God would circumvent the situation and deliver him out of the place of death (6:14–16).

The king did not want to put Daniel in a den of lions, but he had to preserve his throne before the people. He felt that he was left with no other choice. Similarly, there are church leaders today who want to move underdeveloped or carnal leaders out of position but won't because of the fear of them uttering slanderous statements or starting rumors in the middle of assembly of people who come to worship. The king returned to the palace and fasted all night. He would not consent to any musical instruments being played to put him to sleep, and he did not sleep (6:18).

Many leaders have no prudence, due to their unrelated heart

condition that will not permit them to stand up for righteous-ness sake or the things of God. They are fearful or frightened of the physical and emotional vandalizing that man can subject to their ministry or missionary assignment. Remember, the scripture that tells us not to fear man who can only bring subversion on the body, but fear God who can undermine the body and soul (Luke 12:4). When people are conscious of how they mistreat you and others, they may rise very early while making haste to meet secretly and ploy devious working; others may not be able to sleep the night before due to frantic impulses. Many will have restless nights and joyless days, due to incompleteness of strength and character or unwillingness to stand up for anyone or anything unless it urgently affects their home, family, or friends. Do not be one who walks around with a load of heaviness on your hearts due to mistreatment to innocent individuals, even if they are not in the family of God. You must treat everyone as you would want to be treated or respected. This is the genuine will of Christ, to love your neighbor as yourself. If there is strife or confusion between you and a brother, you should be the bigger person and apologize to make or mend peace between co-laborers.

Children of God who are of good spirit and courageous, God will defend their case and make apparent to man that He is first in their heart and life. One day he or she will come and ask for forgiveness. Why? Because it is the only way a true ambassador can move on, with a clear penitent heart ready to do the work of the Great Progenitor of all things. God is omnipotent, having all power; omnipresent, present everywhere; omniscient, all knowing.

The King Darius made haste to the den of the lions and shouted out with a sorrowful pitch unto Daniel. The king immediately asked Daniel if his God saved him from the mouths of the hungry lions and was He able to save him from the snare of the attacks. The king approached the den and found Daniel untouched and without any detriment. Daniel responded to the king, Yes, God sent guardian angels to shut the mouths of the lions and I am liberated from any harm or danger. God found him innocent and He caused no harm to come to the king (6:19–22).

In the individual testimonies of men like Joseph, Job, and Daniel, God delivered them all, in spite of the fact that tragedy and disaster came into each of their lives as fate or necessity would have it.

Your testimony to lost sheep is to be steadfast when obstacles or challenges come your way, to show the planet that God is able to set you out from under the control or power of another, or to save any and all from physical hurt or harm. Although the king felt hopeless, God gave him joy and hope that Daniel's God was the only true God that is above all other gods.

God will hold the wicked accountable for all the people they try to destroy, sabotage, or wipe out. Keep them in your prayers that God might have mercy. And the wicked that proscribe with authority against the innocent and refuse to receive and learn the Word of God shall be judged. Thus, the king summoned for the men who slandered Daniel unscrupulously and unfavorably and cast them and their entire families into the den of lions. The Master will place the enemy in a den or cave of turmoil and despair, permitting their evil ways and thoughts to devour them and their followers (6:24). God is able and will chastise those who are accusers of their brethren or who wish to undermine the children of God. Because these men will not be prepared when the Day of Judgment comes, although they can dish it out, they may not take persecution themselves. When the tables turn and they are under pressure by the boss and others they work with, they will need you to pray for them or give a word of encouragement in their time of despair. God will render more in your later than the beginning. Things may start as being alone or all by yourself, but God can turn all things around by demonstrating to others what is really inside of your heart—the strong love and enthusiasm of Christ. Daniel prospered in the reign of Darius and Cyprus the Persian (6:28).

God is going to try your heart to see if it is like His, which has the composition or creation make up of Christ's tenderness and lovingkindness. God came to make dreams come true and vision become reality. The same was true for Daniel, God had a great purpose for His servant more than being put in this kingdom to give the king dream interpretations. Daniel was to be living evidence of a steadfast servant and worshiper of his God. And when he did that, God gave him kind regard to operate under the holistic range of information, awareness, and understanding of God's consecrated doctrine.

I can understand some of God's other faithful sons being put into a fiery furnace (Dan. 3). In 2000, I encountered the most inspirational test when I was diagnosed with a blood disorder. The doctors could not understand how I could have sustained so much blood loss without being hospitalized by the time arrived for an emergency doctor visit. When I arrived at the doctor's office my face and skin had become so pale, that the doctor realized just by looking at me that I had lost substantial elemental units of blood. After he performed a physical, he instructed me to go for lab work and come back in two days. While at the lab giving blood, I temporarily passed out and had to remain there for another hour to regain consciousness and mobile use of my limbs. Two days later, I returned to the doctor's office to be told that I had lost so much blood that I needed a blood transfusion. I told the doctor that I had to pray about it and talk it over with my husband. At the time my husband was out of town on a business trip and was unaware of how ill I was. I called him later that night and told him what the doctor recommended. He told me that I should pray about it and he would support my decision. That night my children were over tat my mother's home, and I cried out to the Lord for direction and guidance.

The room became very still. I felt another present in the room. I was the only person in the house at the time. I could feel the presence moving around my bedroom as I was listening to one of my favorite song artists, John P. Kee. He was singing a song from his CD *Any Day* called "I'm Healed." Just as he said, "You are healed," I heard a still and quiet voice say to me, "Daughter, I am going to heal your body. Not by man's way nor by man's prayer or might. Trust in me, and I will heal your body." I was stunned and lacked the mobile capability to move from my desk. I had never received a visitation from the Lord before. I did not know how to respond. I thought to myself, "Should I just sit here or get the heck out of this room?" I turned to look around the room. My legs were paralyzed to the floor, and I could not move from my computer chair. I sat as the Lord began to ministry to me saying, "My daughter, I know the test you have been going through, but I want to give you some joy in the midst of your sorrow. Tears rolled down my face. I thought to myself, "Why would God want to do this for me?" And the Lord said to me, "Daughter, receive your calling and everything will be alright."

I knew exactly what the Lord was talking about, because a year earlier in May 1999, my youngest daughter and I were in a severe car accident that should have taken our lives. When I walked away from the incident, I looked up to heaven and said thank you Father for saving us. That night I receive a visitation from an angel. God called me from the secular job in May

1999 after that car accident, and I refused to hear or accept the assignment. I thought that I had a choice in the matter, that I could say to the Lord that I was not ready, and He would choose someone else. I learned in January of 2000, that when you are called, you do not have a choice in the matter. You have to do it, just like Nike's commercial Just Do It. On April 27, 2004, God did heal my body from the blood disorder without an operation. I am so grateful today that the Lord selected me to be a laborer in the vineyard and a helpful companion to present needful results of an action or effort in aid of His ministry.

Be watchful and prayerful, for the avalanches of life are waiting to overtake you by the cares of this locality. It could be in the form of a large mass of loose snow, earth, and rocks that suddenly and swiftly is sliding down your pathway, roadway, or highway of life. The snow kills or suffocates all the life out of unbroken succession by smothering and eliding you with the cares of the world. The earth or soil can release devastation upon finances and health, causing unconventional hazard. The rocks can cause ruin or catastrophe to your homestead and bankruptcy to assets, totally demolishing all frail and delicate remains. These mishaps caused by nature will bring one back into a reality check of why we need God and why we should call on the name of Jesus in time of trouble.

The Lord can sustain your joy during any form of storm of life. God can undo the effects of the storm of driving snow and very frigid winds caused by life's blizzard, which would defeat your serenity and enjoyment in the Lord.

As a parent, I think the most trying storm in life is when we have to bestow tough love to our children. Especially, when we witness outside forces come in and begin to overtake them. We have done everything humanly possible by rearing and nurturing them with love, longsuffering, patience, and guidance according to the admonition of the Lord. Yet, they still prefer to journey down the pathway of darkness entrenched by the ungodly and unrighteous. Instill the Word of God through personal, family, and financial testimonies. Through it all, God is still on the throne waiting for them to see the error of their way and to return to Him. Never forget that our children are loaned or entrusted to us to rear them for only a season. Never forsake or give up on them and continue to love and pray for their salvation and deliverance, because the Lord did not give up on us while we were still serving the prince of darkness and principality of wickedness. God will remove the scales from their eyes to see their way through the valley of death when they are ready to come in for refuge or comfort from the storms of this life. Proverbs 20:11 says, "Even a child is known by his doings, whether his work be pure, and whether it be right." To the fathers and mothers who are constantly trying to justify the deeds, actions, and conduct of their children, remember the Word of God says, we owe no man anything but love (Rom. 13:8). Therefore, hold your head up and look to the hills from which come all your help from the Lord. You are going to need that help, for preparation for the next lesson or storm coming down your pathway, highway, or roadway. The storms will never stop or end in this life, but they will decrease as you gain more stimuli and strength to pursue your passion and destiny. You can endure and weather every affliction that the enemy brings your way.

People ask me why I am always so happy and content. I inform them that the unchanging joy of the Lord lives inside of me; no man or incident will take that away. Learn to operate with a brilliant mind and practical ability to think clearly and to act quickly and intelligently in an emergency if you desire to have prolonged or prolific joy residing inside of your body, mind, and soul. Sustaining and propelling joy during the storms of life are vital to all survival plans providing nourishment for inner toughness and durability, protecting and keeping you from the shrewd and unsentimental attacks of the earth and its inhabitants; and joy lasts in spite of hard times.

## SUSTAINING JOY DURING THE STORMS OF LIFE

The wise builder is a judicious consumer and buyer. The wise purchaser shops around before making any irrational or unanswerable buy of worthy land or lot for one's own needs and not for resale or to use in the production of faithful use. Their perception of a first home is not the world's perception of a first home; they are looking for something that represents their character and demeanor of God. They realize that God controls the realtor, loan officer, and closing officer.

The wise builder or steward constructs a spiritual dwelling on sonorous captivation and passion, peaceable and loyal, with elated enthusiasm, using poise and solid inspiring and endearing tender feelings toward the unit members. This unconditional love comes straight from the manufacturer, Jesus Christ, to create and develop a living place fit for the Master's use. So, when the storms and streams of life come to ravage or break away the trenches, the deep furrow plowed against narrow ground of the house will remain to stand the tests of life.

The piers or pavilions are grounded on the coalesced Word of God; each slab is structurally built and covered with the God's Word; a heavy column connected by grace and mercy. The frame or body of the dwelling place has a refined atmosphere expressing glory and reentry wonder, ecstasy, and pleasure, which bring elation to the Father's eyes and ears. The frame is free from bothersome and unfaithful skeletal structure.

The final attachment, the roof is outside on top, covering the dwelling place with pieces of lumber called rafters. Carpenters nail the bottom section of the rafters to the plates at the top of the outside walls. The rafters slant from plates and meet at the ridge board, a board placed at the ridge, or top edge, of the roof. Rafters parallel the weight of the roof, well-founded and exact. The joist supports the weight of the floor (foundation); the home nailed down absolutely in utterance and mirth draped with laughter and joy.

The interior construction includes (1) floors, (2) walls, (3) windows, and (4) doors. The floor has two layers, a lower layer lies at an angle across the floor joist. The upper, finished layer is made from tongue and groove boards. One side of each board has a tongue, or lip, and the other side has a groove, or slot. The tongue of one board fits snugly into the groove of another board. The family members are very cautious of what they say, being observant of the presence of God at all times. They are always pleading and exhorting the Lord to bridle their tongues. They are fully aware that the words that come from their mouth bring forth life and death. "Keep thy tongue from evil, and thy lips from speaking guile" (Ps. 34:13). They realize that this little member or part of the dwelling place could do or cause the most havoc being adulterated to reside such as, slyness, cunningness and craftiness. This dwelling place has no hidden or invisible walls, to obstruct or keep each member from having a productive and healthy form of giving or exchanging of adequate and truthful information.

Proper construction makes it contingent for the head to supervise a devoted and noble residency unto the Lord, licensed with reliance and certainty in the authorized position. The wise builder of dwelling places must furnish the means of subsistence through shelter, for quiet enjoyment, and as a shield from liability of unjust acts or unfair treatment. Alongside is an annex, added as a condition or consequence, which is like a caution or warning to household members to resist (stand against) the devil and he will flee (shun).

The electrical wiring provides lighting and furnishes outlets throughout the dwelling. The electricians install protective innovations called circuit breakers, which automatically cut off the current when too much current passes through a circuit. Otherwise the wire in the fuse melts or blows. The circuit breaker regenerates from the Holy Spirit electrical and magnetic sacrosanct apparatus.

The plumbing is piped through the river of life; that lifeline is connected to the food and water supply by God's Holy Word. To function properly, traps must have outside ventilation; places where unwanted and unclean spirits are disengaged outside of the place of refuge or hospice. The insulation alleviates the amount of heat or cold that passes through walls, floors, and ceilings. When the air around the house is warmer or colder than the air inside, heat passes from the warm air to the cold air. This means that when the trials and test of life come up against this dwelling, it has been weatherproofed by the power and authority of Jesus Christ. This dwelling place is fireproof and waterproof by the blood of the Lamb and in the name of Jesus. There is no weapon formed against this place that will or can stand (Isa. 54:17). Jesus is the center of this dwelling place.

The stewards of this household will grow with intense and unconstrained optimism to the highest or uttermost. Their belief system shares in ultimate good and primarily prevails over woes; they are more than conquerors through Christ Jesus in whatever comes against their dwelling be it physical, mental, spiritual, or moral intrusion of rottenness. They uplift and elevate the Lord with splendor and grandeur commendation for His ample magnanimity and just legislation. They recognize that God has given them the spirit of jubilee, a time for celebrating and solemnizing no longer being in slavery or bondage; they are free moral agents to serve the Lord.

This dwelling place detests evil and adheres to an explanation or interpretation of useful serviceability for the hereditary head of heaven and earth; as things are systematically coming together by God's divine appointment in the third dimensional realm. It is held together by the spirit of heartfelt warmth and cordial hospitality full of vivacious and exuberant explicit force of expression. Jesus notifies the disciples to hear His words considering the wise builder, building his house upon the boulder of Jesus. In addition, when the sorrow descended, super-abundant trials came, and utterance of falsehood damaging to family character or reputation spread and beat upon the house, it did not succumb or scatter into pieces. The house persisted in being unchanging or wavering in decision or purpose, resting on the solid foundation of the Lord (Matt. 7:24–25).

The landscape is a picture representing natural or inland scenery or expanses of natural scenery seen in one view, which is the fruit of the Spirit. The fruit of the Spirit is a final natural element; non-artificial or unaltered by man therefore it is an upstanding and upright feature of character and behavior to this household. No one tries to upstage the other by drawing attention to one's ambitions and accomplishments at the expense of the other family members. They uphold and keep each other from falling by giving moral endorsement and encouragement. The upkeep on this house is done with over high opinion of who resides and dwells within, yet asserting a spirit lack of density or uncommonness.

The master builder or architect will lay reinforced concrete embraced with stable reliance and trustworthy boulders. This builder has devised fitting parts or elements together systematically for many houses based equity; their foundation is able-bodied, healthy, and strong yet amenable, responsive, and submissive to the planner, builder, or creator, the Great Architect, Jesus Christ, whose profession is designing plans for spiritual buildings. The master planner has built, formed, or devised unique and striking but fitting parts or elements together systematically of several earthly houses needing specific care. The blockhouse is a sturdy, incorporated and resolute structure for defense or observation against their enemies. The greenhouse is a building made mainly of glass with heat and humidity regulated for thriving, nurturing, and formulating equanimity, calmness of mind, and evenness of temper and composure. The hothouse is a structure that needs careful treatment and is very delicate; it's the place where most trying and tribulations take place. The outhouse is used for purging and discharging waste that is undesirable and non-exchangeable garbage or repugnant matters and rubbish, all worthless, inadvisable ideas or statements and nonsense thrown away from the spiritual body or vessel. The storehouse is the place where things are stored and reserved for safekeeping, a warehouse for maintaining knowledge acquired through unselfish acts and good deeds. The summerhouse is small and open in a garden or park for providing a shady rest; a house or cottage in the country used during the warmest season in the year, the period or time of growth and development.[1]

There is a metaphor to all this madness or sadness. When talking about natural storms, it is often said, "there is a quiet before the storm." Henceforth, the quiet silence, peace, and tranquility are a deceptive and delusive lure or bait before the sudden violent, raging, and vigorous attacks of Satan. Heed to the warning of 1 Peter 5:7–9, which gives reference to your aggressor, the devil, who walks about as a roaring lion, seeking whom he may devour.

That is why it is important to cast all your cares upon the Lord, for you have brethren who are steadfast in the faith and suffering the same afflictions as yourself. No one knows the size of your storm but God. So don't wait for the onslaught; always have your spiritual guard up and make preparations early by praying and meditating daily. Prepare before the storm, and do not wait for the storm to provoke you to be obedient and servile during a specific crisis.

Rather, this should be apart of your calculated survival plan for weathering or fighting against all perturbation of the atmosphere in which there is strong resistance of water falling or coming down in drops condensed from the moisture in atmosphere along with outburst of rumbling sounds and discharge of change between a cloud and another or cloud to the earth. Clouds float in the lowest part of the atmosphere, called the troposphere where winds, storms, and other features of the earth's weather all take place. This is where the air gets thinner the farther it is from the earth. There are various types of windstorms such as typhoons, hurricanes, cyclone, tornadoes, or tropical storms that cause severe and tremendous damages to one's life, property, or possessions. A cyclone is a low-pressure area in the atmosphere with winds that spiral inward. A cyclone may cover an area or land half as large as the entire United States. A special intense kind of cyclone, usually only 300 yards across, is a tornado rising up. All cyclones have two unique characteristics: (1) the atmospheric pressure is lowest at the center, and (2) the winds spiral in toward the center. Usually, fierce, brutal winds occur with cyclones. The falling in the atmospheric pressure unwontedly, fair or good, is an indication that bad weather is approaching. But if a cyclone forms in dry air, there may not be any cloud formation. A tropical cyclone a serious type of cyclone that occurs over overheated ocean waters in the tropics. These cyclones are called hurricanes if they form in the Atlantic Ocean and typhoons if they form in the Pacific Ocean. They bring winds up to 180 miles an hour, terrific rains, violent thunder, and lightning. The most devastating natural storm is the typhoon, the vehement tropical cyclones that sweep over the Pacific Ocean from the Philippine Islands to Japan and the Coast of China. Similar storms are called hurricanes and they hit the West Indies and the eastern part of the United States. Typhoons are most frequent from July to October. These storms often do great damage in Japan, they travel slowly, but the violent gusty winds within the circle of the typhoon cause tragic destruction. The hurricane is the second powerful and whirling storm that measures several hundred miles in diameter. The winds near the center of a hurricane vigorously blow at speeds of seventy-four miles per hour or more. Many hurricanes have caused widespread death and destruction. A hurricane has two abilities: (1) function with winds that swirl around the eye, which is the calm and silence that is in the center of the storm, and (2) establish storm clouds called wall clouds sound the eye. The strongest force of winds and heaviest rain of a hurricane occur within its wall clouds. The winds and rain emanate with forces of the sea and produce huge tidal and surge waves. These waves, called the storm surge, are a rise in the water level of several feet above normal land levels and cause floods overland. The storm surge can be especially destructive if it occurs at high tide. As the hurricane moves over the land, strong winds and oppressive rain hit an area for many hours. As the eye reaches the area and the rain stops, the atmosphere and air will become calm and at peace. Yet, less than an hour later after the eye passes, the rain and winds will return to mayhem behavior. Meanwhile, the hurricane begins to attenuate as it moves overland, for it needs the warm sea to supply energy by evaporation. The friction or attribution between the land and wind helps use up the storm's energies; but the heavy rain continues even after the winds diminish.

The tornado is a powerful and convolution windstorm, whose winds are the most violent that occurs on the earth. They may whirl around the center of the storm at speeds of more than 300 miles per hour. A tornado is a rotating funnel cloud that extends downward from a mass of dark clouds. Tornadoes strike in the United States, generally around the spring and early summer. The violent weather is produced by a squall line that results when a mass of warm and humid air rises extremely rapidly. When the air increases and more warm air pushes through to replace it, then the ascending air inclines upward and begins to rotate. As the rotation takes place, a tornado is formed. The uncontrollable and recurring succession of change in the wind will blow down almost everything in its path of contact. The explosive force of a tornado can demolish a small building. Therefore, as the tornado passes over a house, it can suck up all the air from around the structure or surface of the foundation of the premises. The tremendous effects of a tornado's uplifting force results from a powerful updraft of air inside the funnel cloud or storm.[2]

Although these storms can uproot one's lives, overturn ambitions, dreams, and goals with heavy forms of commotion, confusion, and turbulence, do not be dismayed by the sizes of the storms of life. All protection or prevention comes from the Holy Spirit. In addition, no one can be storm watching without total coverage and shielding from the Spirit of God, who brings in a friendly, receptive, and solicitude climate.

His serene power hovers and suspends over your locality with a refreshing umbrella of safe conduct, safe guard, and safe-keeping. The waves of circumscription and circumvention may rise and rivers begin to flow against all kinds of obstruction to keep your mind stayed or fixed on Jesus. Even if you are in the valley of lows or mountaintop of highs, rest yourself in the arms and bosom of Christ.

The wise builder places storm shutters to protect the home-stead from unwanted, undesirable, and unpleasant foreign debris, repulsive nonsense, and insensitive statements. There is no power given to any man or organization to stop or cease the unaltered calamities or inborn tragedies. Prayer is one concept or device for moving the heart of God with a supernatural shutter or hinge. Anything on which matters turn or depend arrives by way of entreaty, persistent reflection, loyalty, deep preference, and humble request to the Father.

This provides shelter from disagreeable and exposable atmospheric conditions against windward and ailing blows of life. Be a wise builder who is nestled down comfortably and snuggled in the upright comfort and fondness of the Lord, who has partly hidden them away from petty traps and snares. No one can ever take what God has entrusted in your care; hold on to His everlasting power. Allow God to sweep your home regularly of foul devilish guests, and keep it consecrated and venerated unto the Great and Mighty King. There is no false sense of security for those who dwell in the secret place of God. In the time of trouble He shall hide you in His pavilion, the secret tabernacle, safe and secure from all forms of danger.

Let's not forget that Sodom and Gomorrah were destroyed by a rain of fire and brimstone for refusing God's unmerited favor and disposition of forgiveness. The Lord poured out His cup of indignation, anger, and wrath for the outworking acts, injustice

157

deeds, or meanness toward the innocent. They gave little regard to personal laws of retribution given repeatedly upon those who responded unrepentantly to God's justice. Some storms can bring devastating defeat for stubbornly contrary individuals—those lead astray from what is rectified or mistaken through worshiping or serving idol gods or mammon and anyone that perverts the good news. The rain of fire and brimstone represents God's judgment and sentence. Sodom and Gomorrah were sentenced to death for their unrestraint and drastic lascivious observable deportment.

The conclusion of the matter is that the storms in your life, whether of little value or importance, having comparatively less or more investment or capital, intermediate in quality, amount, degree or size, or something that is just taking up space can only last as long as you feed them with negative capacity or reinforcement. Without your attention, anxiety, or aggravation, they will cease to exist. Therefore stay on the boat that is anchored by the Holy Spirit, guided by the intercession and mediation of Christ Jesus, and protected by God's grace and mercy. Regardless of how many enemies may come your way, God will sustain and keep you in exact peace. Stop struggling in life's journey by placing a cloud of vertical structure used to bear during the daytime to protect against the storms, the strong disturbance, or upheaval of a political or social culminates. Never forget to walk with your head held high with humble and meek confidence. The enemy counterattacks and counteractions are no match for neutralizing the seizing and capturing forces of God. There is a place of rest in the storm cellar, an impressive cellar for shelter during frivolous or ominous windstorms, storms with drastic winds, but little or no special benefits, cheers, or acclaim. This cellar has a storm door or window; an extra door or window placed outside the regular one as added protection against winter the coldest season of the year. Hebrews 4:1–11 gives the perfect antidote for shelter during tempest attack, a violent storm with high winds that may be accompanied by rain, hail, or snow. The natural intent of this storm is to entice, provoke, attract or lure the saints of God from the commission of the Lord.

The perfect resident or rest comes with salvation, deliverance, and receiving the promise of ageless reconciliation of agreement with the Heavenly Father. Take heed to God's warnings and cautions, unlike the Israelites in the wilderness who did not receive the exhortation by faith and didn't acclaim rest in the Promise Land. The most essential, basic, intrinsic, and indispensable element, natural and suitable for any environment or situation needed in all homesteads, is Jehovah Jireh. Also never forget that the storms of life are temporary and only last for a season: they are temporal, lasting only for a short time; transitory, not eternal; of this world, not ecclesiastical. They have no substance or bearing on your place in the kingdom or advancing the kingdom's supplication. Remember, you are the temple of God, a holy and sacred vessel honorable for His use.

God can sustain your joy at all times, just keep Jesus Christ as the center of all of your joy. Say to yourself, my house is built on nothing less, than Jesus' love and happiness. For His joy is far above houses, lands, and riches.

> The name of the LORD is a strong tower: the righteous runneth into it, and is safe.
>
> —PROVERBS 18:10

# 5

## JESUS, MY JOY IN THE
## MIDST OF MY TROUBLES

*For your shame you shall have double; and for confusion they
shall rejoice in their portion: therefore in their land they shall
possess the double: everlasting joy shall be unto them.*

—ISAIAH 61:7

WHO COULD BE THE best example of keeping joy in
the midst of dissonance than Jesus? The prophet
Isaiah and John the Baptist both knew that Jesus
would come into the world to save mankind. Isaiah, son of
Amoz, is said to have been the greatest of all writing prophets;
his name means "the Lord saves."

He lived during the same period as the prophets Amos, Hosea,
and Micah, and several kings, including Uzziah. Isaiah's book
unveils the full dimensions of God's judgment and salvation.
He gives illustrations of how God would punish His children
who do not fear Him, but would deliver them in spite of their
sins. The book of Isaiah states that Israel had exceptional arid
justice; they were unrepentant, impenitent, and boldly insolent.
He warned them if they carried on after a warning or interruption in sin, that the judgment day of the Lord would soon

come. And the day would be named The Day of the Lord. The Lord sent word by his prophet that He would have compassion on His people and would rescue them from both the political and spiritual onerousness that they were under. God preserved their joy in the midst of their persecution and captivity by the Babylonians. His love for Israel was far greater than Israel's obsequious desire to be obedient. God message to Israel was peace, protection, and joy in the center of their adversity; God told them if they return to Him that they would no longer be ground by extremely vexatious tyrants. God was going to send Israel the Messiah, who would bring deliverance and salvation with Him.

In the Old Testament, through the prophet Isaiah the Lord began to give His revelation about Jesus, the Messiah, being born in Bethlehem and then of a great king who would seek to kill Him. The world (Satan's realm) wanted to exterminate Jesus, because they knew that Jesus would offer mankind a distinct gift of salvation so they no longer be slaves to pessimism but able to come into the marvelous light. This coruscation would disclose to man eternal life, and the enemy would be defeated if mankind receive this gift; man would chase after Jesus and not him. Therefore, Satan's task would be more intricate because he could not give man any more illusions if they could see God in the flesh. Now man would know and believe in their hearts that God was real and alive. Jesus came to earth and denied Himself any reputation, the One who deserved all praise—the Messiah, the Chosen One, the Prince of Peace, Lord of Lords, King of Kings and the Savior.

In the New Testament, John the Baptist was the son of Elizabeth, the cousin of Jesus' mother, Mary. John the Baptist was the forerunner for the Lord Jesus Christ. He came on the scene preaching and teaching about repentance. He was to prepare mankind's heart to be ready for the Word of God and receive salvation. His gospel message was to admonish the church of the importance of desiring a sinless and purified life; the only way into the Kingdom of Heaven was to be reborn. Not, yet born again, but to have turned from the error of their flagitious ways and lifestyle of sin. He lived a humble and meek life, but he was full of joy. He never compromised even when he was put in prison. John the Baptist never hesitated to preach and teach what the Lord said: that there was judgment coming upon God's people if they didn't repent and turn from the vexatious and perpetrating ways. He was also peripatetic in spreading the gospel as he commuted from place to place.

## OLD TESTAMENT JOY

The prophet Isaiah spoke first about a John the Baptist, the forerunner who sent notice to the church to repent of their sins. In Isaiah 40:3, he also told of the coming of the Son of Man, Jesus Christ. The forethought was told in part of John, who was the loud vocal sound or utterance coming out of overgrown land without shelter to God's people to make ready a specific route or direction for the true Messiah. Everyone should create a rigid or intemperate uninhabited highway for our Lord God.

The prophet Isaiah gave some motivating words for the down trodden, stating that the Lord can keep us when struggles and challenges come to test our faith. Isaiah says to refurbish yourself in the Lord and He shall renew your quality of being strong while your frailty will give way to God's strength. These will ascend on wings as eagles with vigor and speed. They shall move swiftly and not be fatigued, moving along with moderation and not without courage (Isa. 40:31).

Regal children, clashing will come in this life. Proceed to trust in the Lord; in your state of debilitation is when God's strength steps in. If you keep your eyes toward heaven, be like the eagle that soars high in the sky. The eagle soars high and looks low; he can see everything that is coming his way. The same is true for the believer if you look toward heaven; God can send relief on earth. It is remarkable how God can unveil and point out snares or traps that were set by enemies or the adversary.

God came and gave Isaiah a revelation from heaven: there is no man on earth purified or sanctified enough to offer up as a living sacrifice for mankind's debt. God would send to the earth a Deliver from the heavenlies, a true Savior, the chosen Messiah, the High Priest who would expiate the sins of the world by atonement. Jesus Christ, Son of the living God, is the trusted envoy or confidential representative of the Father that will bring reform and is a delight to His soul. He shall enforce understanding to the Gentiles, pagan, or heathen nations who choose to serve the living God. He will not be a typical dominator who leads by loud proclamations; instead, He will bring peace to all nations. The minced and fragile vessel shall not be broken; the fumitory seed will not be extinguished or subdued. He would bring forth a new law of truth of grace and mercy. No man would be able to cause Him to fall or be discouraged on His quest. He would finish His journey on earth. Those who were allocated and placed alone would wait for His lawful legislation to love everyone (Isa. 42:1–4).

God was exposing to his prophet that even though there would be nations of kings, Jesus Christ the Messiah, would be King of kings and Lord of lords. Jesus would be Savior for the world, by making atonement for the sins of mankind. There are no men that can keep you from entering into heaven. So do not allow man to take your joy, for you know one day you will see Jesus. I pray that, if nothing else can give you delight and hope, the good news of seeing Jesus face to face will give you exuding joy in the midst of your turbulence.

Even when the enemy confronts you with the past to keep a slipknot-restricted noose around your neck, do not allow him to reacquire or recapture your joy. Scriptures tell you in Isaiah 43:18–19 not to remember past hurts, pains, sins, and tribulations. Now you have a new life, new memories, new hopes, new dreams, and new visions. Be not mindful of the preceding time or matters, neither consider the affairs known from the past; apportion the awareness of your own reactions and totality of intelligible, comprehensible, and impressions to remind you of the awesomeness of God. Hold in view a new concept or abstract notion that will leap onward, refraining from capricious behavior and brusque and impulsive interchanges in the normal waking state. Things may come as freakish notions; just wait for a determining or compelling command, even though you may be perplexed in the state of breaching God's law and duty. He will send plentiful stream or flow of living water in your valley of death. What the Lord is saying here is to not allow the enemy to keep you in your past, because once you have been born again, you have a new life; God will extemporize your every condition of deficiency. He will give you bread when hungry—the bread of heaven and revelations and visions that will warn how close your foe is. He will give you water when you are thirsty from the fountain of emanating water, which is the Word of God that teaches all things and brings all inspirational things back to your remembrance for encouragement along the pursuit.

There is no one greater than God who dispenses genuine peace, joy, happiness, and love. Do not give anyone God's space in your heart, since He is the only one that will keep you in a time you need to be kept. He is the Anointed One, King of

Israel, the wondrous Redeemer, and marvelous Lord of hosts. He is the beginning and the end, the alpha and omega, the first and the last. Besides Him there is no other holy God. Anyone He calls, He shall attest or certify and set in order over his or her life. He appointed the ancient or people of old to come out of bondage in Egypt. God also controls the future and will reveal Himself to his people when necessary (Isa. 44:6–7).

The same thing God did back then, He is doing today— defending and protecting His children. God will not allow anyone or anything to hurt you for He is your Father and He loves you and will defend you. God is the Great Originator who will go in front of man and make his pathway, highway, and roadway incorruptible. He caused the pieces from the entrance of unashamed insolence and impudence to be discrete by intrusion from the obstructions of cruel and callous world (Isa. 45:2). God is telling Isaiah that there is nothing on the heaven or earth that can end His people. Regardless of where the enemy emerges, the Lord can and will find him, because no one or nothing is greater than He is; He knows all and sees all, for He created everything and everyone. The Lord God will reveal Himself to your opponents who you serve and who you belong too. God will justify you and find you righteous, for His ultimate fulfillment. The Lord God will help you; those who falsely inculpate the righteous will succumb to moths and will be blighted (Isa. 50:8–9). Never forget that the Lord will take care of you, even when you slip and make an oversight. He is there for you, so put all your trust in His hands and permit Him to deliver in His utter trueness and greatness; He was always there for the children of Israel and He will be there for you. God prospered Abraham and multiplied him with plenteous offspring by using Sarah, the wife of Abraham, who was barren. God brought a seed from her body that later become the blessing to many nations to follow. If God was able to stir up a great nation from one individual in the past, then he will surely be able to make Israel a great nation in spite of their present state of banishment. God will send comfort to Zion and the entire devastated region. And He will make her wilderness like Eden, a delightful paradise, and her uncultivated division like the fertile and well cultivated land of the Lord. He will extend joy and gladness to His people with endless hope. They will have praise and thanksgiving while having a vocal utterance of melody (Isa. 51:2–3).

Isaiah was telling the people of Israel that the Lord expected them to have exceeding joy regardless of their dilemmas and He didn't bring them out of Egypt for them to be concern about their own problems and affairs. He required them to be busy with His purpose for them and giving Him praise and worship, an easy assignment as He will always defeat their foes as they arose up against them. The Lord is continually sending angles to watch over them. Now He would send them a Redeemer that would give them the tools to take back from the evil one that which he took from them. He would deliver them from sin and its penalties. The Lord choice was to speak or call out strongly audibly unto the people of God, that there is liberty in Him. Eternal joy shall be His covering alongside causing them to have great pleasure and sensuous satisfaction (Isa. 51:11).

In the book of Isaiah, it is foretold how the children of Israel would be able to regain joy, which was through an ultimate Redeemer. This redeemer would conciliate and gain regard or good will by bringing them back to the Creator through kind acts. God had pity for his wayward children. Isaiah went so far as to reveal what God disclosed to him by narrating to the children of Israel what Jesus would encounter on earth on their behalf. He would be wounded for our transgressions and contusions from current, past, or present iniquities. The chastisement of our peace would be upon His arrival, and with His stripes we are made whole and complete from wretched life (Isa. 53:5). The Lord was fighting for Israel even when they were indefensible; as long as He was their God, no one would be allowed to produce pain or injury to them. As long as you are covered under the blood of Jesus, no weapon that is formed against you will ever prosper. And every tongue that rises up against you in judgment will be condemned, which is the futurity of the servants of the Lord. And their lawful claim is Jesus (Isa. 54:17). Regardless of Israel's insubordination to the Lord, He was a protector and guard over His descendants. If you remain under God's power of reasoning, The Holy Spirit will bridle your actions and conduct.

Isaiah gave the children of Israel the same message that Jesus quoted in Luke 4:16–21, while in the synagogue at Nazareth as a revelatory precept by God. The time was at hand, and they needed to turn to the Lord for full reconciliation and restoration so they could become heirs of the kingdom of God. Jesus was commissioned and anointed by God to preach unspoiled information to the spiritless. He was the task force and call driven to give liberty to the brokenhearted while proclaiming repentance to captives of sin. Making men independent from spiritual and mental bondage would be coming in the year of Jubilee, the satisfactory year of the Lord. The day of vengeance of our God will be soon, and He will soothe the distressful and sorrowful from feelings of worthless. He will also provide them with a gratifying attribute while removing religious and traditional downfalls. The garments of praise for the spirit of heaviness later will be atoning as trees of moral basis and fiber. The concealing of the Lord's agriculture, the work of cultivating the Word of God, producing the results, and raising truth in the field will be His glory of unchangeable strain into revelatory reality (Isa. 61:1–3).

No matter how much deliberate devastation or turbulence came Israel's way, Isaiah was always pointing out to them how important it was for them to keep their joy by praising God and rejoicing to His holy name. As God rejoiced over Israel being His bride, He wanted them to rejoice over Him being their bridegroom with thanksgiving and commendation. It was an honor and privilege for them to be selected as His bride. God had many nations to choose for His bride, but He chose Israel. It was a blessing for them that He choose them, since He saw their offerings coming from a stiff necked and frigid hearted group of people. He continued to love them when they forsake Him, turned their backs on Him, and were congested with sin. Nevertheless, He was there waiting with open arms to resume them back to His favor. He never gave up on them, even when it didn't seem as though they would ever turn from the error of their ways or repent. God loves you the same way, even when you appear to not be listening to His instruction or receiving His guidance, He is there with open arms waiting for you to return back home like the prodigal sons and daughters you are. Every child of God was unclean and unrighteous in a filthy and dehumanized state without the blood of Jesus; and without it, we would become inhuman or machinelike. His passion, temperament, or attitude offers forgiveness of sins and debts (Isa. 64:6).

As the prophet Isaiah concludes his message to Israel, he tells them that there will be a joy in the new age through Jesus Christ. He fully understood how Israel felt for he was living under the same conditions, but unlike the Israelites who choose to throw out God's healing for the land. Isaiah reminded them to sing a song of joy from their hearts, although they had a broken spirit which their disobedience had brought about, not the penalty imposed on them by the Lord for their wrongdoings (Isa. 65:14). Isaiah kept his mind heaven bound and his trust in the Lord. God had given him true revelation, and he knew that Jesus would come to take away all the pain and sorrow of this old world and give believers a new environment full of joy and peace. The Lord told Isaiah He was going to create a new heaven and earth; no longer would the children of Israel have to remember the things of their past. God did not create them to mumble and complain during tribulations, but to be people of gaiety spirits at all times (Isa. 65:17–18).

There is a lesson from what Isaiah was referencing to the Israelites in the above scriptures—Jesus would soon come and pass out the joy that would surpass all their understanding. Moreover, if they would keep their trust in the Lord, He would sustain them and keep them in the midst of their trials. God was going to give the children of Jerusalem a new gift in the form of Jesus through His birth and death.

## New Testament Joy

The name John means "the Lord is gracious." However, John got his title "the Baptist" or "the Baptizer" from his ministry of baptizing those who came to him in repentance. John lived in the wilderness west of the Dead Sea. He was son of Zacharias. His entire ministry focused on repentance and remission of sins through baptism. The Jews knew of baptism for Gentile converts, but had not heard that the descendants of Abraham under the Jewish law needed to receive water baptism and give repentance of sins. The Jews did not want to accept that they had to repent, which involved making an open confession. John's emphasis on repentance stirred up and called to mind what the prophets of old said. God gave revelation to the prophets that

Israel would have to repent from their sinful nature and return unto Him.

John was a simple man with long hair, with camel's skin for his clothes, subsisting on locusts and wild honey. He first began his preaching in the wilderness of Judea, telling men to recognize their need for repentance in the sight and presence of God and man.

He preached saying that there was another that would come that he (John) would not be worthy of unloosing His shoes. He was aware that all he could give them was natural water baptism, but the Mighty One would give them the spiritual baptism of water and of the Holy Ghost. For many years Israel had no prophets and no one to pass on God's mandate; it was as if this had been erased from their minds and hearts. Maybe that was why John's preaching seemed to be so irruptive and untimely compared to their previous lifestyles.

Everyday John had plethoric joy, preaching the gospel of Jesus Christ. He never defaulted from the piece of work he had to do, until his imprisonment for speaking the truth to the vile King Herod and Queen Herodias. The queen was very annoyed by John revealing her sin openly, and she became fierce and full of malice. John told evil king Herod that he was breaking the Jewish law by being with his uncle's wife. Herod wanted to kill John, but he couldn't because John was a holy man, so he put him in prison. Herodias was so driven by aversion toward John the Baptist that she used her daughter, Salome, to dance for Herod while he was intoxicated and manipulated him into murdering John the Baptist. Salome danced so seductively for Herod and his guests, that he offered her anything she wanted and she consulted with her tyrant mother who asked John the Baptist's head on a platter. Herod, a wretched man that feared men more than God, granted Salome's request from her mother.

171

In repugnance, John was executed—one who was industrious and unpretentious, blissfully being about his Master's business.

John the Baptist died preaching and speaking the truth. Someone may ask how you know that John the Baptist was a patriot, one who loves and loyally or zealously supports the gospel. Because he stayed on his course; preaching repentance was the only occupation the Scriptures revealed he had—unlike some who will receive multiple degrees and still be not able to make career or vocation choices.

You must be able to comprehend how important it is for you to repent and turn from your obnoxious ways. After losing the presence of joy, you should be able to sense something is internally wrong with your earthly vessel by the way you communicate with others. Something may be wrong with your love and peace if the valley experience is longer than the mountaintop event. If you feel that you have lost your joy, it means that something is wrong in your spiritual root or foundation. Joy has been overtaken with something else; or other forms of offense may exist, such as unforgiveness, bitterness, or resentment. These pieces of fruit are integrals to maintain joy in the midst of everything; they are maintenance tools for rejoicing.

God gave the new church another gift through the death and ascension of Christ; if Jesus never left the earth, then the Holy Spirit would have not been sent to indwell in the hearts of all men. Unlike Jesus and the disciples who could only reach or touch the lives of few, the Holy Spirit is able to dwell in the hearts of those who desire to be children of God. Suffering brings forth the greatest or highest degree of joy through a true heart, where undivided and inseparable allegiance is located farther within the basic or essential nature. Suffering provides thorough and unqualified assurance of faith, which knows no hesitation in trusting and relying on and following

Christ. Emotions, strong feelings, and excitement accompanied by personality attributes are dispersed from a morally vitiated conscience and total freedom from a sense of guilt.

## SUFFERING BRINGS JOY

Later in the Scriptures, Paul tells the church of Corinth that they are expected to undergo ache and disarranged pain for Jesus Christ. In 2 Corinthians 6:3–6, Paul is concerned that he lived an exemplary life since he did not want the ministry denigrated. He verified to them that his teachings was not serving one's own selfish welfare at the expense of others but for the sake of the holistic ministry, he endured it all with patience, calamity, natural causation, and distress. He also was beaten, imprisoned, greatly feverish, hard working, abstained from eating, and a watchman. He gave up prestige and honor. He was exonerated of sin or guilt, long and patient endurance of trials, sameness of feeling accompanied by the Holy Ghost with genuine and sincere love.

Paul acknowledged that he was given an affliction in his body so he would not become elevated or high minded but kept humble to preach the gospel. He went to the Lord three times about removing the affliction but the Lord refused to do so, which He explained to Paul. He understood that the Lord would keep him and he instructed his followers that it is better to glory in your infirmities and depend on the strength of Christ than to trust in their own strength, which can only bring mayhem. He was a living testimony of someone rejoicing and taking pleasure in infirmities, reproaches, necessities, and persecutions for Christ's sake. Early in Paul's journeying he learned to put himself in the hands of the Mighty Conqueror, who delivered him through it all (2 Cor. 12:9–10).

Later in the text, Paul, like John the Baptist, entreated them to repent before it was too late. In fact, Paul wanted them to have repented prior to his arrival. The Corinthians were back to their old ways of dealing in debates and displaying envy, wrath, strife, backbiting, whispering, disruption, and confusion. Paul prayed that they would heed his warning; but at his arrival if there was no peace, he would take a case against them. Paul was agitated that many had returned unto uncleanness, fornication, and licentious acts rather than heeding to his instructions of godly sorrow or repentance. He felt and expressed grievance for their fruitless and obstinate souls (2 Cor. 12:19–21).

Outside of being a preacher, preceptor, and scholar, Paul was most importantly a reliable mentor to Timothy and Titus alongside many more. He was proud and full of joy to hear the good news from Titus regarding the church of Corinth's spiritual maturity in staying true to their call of the gospel of Jesus Christ. He was a mentor who was struggling with a few personal mishaps in the commencement of his ministry, who became bold in his teachings of moral character and the importance of mentorship.

Jesus is your joy in the midst of all your matters. The Father said He will never leave you nor forsake you, and Jesus is your advocate and makes intercession to the Father. Unlike Israel, who had no one to make intercession for them, Jesus came to sustain God's people. He has no discordant interest, conflict between obligation to the public or for self-interest, when it comes to interceding for His bride. As the cases of elected officials who own stock in a company seeking government contracts, there is no one above the Great Investor, who upholds or holds all power. The word of the Father has the last say in all decision-making on heaven and earth. When there is confidence and assurance that Jesus is vindicating our case before any court of law and order, it gives us much joy.

The Holy Spirit is the midwife that helps each believer with the birth of eternal joy. This eternal joy may come during daily or constant affliction, which comes to injure or distress the spirit man. During times of great misery or distress that comes from oppression, affliction, or trial, or while being made the object of scornful laughter by others jokes or mocking, the joy of Jesus is the perfect medicine.

## JOY IS JUST A PRAYER AWAY

Prayer refers to reverent words and thoughts directed towards God by way of worship. Prayer is man's universal means of communicating with the heavenly Father; it's the way He brings His celestial will into being on earth. Prayer involves the Trinity—the Father, the Son, and the Holy Ghost. People pray to ask for spiritual benefits and physical needs for others as well as themselves, their family, and loved ones. Also they offer praise, thanksgiving, or adoration to God, the object and subject of worship. Prayers are also petitions used for spiritual warfare against the wiles of the intimidator. Every Christian has an obligation, responsibility, and accountability to pray for others and self. Prayers may take the form of speech, song, dance of noiseless reverence or utterance. Some people kneel while praying or bow, lay prostrate, stand, or spread out stretched hands. In praying, imploring may be used or a shortened form of directly requesting and making supplication to the Father in the name of Jesus. Prayer is the primitive goal in the life of the believer; nothing can be accomplished without fervent and sincere prayer. Prayer is viewed as the most important or significant form of worship throughout the field of activity or influence; most people have regular prayer time designated during both corporate and private services. Individuals may also offer private prayers that express personal thoughts. Contemplation is done before praying so that one can concentrate only on the object of worship: God.

There are many prayers used in the lives of believers, but we have a few that have always helped us through trying and hard times. A sincere prayer becomes God's own words, alive from within your inner being and parts. The prayer of praise and thanksgiving opens the heart and allows joy to come from within the spirit man, releasing gratitude and unconditional love. Prayer is praise to the Lord for deliverance and instruction in godliness. Praise commonly leads to a call to worship and offer thanks from all faithful supporters of the Lord. His servants have reasons to rejoice and praise Him for providing unfailing protection and shelter from the storms of life. Prayer reflects the goodness of triumphant victory over one's iniquitous battles. As you enter into the very presence of God, with praise as the admission ticket, you respond with joy to His benefits and show bestowed admiration and grace to the King. There is a multiplicity of praise applications that can be rendered up to express one's blissful appreciation for His glory in your life. Some of the Hebrew words and applications of these are: *twoadah*—sacrifice of thanksgiving or praise (bowing); *yadah*—outward hands held toward the heavens (standing); *barak*—blessing the Lord with praise and thanks for His abundance of blessings (kneeling); *halal*—dancing and celebration (standing); *zamar*—praising and celebrating with instruments and ensembles (standing); *tehillah*—psalms, hymns, and dance with expressive jubilation (standing); and *shabach*—praise, adoration, and devotion (bowing, kneeling, or prostrate).

The poignant prayer of a soul deeply troubled by the fragility of human life reminds us of by the present illness through which God is rebuking humanity for transgressions. This prayer in times of illness helps acknowledge sin and express deep trust in

God. The poignant prayer for confession and forgiveness must be done before making intercession or petition on the behalf of others or self. Confession must be made in order to acknowledge or disclose the admission of guilt or sin. The confession of sins in sacrament or penance must happen before forgiveness can take place. A sinful lifestyle will cause much punitive damage or exemplary expense. This may result from inconvenience of just privileges, hazards beyond actual loss, or imposed delay to obey the voice and will of God. Later giving acceptable statement of one's religious belief openly by telling one's transgression to God in worship service or in private, this forgiveness prayer must be offered because unforgiveness breaks down full communication with the Lord. Unforgiveness will desensitize your spiritual being and side track thoughts of conviction, disappointment, or fault. Forgiveness will bring godly sorrow or ethical remorse, a deep and torturing sense of guilt over wrongdoings. Once you forgive others, God is faithful and righteous to forgive you of your sins and cleanse away unrighteousness. Forgiveness will help you give up resentment against or the urge to punish others for their evil misgivings. You have a liking or preference to pardon or overlook an offense of others.

The prayer for joy is making a solemn vow to praise Him for amnesty and sanitization, accompanied by training and pardon. Pardon follows praise; do not subject your moral senses to perverted and irrational feelings, judgments, opinions, and views. Prayer for freedom from all physical matters in spite of corruptible intention helps us remain steadfast, faithful, and willing with a portending spirit of servitude. The joy of our salvation will return to gladden our polluted soul, and it is by His Spirit that God gives His people a new heart and new spirit to live by His will. Only those who know and do the Lord's will can expect to receive auspicious responses to their prayers.

There is a confident prayer to God to deliver from all those who conspire to bring one down; this prayer presupposes the Lord's covenant with His people. There are prayers for liberation from deadly perils and threats of unfriendly and defying enemies, for escape and rescue when confronted by conspiracies and unlawful or infested ploys of powerful and tyrannous individuals. The heart of prayer itself is found to be exuberant, full of life, and nourished with vitality. One must come before the Lord with childlike faith with specific request and knowing how much He desires to give good gifts to His children. Make certain your petition is properly directed and motivated, bringing glory to Him, asking in faith without dubious reaction or having double-mindedness.

A prayer for understanding and patient acceptance of the conciseness of life is a modest prayer, granted for relief from present voices of disapproval or reprimand. There is a terse prayer of mercy when seriously ill and the illness is related to sin. Enemies will greet the prospect of death with malicious glee and betrayal. The prayer of deliverance is used when threatened by ferocious enemies of darkness composing danger. This is followed by a time from daybreak to midday of recovery based on faith bearing fruit, which pleases the Lord. Pray and communicate with God in confidence, giving Him absolute freedom to speak and provide clear direction, broad wisdom, generous knowledge, fortified strength, and tremendous protection. Prayer is God's way of setting sovereignty on the earth, working through people, not working around them. It is a great defense mechanism to protect and shield the mind from any behavior unconsciously used by pestiferous influence. This is how you can capsize or else guard yourself against menial past feelings which are under attack, as you have been deemed not guilty by the colossal Arbitrator. Prayer is a great implemented instrument, tool, utensil, or weapon in fighting spiritual warfare; it is a wonderful intellectual sustenance for the body, mind, and soul.

Make an imperative and urgent prayer for God's help when impended by obstructions or oppositions, pleading for instantaneous support and guidance. Also, request that the Lord make haste to save you from dilemmas and unpleasant alternatives and request God's continuing help in epochs of vulnerability. Through prayer, God reveals mysteries to His people during times of great and sore troubles, while not exempting hardship from them. Prayer, along with praise, is another vital disciplinary tool that is key to successful spiritual warfare; it is one of the most prevailing weapons made readily available to the believer. Praying is an act of one's own will, whether praying in the Spirit or with utterance of understanding. Praying in the Spirit has an authority of heaven behind it, being prompted by the Holy Spirit it overlays unseen or foreseen dangers. Pray interminably and humbly with prayer and supplication in the Spirit, as vigilant watchmen coming before the Lord having or showing a consciousness of one's lack of something needful for completeness or shortcoming. This gives easement—the right to operate under unction of the Holy Ghost—releasing earnest and heartfelt prayers.

The concept of prayer warriors has eluded many, and they adjoin to praying in selfishness, boasting, and pestiferousness. Prayer warriors are to be the forerunners and interceptive messengers for the body of Christ, capable to overcome with triumphant victory the psychological, physical, or moral forces and attacks from adversaries. With the power of the Lord, they can successfully disregard, resist, and outride the uncomfortable and awkward arousal or constrained disturbance resulting from opposing impulses. Boastful and vainglorious prayers serve to communicate random, repetitious, and redundant lyrics or libretto for a captivated audience. Evil inventors pray to air out others' secrets or dirty laundry, often for retaliation and revenge. In the past the Lord would have abandoned individuals for a season while they learned their lessons; but today the blood of Jesus covers the uncultured and unlearned. Prayer is a time for making preparations for removal of sins and impurities of the heart, the center of emotions and personality accredits. Then we shall be ready and receptive to experience God's lesson or rule. Those who are God chasers or pursuers offer prayers of earnestness and seriousness, not ceasing until they receive a breakthrough or deliverance. Prayers enhance the concentration of a free thinker, a person who forms his or her opinion about one's relationship independently of a superficial tradition, authority, or established belief. After having walked in obscurity, lack of understanding, or with a memory filled by a filthy cloud of pessimism, the joy of Jesus Christ is our greatest reward.

## THE JOY OF JESUS

On the Sermon on the Mount, Jesus gave the beatitudes to His disciples, which told them to rejoice and leap for joy, because their reward would be in heaven for the similar and polite ways of social behavior as their forefathers did to the prophets (Luke 6:23). Jesus related to the disciples that they should rejoice that their names are written in the book of Heaven (10:20).

In the parable of the lost sheep, Jesus gives an example of how the body of Christ should rejoice when the lost come into fellowship or return into the fold. God has great concern and joy at the sinner's repentance more than the religious ones who feel no need to have repentance and see it as invalid and needless (15:6–7).

In the parable of the lost piece of silver, a woman lost a coin in her house and had to use a lighted candle to find it. When the woman found her lost coin, she wanted her friends and family members to rejoice with her. The same is true in the spirit of the angels in heaven; they rejoice when one wrongdoer repents and comes into the kingdom of God. There should be a quake on earth as well as in heaven (15:8–10).

The parable of the lost son or prodigal son, tells the believer that we should be waiting with open arms when another leaves from the fold and becomes captivated by bewitching new methods of this era. We should frolic when the estranged child of God comes back into the congregation or flock (15:32).

God wants his children to have a heart like Jesus by desiring that no man should perish but all be saved. How do you know that Jesus is in the midst of all your annoyances? In the parable of the good shepherd, Jesus describes to the disciples how a good shepherd gives his life his sheep. Jesus exhibits the dissimilitude between a good shepherd and a bad shepherd. The good shepherd is concerned about the sheep's salvation and deliverance, but the bad shepherd that is hired is only concerned about his wages. The hireling is mindless about the salvation and deliverance of God's people; he or she is in it for the money. The hireling will run from responsibility and won't be held accountable for the body of Christ. But Jesus, the Good Shepherd, loves and cares about his sheep. Jesus will be their joy in the midst of discomfort; His sheep know Him and trust in Him. Jesus acknowledges that He came to lose His life for the lost and unbelievers who are in need of hearing the gospel of Jesus Christ and want salvation (John 10:11–18).

Just as those of the world abhorred and despised Christ, they will lower your spirit and cast you aside as unpopular and unprofitable for their advancement. The children of God are to have love for everyone as He did, especially the brethen. Jesus wanted them to understand that they must bring forth fruit through joy and pain. Moreover, through it all, the fullness of His joy will remain within us at all times (15:11).

Jesus would be leaving them soon; they were to maintain their joy in the midst of all their sorrow. Jesus was aware that He couldn't tell the disciples that He was going to be crucified soon, because they might have interfered with His terminal destination. Henceforth, He told them that He would not be with them much longer and He wanted them to trust and believe in what He had taught them. Sometimes the world will rejoice in your sorrow and mourning, but rejoice, for your sorrow will be turned into joy (16:20). He didn't want them to grieve over their loss of having Him on earth in the flesh, but to have joy that they would finish their course. Jesus told them that they would have tribulation in the world, but in Him, they would have joy. Therefore, He wanted them to put all their trust in Him and not in what the world would bring against them. Trials are going to come until the Day of Judgment, but Jesus told them that He has prevailed in the world with exceeding inspiration (16:33). Jesus prayed for the disciples that none of them would be lost or overtaken by temptation. He stressed the importance of not reclaiming their old ways or compromising to perpetrate mayhem. Jesus went to the Father to ask God to keep them while they were in the world, that the evil one could not overtake them. He prayed that they would become one with each other as He and the Father were One with fulfilled joy (17:11–13).

The joy of Jesus was what added souls daily to the body of Christ through their steadfastness and obedience of communion of the gospel. The fellowship and oneness in the early church was about dispensing the fruits of everyone's labor among the brethren in the spirit of gratefulness. The earlier church had the joy of Jesus. They broke bread from house to house eating together with gladness and single heartedness, alongside of praising God and having partiality in the company of all people (Acts 2:46–47).

The Father in heaven protects you against demonic altercations by dispatching guardian angels all around His children. Nebuchadnezzar spoke a blessing on Shadrach, Meshach, and Abednego who had guardians sent from God to protect and deliver them while in the unrestrained or uncontrolled hot furnace. Because they refused to give up trusting and believing in the living God and chose not to serve or worship another god, they were a great testimony (Dan. 3:28).

A true and beatific life of oneness comes when there is no more pestering and uneasiness in one's life; understanding retribution connotes relief for the righteous as well as punishment for the unrighteous. Paul, in his spiritual travels, came to places of discomposure and unrest, therefore he had apathy for suffering (2 Thess. 1:4–7). We all will come to forks in the road, where there is a choice to make between serving God with gladness or serving God with deep tearfulness. I will make the choice many of my brothers and sisters of the Bible did: I will serve the Lord with pain, suffering, weakness, misery, or defeat with a spirit of glee.

Jesus sits on the right hand of the Father making intercession for His bride daily. We are not making this trip alone; Jesus said that He would never abandon us nor forsake us (Heb. 13:5). There is nothing in the world that can disconnect us from the love of Christ; not improbable calamity, harassment, persecution, starvation or thirst, nakedness, jeopardy, or bereavement. Even, many of you are feeling like butchered sheep among wolves as gales preying all day long (Rom. 8:35–36). Jesus is the

Tribune and Good Shepherd holding the staff of peace, perseverance, and purity to protect His sheep from the abysmal and abominate wolves.

Jesus has dual role for the body of Christ. As the mediator, He intervenes on the behalf of the defendants while intercepting and taking the prayers and petitions to the Father with love and mercy (1 Tim. 2:5). As the prosecutor, He presents the case in front of the jurors of the world who attempt or try God's people. The great Defense Attorney stands before the mercy of the Judge and the court, God and the heavenly angels, proceeding over the cases of the saints made by their false accusers, the devil and world. He reminds them of God's new testament to the church, that redemption came and the debt was fully paid for all of man's transgressions. The saints of God have an opportunity to receive the promise of an infinite inheritance of mercy and grace (Heb. 9:15).

In contrast to what you may believe, a spiritual war is going on within your mind daily. The Prince of Darkness is trying to defeat your will power with wasteful thoughts, acts, and deeds. You have no choice but to let Jesus get in the midst of all your affairs. Jesus came to give God's creation joy through eternal salvation and restoration by bringing reconciliation back to the Father and mankind. There is reassured joy in the midst of all your calamities.

# 6

## MISERY, THE THIEF OF JOY

*And whatsoever mine eyes desired I kept not from them, I
withheld not my heart from any joy; for my heart rejoiced in
all my labour: and this was my portion of all my labour.*

—ECCLESIASTES 2:10

THERE IS A SAYING in the world: misery loves company.
That saying is very true. Individuals who suffer from
the state of misery want others to be bleak, dismal,
dreary, and melancholy. They have no desire for others to have
joy unless it is present within their area of operation. In general
they are always speaking about pessimism and atrabilious
outcomes.

The *Webster's Dictionary* defines *misery* as a condition
of great wretchedness or suffering, because of pain, sorrow,
poverty, etc.; distress; a cause of such suffering; pain, sorrow,
poverty, squalor (filth), etc. Anyone can tell by this definition
that anybody in this condition would appear to be ill tempered
and dismal. It is vitally important to discard this stipulation
or provisional part of one's character as a believer. Self-discipline or fortitude deficit will lead to self-depravity, self-defeat,
and self-termination. There is no life that can come from this

prerequisite. This is the first sign of illness and ailment within your supernatural house. The Holy Spirit can come in, do a clean sweep, and extinguish all moral impurities. You must comprehend that the dangers of staying in this state can become contagious within the vestment walls of Christ.

## THE CURSE OF SORROW—MISERY

The first sign of misery came from the curse God put upon Adam and Eve after their act of dispraise and degradation in the Garden of Eden. Adonai, Lord of the Old Testament, dispossessed their rights as ambassadors of the land of excellence and perfection and gave them hard to bear and scarce manual work. God cast them out into a land of desolation and loneliness in disjunction from His daily interchangeable sharing and endowment.

His harsh treatment to Eve was that she would have much sorrow and grief during her time of conception and labor. Her undergoing of childbirth would be very laborious, painful, and aching. Her first desire would be to please her husband and his needs. Her husband would have headship, the position of authority and chief leadership in their household. She would experience anguish and agony rather than alloyed joy and blessings without persecution (Gen. 3:16). Adam's labor would be tedious and tiresome lacking the competence to tarry during his days of on earth. He would have to till and work the land in raising and producing crops (v. 17). He would cultivate and manufacture sufficient resource to supply the needs of his family daily. Through the aid of the Holy Spirit, he would be able to furnish a source of strength and expertness within himself to supervise and oversee the security and defense for his family.

Simon, the sorcerer, was another who loathed sorrow with the root of the fermentation of rising from misery. Simon said he desired to be baptized, yet it was tricky to know whether his faith was genuine. Simon told Peter that he believed in their ministry, but his heart was impure in the sight of the Almighty. Simon was attracted to the laying on of hands and the empowerment gift of the Holy Ghost. From the day of Pentecost, only those who belonged to Christ received the Holy Spirit. To others outside of the church, it yet had been made manifest. Many people desired to have something that was new feeling and that would make them be seen by others as special and unique. They were looking for acceptance and appreciation before man, doing anything to be a part of the in-crowd at any price. Simon was so intrigued by this impartation, that he offered the apostles money for the transformation. Peter explained to Simon that this gift cannot be purchased, it comes only by way of believing and accepting Jesus Christ as one's personal Savior. The Lord knows the heart of all men and knew Simon's heart was dull and uninspiring. Simon and all his worth was to perish or be ill fated. He needed to repent for his misused or misdirected intentions and pray that the Lord might have mercy on his soul, that his transgression might be forgiven. Peter told him that his art was in gall of bitterness and in the bond of iniquity. Simon beckoned to Peter to pray for him that God's omen would not come upon him (Acts 8:18–24).

No matter how amazing someone's gift appears to intrigue your mind, what God has for you is for you. You have no real reception or inkling of how much time they have to invest in praying, fasting, and meditating. The word says, "To whom much is given, from him much will be required" (Luke 12:48). That means the more that is given or permeated by God, the greater indebtedness for favor and service.

## Destined for a Life of Misery

In the Old Testament, Jezebel was an individual possessed by a miserable spirit. She did evil in the sight of the Lord. Jezebel was the daughter of Ethbaal, king of the Zidonians, a king and priest of Baal worshipers. She desired to serve and worship Baal (1 Kings 16:31). She was uncircumcised in the things of God and brought more demonic spirits into the nation of Israel. The Jezebel spirit originated in the God of Eden, but it reigns today in the lives of individuals with insecurity or power control issues. These people are prime examples of miserable persons with a preponderate and predominant power over inferior or pitiable people—those afraid of conflict, easily influenced, or immature in understanding the will or Word of God.

Many believers today are the same way, they do not realize that disobedience, and non-submission to authority and leadership is a sin of indifference to God. God placed leaders over His people to give them revelation, instruction, direction, and guidance. If you are in an assemblage and you cannot accept or respect the leadership from your pastor, you need to pray and seek the Lord for personal guidance and instruction. Never move from a congregation to another solely based on emotions and feelings; this could jeopardize or postpone your spiritual growth as well as blessings. The spirit of misery will follow you to the next body of faith as well, making everyone there pitiable as you strive to get back at people who hurt you or caused you pain at the last house of fellowship. You are commanded to overlook the delinquency and wrongs of others, often trained to forgive but not forget which results in taking revenge at a later time and place. This will only allow the spirit of misery, villainy, and miscreant to harbor within your heart.

## THE MISERABLE SPIRIT OF JEZEBEL

When Ahab married Jezebel, he brought in a chronic spirit of corruption and unmoral practices brought to Israel due to Jezebel's ungodly beliefs and customs. She served Baal and wanted to convert Israel from serving God into serving Baal bringing customs such as giving human sacrifices and building temples in honor of his name. She was determined to bring idolatry into the hearts and minds of God's people. Ahab allowed this to take place, so God brought a three-year famine in the land of Israel. Elijah was sent to confront him about his sinful decision and tell him what it would cost his people. But Ahab refused to return back to God because he feared or loved his wife more than God of Israel.

Jezebel brought a lot of pain and suffering on God's people. She had one hundred prophets murdered because she was full of malice, and spoke words of prevarication and contempt. Later she would expire from a gruesome and direful death, as wild dogs would eat the remains of her decomposing body. Given the same prophecy as her husband, she failed to heed or yield to the voice or command of the Lord. Nothing moved her to repentance due to a cold heart of wax and ill-disposed superego, which would be the death of her and anyone that disowned to hear or receive the warnings of the Lord (1 Kings 16:30–21:24).

Many people who are miserable never want to deal with their personal condition or state of mind. They will make your life hectic if allowed, while not dealing with the unrealistic issues in their adverse will and faulty ways. Individuals with a Jezebel spirit may never want to be cordial, let alone joyful; they are persuasive, imperious, manipulative, and controlling. A person with a Jezebel spirit is overtaken with loneliness, possibly from being smothered by unnatural behavior caused by the inner child expenditures and issues, such as defection or abandonment of loyalty, causing stifle inland freedom. This inner character fault will produce cheating action or trickery to followers subjecting them to spiritual death. They are in need of intercessory prayer for deliverance and healing to come into their lives. They will bring secret and ill natured events in their lives, meanwhile becoming unconscious of their reviling lifestyle and influence.

Jehu met with Joram (or Jehoram) and told him that there would be no peace in the northern land as long as his mother licensed prostitution and black magic. Both are punishable by death (2 Kings 9:22). If you are not cautious, you will be drawn into the same condoling party. On the other hand, if you do use wisdom and discernment, God will display how to refuse or to cooperate with those operating under the influence of a Jezebel's fraudulent profane spirit that brings in the spirit of death. They will cause you to sin and have blood on your hands and not choose to consult with God first. They are bearers of mischievous news, which comes from passive events and happenings. Jehu became inflamed and sore with wrath and hit Jehoram with an arrow that went straight through his heart and into the chariot behind him (2 Kings 9:24). Jehu was like his father, mesmerized by his mother's enchanting spell, and felt the need to protect her name, when in all truthfulness she was a miserable and segregated person. She was a very evil mother providing him with infelicitous and warped counseling. There is judgment for maleficent and aggressive counselors and advisers who are shrewdly unsentimental and insensible to the practical illuminating facts of God's will and way.

God is going to bring judgment for those causing pain and suffering to come upon His children. They cannot get around their day of chastisement if they're under submission or subjugation of this demonic stronghold. Jehu murdered Joram, king of Israel, and Ahaziah, king of Judah, because of the evil they had done against the Lord God. In spite of the fact that his father's blood was not spilled on Naboth's land, the burial of Joram there providentially fulfilled the foreknowledge of Elijah. (2 Kings 9:23–26).

The Jezebel and Ahab spirits will cause you to lose your *authority*, the power or right delegated to children of God to be heirs of the kingdom of God; your *integrity* of having sound, righteous, veracious, and sincere discernment between good and evil and right and wrong; and the *anointing* that breaks the yoke of bondage and strongholds in believers lives, which makes or declares what is holy and unholy by being set apart from things that are not of God. Individuals with a Jezebel spirit are in denial and refuse to obey those who have authority, while revolting against leadership. One reason they will repel leadership is that they want to be in charge and make all the decisions.

They cannot be trusted for they have a murderous spirit that has to influence everyone with which they come in contact. This murderous spirit is a liar, asperser, backbiter, and divider of all distinguishing features and imperfections to neutralize authentic worship and fellowship. Jehu was not afraid. Unlike the men before him, Joram and Ahaziah, he was confident he could put a stop to Jezebel's perpetrated dealings. Jezebel saw Jehu approaching the palace from her bedroom window and began putting on makeup as a last counter measure to entice or tempt Jehu into sparing her life. She told Jehu that his fate would be just like Zimri, as he came to kill her. Zimri seized the throne of Elah by assassination and annihilated the entire house of Baasha. Zimri ruled for only seven days before her late husband, Ahab, father Omri dethroned him. Jehu entered into the gate and called her attendants to throw her down from her bedroom window into the street (2 Kings 9:30–33).

This spirit of Jezebel is not a spirit from God, but a form of witchcraft; henceforth, it does not allow the recipients to think on their own. God gives each of his children a free will and none are forced or bound by His superior rules or regulations. They are freewill agents who have liberty to choose to serve God or man without any stipulation. But each choice has a concluding destination. A person with a Jezebel spirit is always recruiting others to seduce or con with her sly and crafty ways. This rotten spirit and demonic stronghold can grate you in various ways. Many people are afflicted with spiritual blindness and hearing, deceiving spirits, lying spirits, spirits of pride, prurient, suicide, homicide, and many more. The primary function of these spirits is to afflict with cruelty and hardship by possessing residency within an individual for a season or even a lifetime. Many people suffer from a spirit of depression, which will keep the secluded or recluse person raffish in spirit, gloomy and dejected from the realities of life. These people never seem to fit in anywhere seeing that they are daily contending with confidential drama and strife.

Others may suffer from a spirit of submersion, which means they have learned how to hold back all their pain and suffering. They will never talk about them or address them openly. Meanwhile, others will inherit their problems because they are always in a state of transference. They will not relinquish or yield past or present hurts to the Lord, causing present situations to cause pain on others, subconsciously or unconsciously.

Jehu killed everyone in the house of Ahab: his warriors, kindred, and priests, until there was no one left to carry on his lineage (2 Kings 10:11). The people took down the images of Baal and burned them. They demolished all images of Baal and the house for idol worshiping then turned it into a draught house. When everything was over there was no remembrance of Baal in the land of Israel (2 Kings 10:19–28).

Jehu was the Lord's instrument to bring judgment on the house of Ahab, for which he was commended. Jehu's family line continued like the Lord promised for four generations (2 Kings 10:30). Men like Jehoahaz, Jehoash, Jeroboam III, and Zechariah reigned during his family kinship. Jehu had humble beginnings, but later made egocentric potentialities and ambition. Jehu had to overthrow the extreme self-pride and boastfully unsavory homestead of Ahab. After accomplishing the task of the Lord, he didn't pay close attention to following Elohim's holy commandments with all his heart. Later he returned to the sins of Jeroboam, who made all Israel violate the religious and moral laws of the God. The land of Israel was reduced in size and overthrown by Hazael with hard and striking intrusion. Hazael subdued everything from coast to coast (2 Kings 10:31–32). Never fail to realize that negative communication and association can seduce and rob your spirit of positive thinking, creative reasoning, and euphonious livelihood.

Grief bearers are the thieves of joy that keep one as a hostage, isolated and unhappy at being alone. This is why you must be very dependent on the Holy Spirit as your comforter. If you want to be delivered from the state of misery, you must do everything pleasing and satisfying to God and not man, while denying yourself as well. Saints of God, don't become overbearing, having or showing great pride in oneself, and contempt or reproof for others. In the days of victory, having this trait in your life will never help you get rid of misery, and it will become like a grim reaper over your destiny.

## Misery, the Grim Reaper

Misery is like the grim reaper. It pervades and plants unclean ignoble and abominable spirits that will devastate the physical, mental, and spiritual man. It is a spirit that instills productive pain and sorrow into unknowing and receptive victims. This pain causes the individual to have panic and paranoia, concealing them in spiritual drought or immaturity.

Misery will come in to infiltrate and pollute the body of Christ and instill odium, mistrust, and insecurity among the brethren. They are at each other's throats and backbiting without concern for others emotional convenience, within the sanctuary. Misery is a thief; it will come in the front or back door while distracting the members with petty indifferences and inconsonance. Misery can make accommodation for the spirit of poverty and squalor in your life. The poverty spirit will overbear your mind into believing that you are inadequate in comparison to others around. The spirit of squalor leaves you preoccupied and numb with the feelings of wretchedness and disinclination, since you have no need of God to supply your needs or wants and say that you have accomplished everything on your own. By not giving God the glory for your riches, you are viewed as a wretched, miserable, lame and poor, blind and naked. The Lord will reprove and suppress you from redundant or impetuous behavior that consumes and impedes you with economical wealth, industrious enterprise, or fame in this world, once you are determined to repent and return to your first love, God.

When at the point of needing a strikingly important advance or discovery, the Lord will expunge the host spirit of misery and subrogate it with the spirit of joy. Joy will lead to prosperity, purity, and peace. Spiritual prosperity will enrich and nurture your inner man with practical logic from God, outside of one's nature or heredity. Purity will cleanse and clear the body from all unpurified and unrefined thoughts, which would puzzle the spiritual man from achieving his temporal assignments. It also brings freedom from unfavorable, inferior, or unnecessary substance, removal of dirtiness and rottenness, and freedom from elements regarded as sabotaging. Peace will bring exemption or liberation from the control of evil and despotic powers and peaceable and not antagonistic association or affliction with others, as well as your enemies. Without the impartation of peace and the impassive and tranquilizing injection of serenity and calmness, you will persist to be a miserable person seeking companionship with closely acquainted and intimate association with familiar spirits instead of congenial, amicable, and compatible spirits, who are kin and relatives of the body of Christ.

## MISERY LOVES COMPANY

In the New Testament, Saul was a Jew by birth and was born a few years before the birth of Jesus Christ. He was born in Tarsus, a city in Cilicia (now part of Turkey). He grew up exposed to both his family's Jewish religious heritage and the non-Jewish culture around him. As a youth, Paul went to Jerusalem and studied under the scholar and rabbi, Gamaliel.

Saul was a very miserable and driven man. He formulated orders to bind or butcher all the disciples of the Lord and sent them to the high priest's in the surrounding towns. The letters went from Damascus to Jerusalem into all the synagogues. When he came and found any followers of Jesus, he would be make certain that they were bound or brutally killed, whether man or woman (Acts 9:1–2). Saul was full of fury or uncontrolled anger that resulted in him persecuting and murdering many Jews before his conversion. Saul's miserable spirit led him to be very resentful to the Jewish community that believed Jesus was the Messiah and Savior. His heart of ignorance promoted him to slaughter brutally innocent men and women without any deliberation.

Miserable people are thoughtless and reckless about how they mistreat others to the extent that they feel most of the people they hurt deserve it, taking vengeance or revenge for what someone in their past has done or someone in their present is doing. Paul began a journey on a road to Damascus when an unforeseen light shone down from heaven. He was frightened, fell down on his knees, and listened to the voice from heaven. The voice audibly spoke and asked, "Saul, why are you persecuting Me?" (Acts 9:4, NKJV). Paul asks who is speaking. The Lord replies that he is Jesus who Saul afflicted with insensitivity. He told him he was striking abruptly against thorns. Paul understood from that moment that he was in the presence of a deity and became receptive to the voice of Jesus. Paul was persecuting Jesus, and the church is a part of His body, the completely physical substance of Christ (v. 3–5). There will come a time in their lives when the Lord may desire to use them as messengers of the gospel when they become fatigued of doing wretched things and turn from evil.

You have the same chance or choice as Saul, to become a new creature in Christ or go on in a specified course of sin. You can follow the straight street and follow the directions of the Lord, or disobey the Lord's voice. Saul was given insight and intuition to his future destiny. It will remain your choice to stay in sin or adhere to the voice of the Lord and no longer be in a place of judgment to receive punishment for your abet misfeasance. The Lord selected Ananias to lay hands on Saul and impart the Holy Ghost in the name of Jesus upon him. Ananias didn't believe that Saul would change after the gift of the Holy Ghost, but he was obedient to the command of God. Others will not believe that you have changed, since many have grown accustomed to your abject and joyless state. You must trust the Lord; He will change the way you walk and talk and make you a new creature in Christ Jesus. You must select to observe closely Jesus words so He will save your soul from the lake of fire (hell) or damnation.

Saul was a murderer of God's chosen people, yet was a chosen vessel to do the work of saving and delivering His Word to pagans, kings, and unsaved children of Israel. Although you have a blotted or blemish past, God can still use you for the work of the ministry. How? If you have a heart repentant with a godly sorrow that is willing suffer for Christ's sake. You may feel some days that you can't do it by yourself; and you are right, you can't do it by yourself. God is our General who has never lost a war or battle; He will get in the middle of our warfare to defend us without a second thought.

After Ananias put his hands on Saul, he rapidly received his sight and was filled with the Holy Ghost. The Lord may divulge your purpose and commission through another—a prophet or intercessor that will touch you and agree with you to release the power of joy into your life. It will be an uphill conquest, so take it one day at a time. You must not lose hope; it may take some time for others to accept the transformation, but give them some time to see how God can work miracles.

Misery feeds on others' pain, sorrow, and suffering. It is friendly in passing off as a deceptive imposter or false impersonator, giving orders with authority after finding out private or secret information or data of others. It will begin a relatively unimportant and insolent detailed crusade to sanction contention or discordant and to coerce control on the unwatchful homes of the brethren. This spirit can embark and subvert households with non-prudent clarity. It comes or moves slowly, gradually, or silently into homes of foolish women burdened with too much time on their hands and not enough purposeful vision, taken off course by lustful desires.

This house is not a dwelling place for the Spirit of the Lord, for the Word of God states that He will not dwell in any unclean thing or vessel. The house of misery does love company; this homestead has been sanctioned for excommunication of members who stand up for righteous sake. Excommunication is one of the most strict or harsh penalties that any religious body can impose on any individual or member. During the earlier church years, it was used only for the most serious or heinous offenses or violations of the religious rule or law. Today it is used to keep others out of ministries or auxiliaries that are run or operated by the mass minorities or cliques—those who refuse to cease from practicing unseen or ungodly behaviors or lifestyles. In some religions, an excommunicated person may not participate in any of the religious ceremonies. Today one is prohibited by the mass or majority to be apart of various ministries or boards if not accepted. Some religions may or will prohibit other members from associating with the ex-communicated party. No one is allowed or permitted to have any association with or communication with the isolated, scorned, or rebuked brethren, even though their offence has no basis in ungodly morals or principles. In many cases there has been a personal difference or issue with the party within the group who makes the decision to disassociate every club associate from affliction with that person.

This form of hatred, jealousy, insecurity, and envy has spread very rapidly within the people of God, with the basis being parties who not being delivered from covetous desires or impulses. These members live day to day imprudent of suggestiveness, without sound ability and facility and lacking reasonable impression or perception while establishing a residence of great wretchedness or distress.

## THE HOUSE OF MISERY

The foolish builder's dwelling place is constructed on a breakable and inferior foundation that is foisted upon fervidness, malevolent, and malignant homebuyers. The lot was purchased from an underhanded and avaricious seller and the homebuyers didn't seek the Lord's guidance or direction before selecting this place of future residency.

The foundation was built on shaky and jittery ground from the beginning, due to the construction workers not properly excavating or digging holes or trenches for the footings, the lowest part of the foundation. These trenches are encased or fortified with a ditch or ditches. The ditches may cause derailment, desertion or failure of peripheral vision. The footings support each wall laden with chains of opprobrium and reproachful contempt.

They are made by pouring solid mass into evasive wood or steel forms that each worker places below the frost line, or the depth to which the ground freezes. The dwelling is unprotected from freezing temperatures and weathering storms of life due to being sacrilegious and supercilious causing the frame like barriers to have perceptible existence. The building material of sand (trials) and gravel (Word of God) bonded with cement (Holy Spirit) forms into a hard substance (faith) to stand against splits or breaks (temptation) in the foundational slab was not constructed correctly.

The basement, the lowest story of the dwelling places below the main floor and wholly or partly below the surface of the ground, has many secretive and reticent thoughts hidden. This keeps them withdrawn and unwilling to be reticulate with others.

The piers are grounded on shallow, deplorable, and lamentable structures that are substantial and mince with an unsound lack of depth of character or intellect. The slabs are not properly raised above the ground on concrete supporters; they are lying indirectly on the ground. The slab is monotonous, coarse, and equitably heartless and lifeless.

The ground has not been graded, or leveled with filler, credible, probable, and promising stone—the Cornerstone, Jesus Christ. The cornerstone is a stone laid in the corner of the edifice which is the foundational. Having Jesus Christ as the Cornerstone will prohibit any mayhem or mutilation from coming through any slab that is made by man's hands.

The frame is the skeleton around which the rest of the house is built. After the footings and foundation have been formed, workers bolt wooden sills, or base plates, to the foundation. The family unit framework has hidden private happenings along with surprising experiences. The sills support the outside walls but due to indulging outside influences, the dwelling place, foundation is unsystematic and riotous.

The sheathing, or inner layer of the outside walls, may be wood, fiberboard, or plasterboard nailed to the studs. Sometimes builders tack tarpaper to the sheathing before adding the ridings, or outer layer. Siding may be wood, asbestos shingles, brick and masonry, or aluminum placed directly over the sheathing or tarpaper. The sheathing and siding are disparate and incongruous by a calamitous and ruinous surface.

The roof is the final attachment that seals the top of the home with catastrophe and culminating events of drama in day-to-day life. The rafters or beams are slope from the ridge of the roof to the eaves with laxness, not thinking before they act or speak. They are uncovered with inappropriate joists causing them to behave or act in shock, amazement, or confusion against the attacks of the opponent or adversary. The ridge board was placed with thoughtlessness, lack of attention, and precision. The ridge board has a corrupt slope that falls downward into the abyss, surrendering daily to obeisance and utterance.

The interior surface is full of bewilderment and disorientation, many times dismissing each other's conscience to experience physical sensation and sending members away feeling dispirited and unloved. The members are frequently perturbed with normal function or operation while without the capability to have general stimulation of joy and happiness. They are unable to express their sensual belief that Jesus Christ is Lord and Savior without being openly reproved, scorned, or outcast.

The electrical wiring in this place is hazardous, degenerated, illogical, and a malfunctioning vessel. The circuit breaker is possessed by deranged and insane spirits, causing the individuals within the dwelling place to display happiness one day and tearfulness the next day. They are on a superficial amusement ride on which small insurmountable barriers cause a slightly sharp decline and intensified behavioral changes of moods. This will never pass inspection due to the electricians and construction workers being unreliable, untrained, and uneducated regarding the procedures and policies of constructing a house for God's Spirit to indwell. They took many short cuts and did much underhanded planning and devising, leading to a severe power shortage. The power shortage comes in the homestead and causes a major disunion from the power source—the anointing of God provides divine influence, specified force, and legal authority that are regulated from the power structure of the Holy Ghost.

Without the aid of the Holy Ghost, the dwelling place will lack sufficient insulation, which diminishes the amount of heat and cold that passes or sips through the walls, floors, and ceilings. When air around the home becomes warmer or colder than the air inside, heat passes from the warm air to the cold air. In the winter, the heat will pass to the outside and the house will become cold. In the summer, the heat outside passes into the house. Insulation, the Holy Spirit, fills the air spaces in the walls, floors, ceilings, and creates dead-air space. This helps prevent heat from passing through. The Holy Spirit is the insulation to your dwelling place that protects you at all times from all types of disagreeable atmospheric conditions: storms of discord, rain of distrust, or floods of disagreements. Without this protection or defense policy covering the residence, it will be dilapidated when the strong and easily excited outburst of deluging showers come down.

It is impossible for the head to supervise a devoted and honorable residence that is operating with a license of dissidence and discrepancy. The wise builder of dwelling places must furnish the means of subsistence through shelter, quiet enjoyment, and a shield from liability of injustice or candid treatment. The stewards of this household are religious and primitive, confined to primordial practices of condemnation and censorious. They are splenetic people, full of aspiration, who will harm and show traitorous feelings towards others, lacking potential and destination to do the Father's strong and fixed purpose.

There is no celebrating or commemorating of holidays, anniversaries, or festivities due to the dwelling place being succumbed by anguish, nervous anticipation, and discontent. A foolish man will build his house on sand held cohesively by discrepancy, discourtesy, and disintegration, refusing to align with obeying or complying with the Word of God. If the house is built on sand, when the propulsion of assaults, inundation of hatred, otiose or empty talk, boasts or fierce aggravating vibrations came against the house, it can not stand. The house of sand collapsed and great was the loss which was heard by many (Matt. 7:26–27).

They are captive to the misery of the world's tragic events by the news, daily drama, and literary compositions that tell the story by means of dialogue and action. They are intrigued by onset performances and minuets of life series of events, finding them interesting, vivid, and realistic. They are not refracting or reciting the Word of God. Their life course is a neglectful and an uncritical examination coming from the occurrences that fence them within their temporal habitation. This house possesses omens, bipolar faith caught between two opposing opinions or natures, and imitative gifts of others. This house is inhospitable to not only visitors, but also the Holy Ghost.

The Master Builder will construct a house with a refurbish or renovated anointing. This house will have the like mind of Jesus Christ, removing the double mindedness of the evil one. The astounding Planner can heal all aliments, cure all sickness, adapted dysfunctional counsel, and ablate a new heart. After renovation or reconstruction, this house will be certified with joy, peace, and happiness, which will stand the test of time.

## SHAKE OFF MISERY

Saul was later named Paul. Since he successfully obeyed the Lord by preaching the gospel, the Lord gave him a new name. *Paul* means one who is "asked of God." Now he began his ministry, preaching to the pagans. You must have a successful resolution to begin your purpose. Kingdom building is serious and rigorous, requiring making confidential sacrifices, moving toward the altar of grace, and pursuing the Lord at all times.

Paul experienced spiritual blindness, but the Lord deleted the scales from his eyes and he received sight, later to be baptized. He message was the declaration of what he experienced on the road of Damascus—Christ's deity and Messiahship to the lost. (Acts 9:11–21). When scales come off, the superficial perception of good and evil that causes captious and irrational decision-making has been obtruded after undergoing the empowerment of the Holy Ghost. The Holy Ghost will get rid of the unclean, uniform perception or intuition led by the fiendish incitation of nature.

When Paul went to Jerusalem to join the other disciples, they were afraid of him. They remembered his past and were unwilling to believe he was a new creation in Christ. The marvelous Creator has all power in His hands; He can change hearts and minds that were once under the pre-domination of the world system. Barnabas took Paul under his wings and brought him to the apostles, declaring to them the miracle the Lord had performed with their brother Paul. After his speech, the apostles preached boldly that day in Damascus (vv. 26–27).

This is not a matter that should be taken effortless and rewarded with much delight and candescent gladness. Paul at no time ceased his authorization to perform his duties to the pagan or heathen nation because the men of Israel wouldn't receive his call (13:16).

Paul was one of the most important patriarchs of the early church. He became famous or well known as a missionary and religious founder of many congregations throughout Asia Minor and southeastern Europe. He was under no condition ashamed of the gospel of Christ and the explicit way of salvation. He preached to all that salvation is liberty to everyone that believed, whether the Jew and Greek (Rom. 1:16). Others will know that God has changed your life, but will not be willing to accept true liberty because of your past.

Paul gave projecting and controversial speeches and teachings that angered many of the Jews. Paul was sought after many times to be killed, because they began to grow resentfully envious and suspicious of his preaching format. When the church leaders saw the multitudes that followed Paul's ministry, they were filled with hatred and wrath. They openly spoke out against him, saying he was contradicting and blaspheming the true testament (Acts 13:45). Many Jews begin to mistreat and persecute him and his followers with threats of imprisonment and stoning. The Jews were angry that he spoke the truth, and they became odious and envious. Paul left the city and refused to modulate or accept the principles of iniquitous behavior that was bestowed upon him. He and Barnabas had wholeness in the joy of the Lord and left in the spirit of meekness (v. 52). There will be rivals who will speak out against your denomination and tell others your ministry is debased or counterfeit and your testimony is ill-founded. They will treat you the same, not allowing you to be apart of any ministry within the body of Christ. Hold your head up high, looking to the hills where your help comes from and realizing all your corroboration comes from the Lord.

The Lord watched over Paul and his followers by feeding them with heavenly foresight and foreknowledge, so that they could accomplish their missionary work. A word of encouragement should rest on your lips, ready to speak life into other's lives—definite, constant, and continued news of the gospel of Jesus Christ.

You will never have true joy unless you understand how important it is for you to repent and resist evil. In Romans

7:14–16 it says that the law is spiritual, but we are carnal, sold under sin. All believers have a seed of renegade or defiance in their heart that instructs them to withstand authority or oppose any control. I can't comprehend the struggle within which creates tension, ambivalence, and bewilderment. Paul admits to being rebellious and insubordinate. The Holy Ghost has capability to unfasten essential goodness.

Contrary to what others say, you cannot live in sin and think that the Lord will protect you when trials and troubles come your way. Paul rejoiced in the law of God, but two extruding or impelling elements were travailing within his inner man: one trying to take him back into captivity of sin and the other trying to guide him to follow God's regulations. Paul saw himself as a wretched man and asked the Lord to deliver him from damnation. Deliverance comes from salvation from Jesus Christ, the Savior, not through legalistic effort. Meanwhile, the inner man delights in God (vv. 22–25).

Paul wrote letters to his followers, called the epistles, which were a significant part of the New Testament. These letters were vital to aiding and assisting other believers with their withdrawn struggles and dilemmas that the devil brought their way. Paul clarified a previously determined letter submitted to the church at Corinth regarding lawless living. The Corinthians mistook the first letter, exfoliating the sins of the non-Christians but not addressing the problems of the brethren. Paul was referring to all disorderly and variable individuals; not to have any association or fellowship with these riotous dispositions. He stated to them the importance of having holy conduct, conversation, and association. They are not to keep to company or be closely associated with a fellow believer that is a fornicator, covetous, idolater, complainer, drunkard, or extortionist. He said not to even sup with them, forasmuch as the world would assume the church approved of such disorderly and ungodly living (1 Cor. 5:9–11).

Paul wanted the church at Corinth to understand that the unbelievers were watching them, and they were deporting an unmoral distinctive trait or quality. Since they were calling themselves believers and living like the world, they were giving a false testimony of their faith. He wanted them to be sentient of the influence on the non-believers. They might deem that they could go on to live ungodly and unmoral lives without future consequences or judgment from the Father. The Church of Corinth was not aware how they were tarnishing the true character of Christian lifestyle. Just because we live in the world, we mustn't become like the world. As of today, we are called or chosen to be compassionate leaders, not sentimental guiding heads. The compassionate leader must examine one's spiritual, not emotional, reasons or thoughts, emphasizing sincere understanding and instruction under the unction of the Holy Ghost. The sentimental guiding head operates under emotional feeling rather than spiritual reasoning, easily influenced or manipulated due to working by sight and not by faith. This causes them to have delicate or tender sensibilities. The weapons of a true believer are not over-bearing pride or self-importance but might through God to extract strongholds and the imagination of defenses and onslaughts the perturbing one (2 Cor. 10:3–5). The captious reasoning supplied by the false apostles were trying to shake the faith of the Christians of Corinth. The lordship of Christ will bring man's being under full subjection and liability.

Paul customarily would tell others that although he was called to suffer for his ministry, he would not give up his fight until his task was complete. He was constantly defending his call and ministry because he once persecuted the church of

Jesus Christ. Paul says he would not be like the false teachers who were fools, boasting in their self-centeredness and loquacious accomplishments. Paul gives his personal testimony, being beaten three times with rods for punishment, once stoned, and shipwrecked three times. He journeyed by night and day in the deep against exposure of water, reviling robbers, disagreeable countrymen, strong jeopardy from an irreligious and repugnant city, pestilence, wilderness, untamed seas, and evil among false brethren. He expressed a mood of weariness and painfulness, closely observing while hungry and thirsty, eating very little, and cold and naked. Through all this he took care all the needs of the churches that were entrusted to him by the Lord (2 Cor. 11:19–28).

Paul's testimony for the churches was to have joy in spite of the world's oppositions and diversions; it would be a daily clash, but know confidently that the Lord is there. You are no longer a prisoner of the evil one, but now walk in the vocation and calling of your ministry. Walk in lowliness and meekness knowing that joy is encompassed by longsuffering while forbearing your neighbor's burdens in unity and a bond of peace (Eph. 4:1–3).

Paul writes a letter of encouragement to the church of Philippi as they were being persecuted for their longsuffering in the ministry. He wanted them to carry on again after interruption of humility and unity, and rejoice regardless of circumstances. He warned them to watch out for those who were complaining and mumbling about the ministry work being complicated, for they were improbable laborers of the gospel of Jesus. God's labor is not grievous or utterly revolting, but fortifying and highly pleasing. Subsequently, those who were grumbling were doing it for vainglory and self-reward, not from their heart (Phil. 3:1–3)

Paul was praising and admiring them for their enduring and obedient spirit. The church at Philippi was rejoicing and praising God in the midst of their trials and were not trusting or relying on their vacillating human nature to direct and instruct their hearts when it was time to make sound conclusions. They offered up purebred and candid magistrate, yet explicit and delightful devotion.

Expelling and ejecting sin is an impotent testimony for people who are trapped by the unclean spirit of misery. They can't take pride in presenting themselves unto the Lord, holy and satisfactory as being their reasonable service, since they are unaware what is the service or purpose in this realm. They are no longer concerned about who may be watching their work and witnessing their present state with the enemy. You must not turn away from the doctrine of Jesus Christ, for it should be kept in your heart to aid in times of temptation (Rom. 6:17).

Miserable people want to see you fail, because they are not ready to change their ways or by any means extend grace to whoever is struggling. The light that you are shining is revealing how they really are in Jesus: counterfeit Christians that are perpetrating and imitating the true believers and followers of Christ Jesus. You should passionately pray that they would desire in their hearts and minds to be transformed into new holy and purified creatures. You must grant them the same mercy that Jesus had for you, as a lost sheep gone astray.

Misery is a shrewd and clever stronghold that will bring in other unclean spirits. In Matthew 12:43–45 there is an example of how an unclean spirit can connect to other strongholds. The Word of God says when the unclean spirit left a man, the spirit walked throughout deserted and inhabited places exploring for somewhere to rest. When it could not find an uncultivated and uninhabited recumbent place, it decided to return back to its primordial homestead. Upon its arrival, noticing that the house is still empty, swept clean and dressed up on the outside but with no spiritual substance or fiber on the inside, the unclean spirit went out and brought in more detestable and vile spirits that took up residency in this old nature house. The house was a whitewashed surface dwelling, but still ripe with wretchedness on the inside, where there were now more operable forces.

Misery does want company and will bring other unclean and perverted spirits into the temple. These spirits will send out a capias for your inner man to put it into spiritual bondage without any negotiation, now a hostage to dispirit, unforgiveness, oppression, manipulation, opprobrious, incongruity, and encumbrance. The spirit of depression is sad and dismal and sees no hope. The spirit of unforgiveness is resentful of others and will not grant amnesty to others of misfeasance. The spirit of oppression treats others with cruelty. The spirit of manipulation is controlling and does things for self gain. The spirit of aversion has abstruse reproof toward others, along with strong dislike, reluctance, and unwillingness to cooperate. The spirit of discord and disorder is plain spoken, abrupt, and clashes with everyone while bringing a breach of communal peace and overset of normal function. The spirit of encumbrance supplies hindrance and burdens causing inequality or dissimilitude in quality in incongruity.

The spirit of misery is very incommodious to harbor others; it will never permit peace and joy to cohabitate. This habitude must be replaced with some good spirituality and solid moral strength. Now is the time for you to move from being a child of darkness and walk gracefully into God's glorious light of salvation, in the spirit of goodness, righteousness, and truth. (See Ephesians 5:8–10.)

There are three steps to use to help get rid of the spirit of misery. The first step is walking in godliness; you must have a spirit of excellence, virtue, kindness, and generosity when serving others. The second is walking in probity; you must be just, upright, and moral to everyone. The third step is walking in truth; you must be sincere, honest, and accurate in your dealings with others.

This condition or state of misery is not what God has designed for His children, but the choice is yours. So ask the Lord today why you don't have a new character filed with erudite joy. You negate the aid and bolstering of the brethren by refusing to fellowship and observe how others around you are relying on the Holy Spirit to evoke the crown of joy upon their lives.

Misery is nothing more than a thief and should be treated as an unwanted guest. It will come into your house or dwelling place simply because it does not like being alone. You do not have to be hindered by misery or the unclean spirits that hang around it. This unclean habitude spirit of tragic deadliness and sonorous sorrow brings about death to the spirit of man. Misery is effete and cannot be left untreated; the unction of the Holy Spirit is needed to irradiate such a stronghold from the extended range of a fluctuating quantity.

Misery is a plagued character that will afflict and aggravate for many days if you do not learn how to stay away from calamity. It is a dangerous epidemic disease to society and the welfare of society. It is a prevalent and rapidly pervading contagious and infectious ailment within your inner man. It can disguise itself as a friendly and loving comrade, which will infiltrate and steadily take over your mind, filling it with abominating thoughts and ideas. The unclean spirit will bring about a gradual, stealthy, or even abrupt spirit of death.

Misery is an intrusive and unwelcome houseguest; the longer it stays the longer you will be hostage to your own uncleanness.

The longer it resides and takes residency in the home, the sooner it will become a house intruder instead of a houseguest. It will infringe or desecrate from the benefits of beatific and bountiful living.

The Word of God states that the wages of sin is death, but the gift of God is eternity through Christ Jesus (Rom. 6:23). You have the choice today of life with Jesus. It is better to go to the house of the sorrowful than to go to the house of religious festival, for that is the end of all men living according to the elaborate richness of their hearts. Sorrow or plaintiveness is better than laughter, for by the sadness of the countenance the heart is made better. The heart of earthly or secular wisdom is in the house of acute sorrow, but the heart of the house of merriment is enriched with absurdity in a godly range of information sprinkled down from above (Eccles. 7:2–4).

Better is the end of a thing than the inception thereof; and the patient in spirit is better than the proud in spirit. Be not hasty in your spirit to be angry, for anger rests in the bosom of fools (vv. 8–9). Make peace with the brethren and try to live peaceable with all men, for a life without restraint will lead to destruction and death of all who are involved or influenced by its depraved system for survival. The world system teaches and devises circuitous ways to achieve wealth, through deceitful and mischief plots and schemes of the heart. Some use a formation of slander to create distrust or discord that culminates in alienation and possible insanity, if you are not cautious and prayerful. Nonetheless, God's system comes with prolonged and healthy days.

In many cases the wicked appear to be strong and prosperous, but that is not so, for everything that goes up must come down. It is God's will for the righteous to be prosperous and happy in the Lord. The Word of God warns those who inhabit pride, hatred, and disgust in their heart that it is an abomination. Everyone operating under the direction or guidance of exaggerated self-esteem have been informed and warned that pride goes before destruction. The contumely spirit shows scornful insult, haughty rudeness, and humiliating treatment. Child of God, do not be dismayed; overwhelming pride in oneself and willful disobedience toward God go before every sudden fall, unseen breakdown, or every contentious quarrel. The spirit of the humble, meek, and gentle is the course of action or procedure to true spiritual integrity. No man is to share his spoils with the arrogant and overweening.

Do not be foolish and become prey to their snares and nets of deception and deceit of the ungodly. The soul of man has God's moral awareness of right and wrong, good and evil, justice and injustice, righteousness and unrighteous. This conscious mind of thoughts, feelings, and impression of God is called the Holy Spirit. The Holy Spirit holds the flashlight that searches all the inward and deep notions within the inner parts of man's soul— moral, emotional, and spiritual character.

## 7

# GREED, THE DESTROYER OF JOY

*But this I say, He which soweth sparingly shall reap also sparingly; and he which soweth bountifully shall reap also bountifully. Every man according as he purposeth in his heart, so let him give; not grudgingly, or of necessity: for God loveth a cheerful giver.*

—2 CORINTHIANS 9:6–7

THERE ARE MANY IN early or youthful graves that tried to access the riches of this world. They failed to realize or understand that God is the giver of all good and perfect gifts. Greed will challenge all signs of cheerfulness and joy, for many will never have anyone to share their ambitions, fame, and wealth with.

Greed is defined as extreme aspiration for getting or having excessive or insatiable desire for wealth or prestige. A greedy person is rapacious, taking or seizing property, possessions, or belongings by force, or plundering in any matter, occurrences, or things, many times making or arousing public controversy. They desire greater amounts, quantities, or degrees beyond necessities or obligations. They crave something additional or further than what is rightfully earned or merited. They are avaricious, having great desire toward elusive wealth and erroneous riches. This behavior is percolated into the unclean actions of a person suffering from gluttony, having too strong of a craving for food or drink. They appear to be intensely petulant or anxious and show an appetency to be successful, famous, powerful, and wealthy. They ambush others with unclear, indefinite, or vague conceptions. Many people work all of their lives and die trying to destroy others or take over opposing challengers or competitors. Whenever the opportunity comes for them to bless or help someone else, they are too busy trying to obtain and receive everything for themselves and their families—they suffer from the *me* and *myself* syndrome. They never concern themselves with other's cares and concerns, since it is not advantageous to their livelihood. If they were to put too much focus on the sick, the hungry, the naked, or the homeless, it might cost them something that they were not willing to let go—money, honor, or prestige. They will set perilous exposure to harmful or hurtful snares and pernicious traps for God's people.

The Word of God says to take close observation and attentive responses to false accusers and to also put careful guard around one's soul—to be awake and observant of all surrounding affairs, concerns, or matters. Also, we must use prayerful, imploring, condensed, concise, and unrestrained in speech and heartfelt requests or pleas for others and ourselves. If we keep our minds on the Lord, He will keep us in perfect peace.

In the Old Testament there was a man named Ahab. He was a very wretched person. He only concerned himself with the propensity of his heart. His lifetime was marked by great political changes and serious spiritual unrest during the time when the growing menace of Assyria caused Syria and Palestine to forget their political rivalries. Later, Ahab's daughter married Joram, the king of Judah. Temporary peace brought prosperity and enabled Ahab to do much building in the new Israelite capital of Samaria. But the customs of his wife,

Jezebel, offended the Israelites and were sharply denounced by the prophet Elijah. The peace with Syria soon broke down, and Ahab was killed in an attack against a Syrian garrison at a military post or station east of the River Jordan. Ahab was iniquitous and his greed caused him to forsake the kingdom and lose his life and salvation.

## GREED, THE PRETENTIOUS SPIRIT OF AHAB

After the fall of Adam, man became the head priest of his own home as commanded by God. Ahab failed to operate under the authority that God had given to him, since he was bewitched and enchanted by the perpetrate seduction of his wife, Jezebel. Inevitably, Ahab was not following the will of God; therefore, his wife could not be converted by his testimony of faith. Ahab was not living according to the Law of Moses. He was under a generational curse left upon him by his father. His father was a wicked and indecent king and leader to the nation of Israel, so it was learned behavior.

First, let us discuss the spirit of Ahab, which was a spirit of control, covetousness, ravenousness, and jealousy. Ahab was the son of Omri, who sinned more than all the kings before him whose sons sinned greater in number than his father. He was the king of Israel in Samaria for twenty-two years. It appeared that he walked in the sins of Jeroboam the son of Nebat, as second nature and learned behavior from his father, Omri (1 Kings 16:25–28). People with controlling spirits must always be in the spotlight of power. Many of them will believe that because they go to church, that they can mistreat God's people and not receive chastisement for their sordid ways. Ahab would not repent when the famine came upon the land and he remained in leadership. He decided to take another route by having his soldiers to look for food and water. The soldiers looked for a brook and grass to feed the horses and mules so they would not lose all the animals due to lack of proper nourishment (18:5).

Voracious people will easily investigate shortcomings of others when they are looking for self-condolence rather than turning to God and repenting. They will never deal with their crises themselves. Furthermore, they will recruit others and draw them into their web of sorrow. They never want to accept responsibility for their own actions, while stating that others are lackadaisical and not eager or willing to work or exert themselves as they did because they are slothful and sluggish. There is no defense to use when dealing with an avid person who refuses positive encouragement and insists on being avaricious. Avarice is a choice of their character, for they desire or crave all things pertinent and relevant in life.

Life is not a fantasy as in romance novels; there will be some good and some bad days, but we must make the best out of each, for tomorrow is not promised to anyone. Elijah was not self-centered or self-seeking, but shared with Ahab that there was an abundance of rain to come and take away the drought from all of Israel (v. 41). This is a fantasy life for a plundering person, who thinks all particular course of action or line of action will bring them greater or extravagant affluence. They bound ahead of others with abundance and richness due to wretched plotting, planning, or scheming. Elijah went to the top of Mount Carmel and prayed for the curse to be removed now that the people were convinced that Jehovah was the living and true Elohim (v. 42). You can give a testimony all day long; but people will continue to have this despondent cloud heaped over their heads until they decide to make a difference in their own lives or choose to not be joyless any longer.

Believers cannot remain fixed in a state or engaged in unlawful habitual misdemeanors or behaviors, for they will be unable to see the good in anything, even when they see a miracle right before their very eyes. They operate with absence of belief and have unfavorable opinion about the miracles of God. Many will share the misfortune of others before they share the good; they are tedious and unable to see hope in anything. Jezebel sent messengers to Elijah, threatening that she would kill him as he had killed the prophets of her gods (19:2).

This is not the will of God for His children; God wants us to have hope and revivifying disposition of joy. But we must repent, turn from our appalling or dismaying ways, and then take ownership of peace and joy. We cannot take all of our problems and worries to man; they will never have the true and just answers for our deliverance. Many will tell you that need not repent about, justifying your actions and misdeeds.

Immature Christians cannot help someone who has a gluttonous spirit, because they are uninformed that they are Monopoly pieces that have been placed in the middle of demonic influence or possession and prayer is the only way of deliverance or escape. You cannot afford to become like Elijah, giving up right when God has magnified you before the very eyes of your enemies. God will uncover to them that He is the only one that has absolute control over your life; don't lose hope or fret. The Father is on the scene and He is ready to take on the world just for you to have rendering joy. Elijah allowed his joy to escape by hiding in a cave from one evil and wretched woman, Jezebel (v. 9).

There will come a time in everyone's life when the Lord will ask why you are giving up so quickly without a fight. What will you say to Him? My enemies have become too many or too great, or I fear man more than the Almighty God. The combat or war is not yours, it is the Lord's, who is robust and a powerhouse. You are not alone; there are many others who are combating evil in this warfare for the same cause. Not everyone has retreated backward in the method of the deplorable one (v. 18).

Greedy people will still use transference to others because they are in need of deliverance; do not be filled with alarm, but keep them in prayer for many never realize their misguidance. Some people have no inkling of what all their craftiness and sordid inventions will cost them in the end. They will not consider what their end will be or what they will have to answer to at the time of judgment. They must get or gain by their own effort or actions more stocks, bonds, and mutual funds, even if they have to take them from someone else. By seizing the moment, they can do this by giving employees smaller raises, lesser bonuses, and fewer incentives. Even so, remember there is nothing that is done in the dark that God will not bring to the apparent light. Some are eagerly looking to see what they can get out of others at someone else's expense, uncaring and uncompassionate about how they misuse or mistreat others in order to meet their needs. They are heedless about outcome no matter the kind of pain it will cause others, as long as they are on top.

Ahab was one who did not understand or care about others' welfare; he wanted what he wanted when he wanted it. He was like an addict, craving that quick fix of satisfaction and then going on to the next fix or want. Greed is like a chief appalling spirit, going around exploring for more riches, valuable holdings, money, and property to acquire. Ahab saw Naboth's vineyard at a convenient location near his home and coveted it for a garden of herbs. Although Naboth was unwilling to receive another piece of land in commutation or any amount of money for the purchase, this didn't concern Ahab. He was a voracious and selfish man who was unconcerned about Naboth or his family and how they would feel if he just sold their vineyard at the spree of the moment (21:2). The vineyard was a part of his family's legal inheritance besides the great sentimental value that would be left to his heirs; it valued more than any piece of property, no matter how large. He told Ahab the Lord would rule against him to give or sell the property since his father left it as an bequest to him and his family (v. 3). He had abundant natural resources and well-supplied riches, wealth and land, also abounding in all things.

Naboth declined to sell the land to Ahab, so Ahab became very angry and went home and told his wife Jezebel about the discrepancy between the two. These where two individuals who refused to deal with their own deficiencies, inadequacies, and limitations, but rather made excuses for them, causing a man to not only loose his inheritance but his life. Ahab was an avidly immoral person who had an intense desire or craving for another's earthly possession, and was willing to bring spiritual bankruptcy or destitution in Naboth's life to attain his property.

Greedy (malicious) individuals look for defects in your character and integrity to justify their ruthless and hostile treatment. Others, who become victims of their transference, misleadingly sided with their repulsive deeds and ways. Many people will defend their anomalous manner by not taking the blame for their inadequacies, and releasing them on to others. Individuals who are content in praising, worshiping, honoring, and loving God whether they are abased or abound, obfuscate the ungodly. Praise God in humility with a reputable condition or rank, having or demonstrating a moderate opinion of your own value or abilities, and being an individual who is lowly and unpretentious. Jesus said whosoever shall exalt himself shall be humiliated and anyone that humbles himself shall be sublime

(Matt. 23:12). There are those may try to bring you down to mock and mire you by sabotaging your reputation and affiliation with others.

When Ahab returned to his house, he became heavy-hearted and displeased with the words of Naboth, the Jezreelite. Ahab rested his head, turned his face to the wall, and would not eat anything. Ahab was having a temper tantrum because Naboth wouldn't give away his family inheritance from the Lord. He began telling Jezebel about his request for Naboth's vineyard and how he had been refused of his offer of money or exchange.

Ahab told the story, but he left out one factor: that the vineyard was an heirloom for Naboth's family. By leaving out one minor fact, it could have made the difference when making the decision to take Naboth's vineyard instead of searching for another. He managed to control his wife artfully into thinking that Naboth was inhospitable and ill-mannered to him when he requested to buy his vineyard, setting entrapment for his wife to side with him, knowing how wretched she was. Jezebel fabricated a monstrous plan to take control of Naboth's vineyard permanently (1 Kings 21:4–16). Foremost, Naboth was forbidden by the Lord to sell or give the land away; secondly, it provided the livelihood for his family.

Cold and cutting individuals are always behind impish, inveterate conduct and don't care about having all the facts; they live to cause habitual dishonest management. They are relentless, disagreeably crude, and gloomy, overspread with or enveloped in darkness or vagueness regarding any specified materials of concern. Many are cheerless and hopeless of their tomorrow, meanwhile substituting a sentence of condemnation accompanied by morose or dejection of the present entity. A little disarray gets their creative juice flowing. Those who are cursed with the unclean spirit of Jezebel are capable of moving with great exploration to extract naive blood of another brother while devastation and greed are in their eyes and heart. They are unable to assess footsteps to peace lacking awe and reverent honor of God (Rom. 3:16–18).

Jezebel had enough information to come up with a pulverizing scheme for Naboth. Jezebel, with Ahab's indirect consent, took retaliation in her own hands to pay Naboth back for refusing her husband's fulfillment of the consummation of his own aspiration and request for another man's acquisition. She commenced and forged letters with Ahab's signature soon afterward sealed them with his signet. She sent the letters to all the elders and nobles of Ahab's city (1 Kings 21:8).

There is nothing that a greedy heart would not do to possess whatever it desires, craves, or longs for. Many seek opportune moments to accumulate contraband—a well-timed moment to take custody someone else's personal or private possession of by illegal authority or forcibly control or quickly without warrant and devoid of a legal acquittal. Many will confiscate and seize private property for their own treasury by smuggling goods that are forbidden by law to be imported and exported into the community and enjoin with unlawful or prohibited traders or barterers who distribute illicit or illegal property or things that have been allotted or deemed as stolen merchandise.

These actions of greedy persons are pathetic, when in all actuality they desire things or something that belongs to another, which is considered to be covetous. Their heart is full of greed and avarice for wealth, riches, houses, and land. The Word of God says that a covetous person acclaims no prominent landscape from the region of God (1 Cor. 6:10). The rapacious person wants all things and puts these things in the place of God, thereby committing idolatry. The person who persists in greed has excommunicated himself from God, therefore excluding himself from the royal priesthood (Eph. 5:5). In the last days perilous times "men shall be lovers of their own selves, covetous, boasters, proud, blasphemers, disobedient to parents, unthankful, unholy" (2 Tim. 3:2).

Ahab was given a free will. He could have decided to repent and turn from serving Baal gods and be the man in his household. But he was an enervate and verdant man craving everything and all things. Ahab was responsible for an innocent man being murdered and then taking possession of his family asset. Ahab persisted on being deviant before the Lord; furthermore, he was in trouble for killing another and confiscating his property fraudulently. The Lord sent Elijah the Tishbite to give Ahab a word of prophecy for his cruel transgression of peculation of Naboth's vineyard and having him stoned to death. The prophet Elijah told Ahab the same fate that he and Jezebel placed on Naboth would come to pass for the two of them. Ahab was unwilling to accept the responsibility for taking an innocent man's life with little thought or regard for his family. He was like so many people who try to justify their unlawfulness by asking a question of disbelief and not accepting their actions. However, Elijah told Ahab that his deed was sordid in the sight of the Lord, therein his issue was with the Great King (1 Kings 21:19–24). Anything that is found displeasing, disgusting, and unacceptable before Lord's sight should be the same in sight of the children of the Most High God.

Greedy people are always looking for a retractable way gain or possess everything within their clutches. Ahab's selfish actions were the root behavior that would keep Israel under a blood curse and generational omen on Ahab's household since he was not willing to obey the words and the Lord. He would have no more future descendants who would pass on the family's name or heritage nor legacy. In man's eyesight, He might have been noble and powerful, but in God's eyes, he was considered a murderer, liar, erroneous, and wicked. He was a man with no valor or integrity, and he chose to lead the nation of Israel in sin. He did many abominable things including engaging in worship of idol gods, according to the sinning Amorites, that his wife introduced as a custom to the nation of Israel. These were the same individuals the Lord tossed out in front the children of Israel for their immoral practices and morally stained lifestyle. All that Ahab did was for his own egocentric needs.

As a result of hearing these words from the prophet Elijah, he tore off his clothing and put on a cloth of penitence and begun to devote homage to Elohim. He covered himself with sackcloth and fasted, showing his repentant sorrow. Some things are not worth the sacrifice of your soul and reward in heaven for the toiling and laboring in the vineyard, especially if God turns you over to sin and lateral judgment resulting from afflictive heartache. The Wonderful Consoler sent Elijah with another word for Ahab saying since he humbled himself before God, He would not bring atrocity on him. But it would come in the days of his son. Ahab's son will be accursed for his animosity and annihilation of Naboth (1 Kings 21:27–29).

## THE GREED OF THIS WORLD

Before entering into the joy of the Lord, one must be converted from selfish, pensive action and deeds. The Holy Spirit will discard greed and replace it with generosity, willingness to share or give to others, altruism, noble-mindedness, graciousness, and a magnanimous heart. Many think that having things and desiring to be successful, owning a business, or becoming an entrepreneur is unrealistic. Not when God is on your side; all things are possible to those who have unwavering faith.

God's word doesn't state anything evil regarding wealth or

prosperity. But, there is a wariness to be measured in relation
to the love of money, which is the root of all evil. Why? Because
many who coveted and desired zealously other's riches, became
greedy or avaricious. They became perforated through with
much suffering, importunity, or misfortune. Their direction of
movement was for ravenous gain, wealth, or earnings, which
will take away the life of the owners, like Ahab with Naboth.
Someone could forfeit the lives of their household due to taking
advantage of others and being impudent for that with which
God has already blessed them. They are clogged with active
hatred and enmity, evil intent, and grudges. Their actions are
malicious, having provided or caused detriment and danger to
innocent or gullible individuals.

Watch out for those who do evil in the name of the Lord, as
children of God or men and women of God. Leaders, who will
ravenously devour the sheep and never be satisfied with what
God has provided for them or their ministries. They are parsons
engulfing or engrossing the possession and fortune of the sheep,
for one's own welfare or interests with little or no though or
care for the members. The greedy parsons will swallow up the
entire assemblages' tithes, one tenth of the annual produce of
property or annual income paid as a contribution and offerings to support the church or benevolence funds. This spirit is
chiefly derogatory with greedy and grossly obscene riches and
money. They will sell their uprightness, honesty, and sincerity
for an unworthy purpose. They are agents who promote the sale
of the report of the Lord for money without authorization from
God. Many choose to contradict or hinder repentance; they are
given over to a reciprocal lifestyle of lasciviousness, lust, lewd-
ness, and wantonness entrapped by greediness.

## THE LITTLE FOXES THAT SPOIL THE VINE

The little or small, sly treacheries being with cunning expertness in deceiving unsuspecting men or women, and which fool, cheat, lie, or outguess by means of craftiness or slyness, leaving people baffled. The conjugators travel in a cabal or junta hunting together, setting any stratagem or ambush designed to catch or inveigle unsuspicious people, making entrapments to lure others in embarrassing and predicament situations. The predators are crafty, using skillful deception and delusions by temporizing illusive bargains or deals. They are plunders, taking or stealing from people and public agencies by defrauding for selfish gain. They are robbers who subdue others' personal property unlawfully, using force to instill fear, anxiety, or doubt in others; exploiters who profit from the labor of others in an unethical manner.

You must be on the alert and watch with the instincts of a foxhound; a strong and swift creature that is courageous and bold and trained to search accurately, skillfully, or cleverly for particulars during hunting season. There is no time for slumbering or sleeping while still viable in seeking and pursuing a career or interest devoted to the cause of the ministry. The career goal is expedited through life or in an itemized vocation or profession with prompt progress, but sometimes seen as contemptible or despicable in regard to senseless abomination or malicious and hateful spite by another brother. Their goods or territory are defaced, spoiled, and marred, which impairs the enjoyment or quality. Many are deprived of definite or specified belongings due to others, causing physical harm or hurt to offend someone's emotions or competence to experience sensitivity or sensibility, wounding the moral and physical being, or the fragilely broken or contrite spirit of those who are not firm in their mind or purpose. They cause harm to a massive number of people, never once designating loving action that involves sympathy, kindness, or forgiveness. Their observable response to stimulation is unlawful, against moral or ethical standards; lewd, not in similarity with accepted principles of just behavior; and anomalous, not in accordance with the truth or fact. Nothing is done in mutual appropriateness with any legitimate spiritual growth and development or nurturing and fostering. Your attitude must become resolute, unyielding, determined, and resolved with intention and aim promoting godly values, vigilantly prepared to act or be used immediately, right for the intention or occasion and set aside for the exclusive use for the kingdom.

We are the beloved or dearly loved of God; exalt Him with obedience and honor through much and deep affection, endearing arms of peace, yet always pleasing and friendly to the household of faith. You have been defamed by many, your reputation has been attacked by lies and slander, yet never forsaking the undoubting belief in God. You cannot be anyone's spoil or detriment goods that are useless or valueless to the gospel of Jesus Christ. When your nay (no) be nay (no), and yea (yes) be yea (yes), you can be delivered from the greed of this corrupt world system, understanding no man can serve two masters. Keep in mind, you will despise the one and love and uphold the other.

## GREEDY WOLVES IN SHEEP CLOTHING

The worst culprit of them all is the wolf in sheep's clothing, or, vice versa, sheep in wolf's clothing. The wolf in sheep's clothing preys on the trustworthiness, compassion, and credulousness of another's heart, sometimes the senile, for self-satisfaction. They target unsuspecting or unsuspicious individuals to swindle them of money, and even their entire life savings. Another way of describing those wolves are as a group of undomesticated, uncultivated, uncivilized, uncontrolled, unruly, and unlawful people who assault another's sensual aspect (name). They make unlawful threats or unsuccessful attempts to physically harm another with rebellious and refractory temperament or control. They have an unmerciful nature, enjoying other's suffering, callously inducing pain and distress. They become money hungry and greedy, using secret, private, and confidential information to black mail, receive payment extorted to prevent disclosure of hidden sins, insecurities, or habitual shortcomings. They may coerce or approach others with self-serving purpose and pleasure, making sinister and devious advances, proposals, or requests.

The wolf in sheep's clothing sees conflict as a method of getting what one wants, attempting to keep them from being happy or content. Even if it rightfully belongs to someone else, this can be done through having rampant and disrupting outbursts to interrupt the order and peace. They are like parasites that live at others' expense without making any useful contribution or attribution to their homes, community, or local church. Living on or within another from which they derive sustenance causing chaos or ailment. They will libelously and scandalously change or falsify recollections for the under shepherds—those entrusted by the Great Shepherd to watch over the flock of sheep in the field to guard them against attack of wild predators. They will cause internal rivalry, debates, and confusion to distract the ecclesiastics from being about the Father's business.

Sheep are docile individuals easy misguide, to guide wrongly, lead into fallacy, or lead astray. These predators use several strategies: (1) misconduct or mishandle, to handle glaringly bad or angrily, or notoriously and outrageously maleficent;

(2) to misinform, to commute or exchange with incorrectness or disloyal yet deceiving information or data; (3) to mislay, to put down and audaciously treating inferior or below average; (4) to mismanage, to manage or administer flagrancy while misrepresenting, to represent under false pretense or give prevaricated answers and ideas. They use unfriendly training that develops false self-control or orderliness and efficiency in a way of wicked reproach or vituperation in an unprocessed way with blunt refusal to offer help and to reprehend severely, formally, or openly, even in the midst of the congregation or church leaders.

On the other hand, the sheep in wolf's clothing befriend or act as a friend to others to impose retribution or revenge in the form of excruciating, due to past or present hurts and pains. Their main agenda is to get back at those who cause them disgrace, embarrassment, or shame. They feel that the world owes them something, and they will not cease until they accomplish their self-proclaimed mission. The sheep in wolf's clothing sees conflict as competition, a contest or match to enter into rivalry or battle. This is the way to dishonestly get what they really or necessarily want, which may be done through guile or voluminous slyness and cunning in dealing craftily by way of deceit or lying. They will inveigle others deliberately or intentionally doing as they please by cunning, scamming, and scheming others to always get their own way. They also thrive on conflict by way of being antagonistic, incompatible, or self-contradictory and having sharp dissidence or opposition with other members.

These sheep appear to be easily emotional flurried, after opposing impulses or transferences. They fool or entice many because of their domesticated nature or custom and high-spirited pointing toward much courage and nobleness with fueling potentialities. They will be fearless against the strongest Goliath in the crowd, to outwit and test the alertness and intelligence of the bystanders. These undomesticated sheep are self-reliant, relying and having assurance and dependence on themselves and their expertness or superiority. They are not only willful but also prideful, having the nature that resists taking responsibility for any immoral violation of attitudes, behaviors, or habits.

Many are unable to receive help from God, spiritual advisors, or counselors because of prideful standing at the entrance of their soul's pathway. Unable to receive healing due to the needed receptive position is antithetical to the pride causing them not to heed to God's satiable grace. They make conscious choices or decisions to harbor pride, delight, or satisfaction in their own achievements and have exaggerated self-esteem toward foolish pride that holds strong disesteem or rancor toward those who are abased and unusual. It doesn't matter whether they are surreptitiously disguised as a wolf in sheep's clothing or a sheep in wolf's clothing; the only way to encounter God's agape love is to become prostrated with humility before His presence.

Pray and ask the Lord to deliver you from this wretched spirit of greed. Greed will bring personal dilapidation to you and your family, for you must reap what you sow. Greedy persons are sowing depressingly wretched inventions, while focusing on personal aim or goal without giving any forethought to their future. The Father wants sheep that are able to withstand the savage and untamed storms of life while climbing over the trying mounds of frustration, carrying the burdens of life until you reach your destiny.

## Deliver Me From Greed

The Bible gives us an illustrative story about the rich young ruler, a member of an official council or court, who came to Jesus questioning Him on how to become a disciple. He struggled because Jesus told him to give up his worldly possessions. The rich man thought he was worthy to be merited eternal life, but Jesus taught him that it was a gift and could not be earned. Jesus impresses the young man to recognize that his only hope is in total reliance on God, who alone can give eternal life. He also encouraged the young man to consider the full identity and nature of the Holy One. The ruler came with sincerity, keeping the law since his youth, which was a matter of external conformity. The law required internal obedience and discipline, which no one can fully accomplish without the intercession of Christ. The rich young ruler, this young man, kept the holy precepts from the days of his youth and was identified as being known beforehand, being serious minded about the law of God. Jesus wanted the young man to grasp the spiritual revelation of the commandments but through an expression of willing obedience and unconditional love. His primary problem was his false reliance in his prosperity state, for there was no indication that Jesus' direct authoritatively order is meant for all Christians.

Since, in some parts of the world, there is a need for financial aid as well as spiritual nourishment, it applies only to those who have the same spiritual problem as the young ruler—putting earthly possession and wealth of this world before the plan of God. The presence of perpetual life or salvation is a treasure received by following Jesus and cannot only be earned by self-denial, depriving one's material goods, or sacrifice of one's own desires, interests, or pleasures. In forfeiting or neglecting his wealth, the young man would have removed the obstacle that kept him from the saving grace and mercy. The admonition to the rich young ruler was to leave all his earthly possession, put his trust in the Lord, and receive infinite prosperity and joy in knowing Jesus Christ as his Lord and Savior. His tragic decision not to turn away reflected an intensified love for his possessions more than for eternal life (Mark 10:17–22).

There is another story of a lawyer, a well-schooled professional that advised others in matters of conduct established by injunction of the legalistic or a council representing others in the court of jurisprudence. The lawyer was enticing and tempting Jesus with a simple question regarding inheriting eternal life, possibly to cause embarrassment or ridicule to the Master (Luke 10:25–26). Jesus "answering said, Thou shalt love the Lord thy God with all thy heart, and with all thy soul, and with all thy strength, and with all thy mind; and thy neighbour as thyself" (v. 27). The answer to the surreptitious lawyer was to love the Lord with his total being and his neighbor as himself.

Those who have done this are filled with sentimental or indefinite compassion from a spontaneous and altruistic intellectual spirited nature, God Himself. The heart of humility looks to the Holy Spirit to help with apologetic and repentant entreaties for God's unmerited help and lovingkindness in the time of desperate need. In Biblical contexts, the center of the human spirit is the place from which springs intense feelings, devotional suggestions, and dedicated gestures through faithful courage and actions. The heart is the place where the issue of life springs forth. The heart and mind, literately speaking, refer to man's innermost center of conscious life, housing conventional expression of holiness and purity of character and motives.

The rich young ruler or lawyer didn't want true deliverance from his exorbitant desires, greedy indulgence, or appealing lifestyle. You must be free of the adulterants of greed if you have to crave or desire true joy. The only way to gain it is to be born again by the blood of the Lamb, our Savior Jesus Christ. He can give you infinite joy, which cannot be confiscated, redeemed, or stolen by robbers or thieves. These men never received the inheritance of the earth or land, which was to secure their peace in alienated time and supply a sacred entitlement for the children of God that would be redeemable from the sins, transgressions, or wicked acts.

Those who are reassured know their hope is in the Lord and trustingly look to Him. They look to life and its blessings as an immortal gift, an inheritance. They have no need to resort to systematic program for attaining some personal agenda or goal, secretly or underhandedly scheduling or charting by sinister and mysterious means to take someone else's belongings and property. In conclusion, God loves a cheerful giver. One who gives bountifully and freely, graciously and generously sowing, shall also reap bountifully without grudging or out of necessity; giving to help or aid the advancement of the kingdom of God. Those who sow sparingly or meagerly of poor quality or minimal amounts shall also reap sparingly, a small or diminutive reward.

One must receive spiritual freedom from the covetous stronghold of greed and avaricious place of security. Give thanks to God for His unspeakable gift to mankind, Jesus Christ the first giver, who first gave Himself selflessly to a dying and lost world. Giving is a direct and obedient response of gratitude for this marvelous gift of Jesus that goes beyond comprehension or apprehension. The Lord Jesus says, "It is more blessed to give than to receive" (Acts 20:35). Give and it shall be given back to you with financially and beneficially means to aid the kingdom of God with wholesome health, unconstrained joyfulness, and adjoined or blended rewards collectively from overrunning and overflowing results. The privilege of wealth or financial security should be to bless others, such as aiding and supporting the disadvantaged and less fortunate. With this, the Holy Ghost brings satisfaction and happiness along with willing and assenting fulfillment and enjoyment.

The person who is well supplied or provided for through the grace and mercy of God can be delivered from the bondage of greed. This spirit is deadly to the inner man's well being—body, soul, and mind.

## 8

# THE WORLD DID NOT
# GIVE ME THIS JOY

*My brethen, count it all joy when ye fall into divers temptations.*

—JAMES 1:2

THERE ARE MANY THINGS that this world has to offer, but joy is not one of those free gifts you can win through the mail or sweepstake winnings. The world's expression or translation of joy comes with palliate pain and sorrow. Almost every product you purchase or buy has a caution or buyer beware note on the label. Why should you receive your joy unlike most others?

Jeremiah was a priest and prophet of in the Old Testament who was described as a bashful youth who in earlier years received strength and encouragement from the Lord (Jer. 1:6). Just like Jeremiah, many today are not confident and sure when the Lord calls them to carry His message to a dying world. They feel as though the Lord made a mistake and are unsure of being able to handle the task. Remember Jeremiah who was called when he was a youth.

The Lord selected Jeremiah as the prophet for Israel during the reign of Zedekiah, the son of Josiah, king of Judah, who took the children of Jerusalem into captivity in his fifth month. In that, Jeremiah was known as the "weeping prophet" that mumbled and complained on multiple occasions regarding his assignment. He was the messenger of woeful condemnation and conviction, due to many people not receiving God's conditional terms for retribution for their sinful and lustful indignation against the oracles and precepts of His law. He didn't want the Lord to give reprieve to his intimidators, due to their unremitting and cruel treatment of imprisonment.

The Lord spoke these words to Jeremiah: "Before I formed thee in the belly I knew thee; and before thou camest forth out of the womb I sanctified thee, and I ordained thee a prophet unto the nations" (v. 5). God divulged through Jeremiah how He would commission him to carry a message of doom to the nation regardless of whether the people wanted to receive the word from the messenger. God was not concerned with Jeremiah's unreceptive or unrelenting spirit to take on the challenge; he was definitely someone who was picked out to be picked on.

Today the same is true of many who will not take up their cross and follow the Lord for fear of the unknown, what others will think or say, or how family members may eliminate them or receive them. Two things are for certain: you did not choose yourself, and the Lord chooses whom He pleases. His word states that He is no respecter of persons. There is no partiality and candidness with Him. While you are concerned with how others will receive the gospel message, rest assured that someone else is waiting in the breeze to take your place.

The Word of God says, "For many are called, but few are chosen" (Matt. 22:14). A "call" could be for a temporary season, while on the other hand "chosen" could be for a natural life. Jeremiah was not prophesied to regarding his destiny; it was already established. A chosen individual is someone who is picked out by preference or selection, while a called individual is someone that has been convoked or summoned to come, considered, or declared to be used for a specified duty, task, or assignment.

The Lord made a way for Jeremiah as messenger of His Word, and He made a way for the recipients to receive his report. Only God can pave the way for you to be fearless in the service of His commission—that which you are chosen to do. Jeremiah told the Lord that he was but a child and too young to do such a task. Adolescence and lacking skill do not disqualify when God calls; He equips and sustains those He commissions. The world has no power to give; therefore, do not be concerned of their approval or disapproval, for the Lord is with you and will deliver you from the presence of evildoers. God will not permit anyone to stop His purpose before it is fulfilled (Jer. 1:7–8). Life came from God regardless of what the evolution believers say. In the beginning God created the heaven and the earth. The world didn't exist until God formed it during creation and provided life with His enlightenment (Gen. 1).

You shall have enough faith in the Lord to know that your joy doesn't come from man, but from the Lord. God wanted Jeremiah to have the prophetic dominion and ownership to pull out the embedded sin in the lives of God's people by cautioning them of their libidinous and repulsive demeanor and deportment within the gates of the city. Consequently, the people in the city could have restoration, and he was to apply with great energy or effort in speaking the truth with great and powerful anointing that would demolish all wicked thoughts and imaginations.

## Israel's Faithlessness in Joy

Jeremiah began prophesying in Judah during many kings' leadership. An extraordinary event acquired prior to Jeremiah being born, was that king Nebuchadnezzar, a mighty and strong general of warfare and tyrant of the Babylonians, overtook the Egyptians. Nebuchadnezzar besieged Jerusalem on numerous occasions and overthrew their kingdom. Due to their seditious and contumacious spirit, God permitted their enemy to take them into captivity. Jeremiah foretold the captivity of Jehoiachin and his followers and that prediction that was later fulfilled. God was warning Judah and Jerusalem about their coldhearted ways, distant in sympathy and interest and their unwillingness to circumcise their hearts, repent of their infirmities, and turn from gross ways.

The men of Judah and Jerusalem were expected to have openness to the Lord's overtures, a necessity for total commitment to His will. They were disjoined into discontinuous parts or fragments of uncultivated or unplanted basis and not disseminate from the petulance, misfortune, or affliction of the earth. Jeremiah told all the men of Judah and occupancy of Jerusalem to disintegrate all presence of sin from their living and unload all nefarious or unrighteous acts from their hearts. He said to consecrate their hearts for fear that God's vengeful rage would come forward like a strong power and extinguish them along with all sinisterly doings. No man could stand against the Lord's wrath (Jer. 4:3–4).

The prosecutor is throwing outright and false illusions along with provisions that give an illusionary picture of joy and peace, but are not important in this life. How will you enjoy the toys and things you have in life? That is why God wants you to be integrated in Him, and content with His joy. No, God is not saying that you cannot have tangible assets or prosperity. He just wants His children to be equipped with the fruitful spirit first, so they won't stumble and become prey to this world. God knows this world is unreliable and cannot be trusted. How many people don't have enough money in retirement and social security benefits? There are more than you will ever hear or know about that have worked all their lives and do not have enough money or health coverage to sustain them throughout each month. Therefore, responsible individuals, don't put trust in the world, for it will turn its back on you and have you up late at night wondering how you are going to make ends meet.

Judah had to learn the same. They had to leave all their aureate idols and images behind before God would bring them out of captivity. But then He replenished them with His riches, land, and possessions. In the New Testament, a rich young ruler had an unwilling heart, yet he would not renounce his earthly assets; he chose the world rather than heavenly blissful things. Judah commenced to follow the words of the false prophets who served Baal, which led them into immorality and idolatry.

The Lord sent word again by His messenger Jeremiah that before they could pass through the wall between inner and outer court, the children of Israel must amend all unconditioned ways and doings by no longer robbing, murdering, committing adultery, swearing falsely, and burning incense to Baal or chasing after other gods. He wanted them to come to the house of deliverance and repent of all their transgressions and iniquities (Jer. 7:9–11). God's house is holy and no abominable acts should be ignored, overlooked, or tolerated. The sanctuary of God is not a safe haven for anyone with a sinful nature or heart of the ungodly. Never put your trust in false hope or belief. Repentance is necessary before coming into the presence of the Holy One.

Do not fail to listen to the voice of the Lord when He is warning of a day of devastation. If you fall into a reprobate state, He will not hear your cry nor prayers. God is understanding and merciful, but He is also sovereign and a righteous judge; therefore, never take His privileges for granted. God told Jeremiah not to pray for them anymore because they did not want to cease from breaking His sacred covenant and live holy. He would no longer listen to unholy, meaningless and repetitive prayers on their behalf, for they wouldn't detach from the power of darkness (v. 16).

## SURRENDERED JOY

Jeremiah was like so many believers who have heart of passion and love that no man be lost in sin and who cry out to God on behalf of the lost or unsaved. God saw that Judah was no longer respecting or honoring the covenant that was made on Mount Sinai; they had returned back to their sinful ways of idol worshiping. The Lord was going to rescind His promise because Judah was in constant rebellion and challenging His authority and control. They exhibited bipolar tendencies between serving God or Baal and other gods, unable to grasp a conscious servitude to Yahweh (vv. 23–24).

The believer often does the same. God comes in and delivers from a harmful relationship and elevates dignity and esteem. What does the believer do? They turn their backs on the Lord at the first sign of mistreatment; all this comes with the price of the cross—no cross, no crown. Would you rather receive pats on the back from man, which will last until the next person comes to out do you, rather than emphatic approval from God of eternal bliss and jubilee?

There will be disorder in the days to come. You may begin to wonder, like the children of Judah, where the balm is—the pleasurable medicine to heal and soothe all afflictions and distress with comfort. The territory of Gilead was known for its trades and source of spices and herbal medicine. The children of Judah began to cry out to the Lord asking why the medicine for curing, healing, and relieving was not working for their contrite and vulnerable hearts (8:22). The medicine the people need could not be dispensed by man. Judah was in need of spiritual diagnosis to treat, prevent, and heal them from their repugnant living, which is the only treatment that would rescue the people from their wretched position. The people would not recover gradually from illness from any magic potion, only supernatural powers of remission. The remission for sins would come when the people repented with godly compunction.

Until you know clearly the nature or character of the true and living God, you will never be able to receive the joy of the Lord. The children of Judah had a problem receiving the same revelation: its God's way or no way. The Lord God is jealous, which means that no generation will bow down or serve another god. The Lord God is jealous in His disposition, attitude, or feelings toward His creation, and those who blatantly violate His covenant and reject Him as the King of kings and Lord of lords will bring utter destruction upon themselves and their households. He will bestow mercy unto those who love Him and keep His commandments (Exod. 20:5–6).

The Lord God is a consuming fire, even a jealous God (Deut. 4:24). Mayhem and injury inflicted on the disobedient so as to cause decrement of a part or function necessary for self-defense. The people of Judah and Jerusalem would not display self-reproach alongside a profound and repentant sense of guilt over their wrongs committed. The pastors or leaders were uncaring and inflexible, and refused to seek counsel from the Lord for divine instruction and direction. The Lord would not prosper them, and the flocks (followers) would be scattered because of their disobedience (Jer. 10:21). The Word cannot make it any simpler: true godly regret and sorrow must take place before one can have assured joy in the Lord. There is no other way to have constant joy without it coming through the Deliverer, Redeemer, and Savior. Only God is able to uncover all of man's insincere behavior; He will do so to bring you back to reality.

## A City Under Distress

Many times Jeremiah petitioned for Judah and pleaded with the Lord not to punish those who were innocent and didn't know Him, but to spare the unknowing. He wanted God to have mercy on the children of Judah. God gave revelation to Jeremiah that Judah didn't want to come out of bondage, because they didn't want to live consecrated and holy lives. They had fallen under the influences of the enemy and the enormity of their foolish minds. God is a righteous public official with all authority to hear and allege cases in all courts of law; He is a reliable arbiter and umpire. He is ready to listen to the undergoing observation and questions of the defense. Jeremiah's inquired of the Lord how long the wicked would continue to prosper in their ways. Would they resume being peaceful or become more treacherous?

But a sovereign Judge can always reconsider His verdict. The wicked in the land were flourishing, while Jeremiah's fellow citizens were diminished in their own fruit. Jeremiah's countrymen offered all kinds of vain and idle lip service unto the Lord, as they pursued after the ways of Baal. Jeremiah reminded the Lord that He knew His heart and had examined his heart's intents. Jeremiah begged the Lord to return his former plans for the wicked (12:1–3).

God was very upset with the leaders of that day; they were

acting like leeches taking advantage of the people and had meager tolerance. The overseers had deliberately vandalized God's land that was devoted to supply the needs of His people. They had made God's pleasant estate a desolate wilderness (v. 10). The overseers were living unholy and unsacred lifestyles before the people and leading them down a road of ruination by turning them away from God's law and ordinances. These co-conspirators were corrupted leaders, instilling unlawful actions of illegal rules or improper codes of ethics.

The world is in the same state today. Everything that God created is represented in procreation—a man and woman amalgamating in covenant with God through holy matrimony. *Holy* is defined by *Webster's Dictionary* as consecrated, sacred, spirituality pure, sinless, saintly, or giving deep reverence in a religious use. *Matrimony* is defined as the act or rite of marriage; the state of being husband and wife. Even the world's definition is the same as God's.

While many will have you to believe that other options are acceptable, the Bible tells this was one of God's problems with the Judah. Anything outside of God's holy and sacred calculation to replenish the earth comes from the pit. God is not the Father or Author of extreme or slight confusion or vagueness of mind. "For God is not the author of confusion, but of peace, as in all churches of the saints" (1 Cor. 14:33). This is not a matter for controversy but is a moral matter of what is pleasing and desirable before the presence of God.

Later in chapter 10 under subtopic regarding the fragrance of joy there is an illustrative reference of the various fragrances that please God's and odors that displease Him. Your destination in life is not about receiving lustful pleasures, but to bring the lost and scattered back into the fold. Judah was caught up with self-centered pleasure and sensual desires; therefore judgment would come and uncover their untrustworthy and unreliable new methods. The infamous state of their conduct was viewed as grossly shameful—their promiscuous and performance of all sorts of pitiless and disgusting acts on the hills and in the fields. Great sorrow and grief would come upon Jerusalem.

Will you not be purged clean? If so, when shall it be? God's question to Jerusalem was how long they would remain in this disgraceful and disparaging social position. The Lord conferred them to deterge themselves of impurities and extraneous matters of sinfulness. There was yet hope for the descendants of Jerusalem, nonetheless slim, postponement for the supremely great wrath. Return to your true husbandman with a sincere and remorseful heart (Jer. 13:26–27).

The veil of God provides the same coverage today; you do not have to walk around with your head hanging down in ignominy; hold onto God's word with homage and dignity. He will ratify your penance with a penitent sentencing, found to be not guilty. The Word of God tells you not to get all in a rift and worry about the cares of this world.

The Messianic era is associated with Christ's second coming. Paul summarized what will happen prior to the Savior's return. Men will have superior joy and concern for themselves and their own interests, exercising ravenousness and avariciousness, overindulgence pride and bragging, arrogance, speaking irreverently or profanely of God, disobedience to parents, being ungrateful, imprecatory, and execrable. They will be gender confused and lack sexually chastity without continence, peace breakers, and false arraigners. They will have vehemently brutal temperaments, looking down on others as worthless and beneath notice, and be despisers of those that are honorable. They will become traitors, heady, high minded, and lovers of pleasure more than lovers of God. They will have an outward appearance of godliness, but negate the supernatural power of the Holy Ghost. We must turn away from those with these negative, spiritually deadly traits (2 Tim. 3:1–5).

Why go around in a state of contempt and confusion? When the Lord hands are expanded wide to receive His prodigal son or daughter, it's time to come back home. Don't allow yourself to be turned over to a rejected or abandoned way, state, or direction of thinking, feeling discarded and abandoned by God. Who else can take on your conflicts? If the Lord gives up on you, there will be no more triumphant memories, pacific days, gleeful tomorrows, and future happiness. The children of the King certainly heed to the caution, feel regret over past fallacies or omissions, and return to the place of rest.

Jeremiah could see that Judah was beyond deliverance, because the Lord of hope told him so. They were so engulfed in their pleasures that they had no time to rejoice in the Lord. God was in the process of bringing judgment against Judah and removing His promise. Israel had confined to multitudinous acts worse than the forefathers, yet continued walking after their own consumptive imaginations from their pernicious heart, not heeding to the voice of God (Jer. 16:12).

Jeremiah was fulfilling his ministry alone without cohesion from his friends and family. Many times walking this journey alone is what God has planned for your life in this interval of time. While you are waiting to enter into the next season, you must disjoin yourself from those who are not in agreement with your purpose, such as unsaved and unbelieving family members, friends, and loved ones. No one else can be blamed for you not reaching your destiny. The Lord will keep you in His joy, which is greater than the standardized joy that the world offers through in-crowds or cliques. Cursed is the man who trusts and establishes his own soul and heart and digresses from the Lord. Blessed is the man whose trust and hope is the Lord (17:5, 7). Many will shut out or break faith with you for speaking the truth and for choosing to be a disciple of righteousness. Do not be bamboozled even though it appears that pessimist, who believes that the evil in life outweighs the good, is getting way with everything. Know that optimist, who believes that the good in life outweighs the sinisterly, will prevail.

## PRIDE WILL REMOVE JOY

During the time Jeremiah lived there were a lot of tenuous and false pastors leading Judah astray. Jeremiah told the Lord that he had complied with God's laws and commands and shouldn't be considered as one of them. You may feel the same way. You strive daily to be legitimate before the presence of God and things seem to go wrong in your life. Other believers may say you are not living holistic or your testimony is a lie. The Lord has all the facts and will defend your case. He is the public defender, someone acting on the behalf of the people or person for the case that is being presented. Jeremiah didn't have public defender as you do today. Therefore, he was making an appeal for his case before the Lord alone. He was his own advocate and public defender, but God had power of attorney. Jeremiah's sober pledge to serve Him was a legally authorizing statement to act on His behalf.

In contrast, you have Jesus who makes arraignment before the high court of God for the rehearing of your case. Jeremiah was not a careless or reckless prophet and followed God's enactments and precepts, neither longed for pitiful days. He spoke only the unadulterated and lawful truth. He pleaded with the Lord not to bring terror to him and to be his hope. He asked for those that persecuted to be delivered into the hands of catastrophe. He requested that his foes be filled with great fright, but that God would warn him of the endangered days to come. Bring upon the wicked the sunrise of disaster and bring a double downfall of demolition (vv. 16–18).

Jeremiah became a little personal in his prayer to the Lord; he wanted God to destroy everyone that spoke discourtesy and ill mannered against him. He was at his breaking point and unable to see relief for himself in the future unless God reacted soon in his defense. He could no longer wait for his pending freedom; he wanted vengeance taken upon his foes and accusers.

Jesus is the eminent defender who wants you to have the same desire to pray for your enemies as He did; not to want them to be overrun fatally, but be delivered. All the repulsive, degrading and morally base deeds and progressions that go contrary to the Word of God or to His expectations in your life, resulting in disadvantage or harm that could hinder your empowerment are to be forgiven. Regardless of all the slandering, gossiping, and lying, God is still in control and every equivocated, fabricated and unjust word spoken against you will return back to the sender; just like a boomerang. It is something that goes contrary to the expectation of its originator and results in his disadvantage or harm.

Jeremiah was faced with the same dilemma; the leaders of his day were using every single wretched device. They could not find any delinquency in his living, his counseling, or his prophecies; therefore, they manufactured false impressions and unfurled and uninformed stories to wreck his upright reputation (18:18). Jeremiah was ridiculed for speaking the truth and they did not want to hear him since they weren't already to leave the ways of the world and lifestyles with which they had grown familiar.

Your enemies may become great, but the Lord insists that you hold to His first commandment that is to love your enemies, returning good for evil. God will be your Protector. To take vengeance on your own behalf is wrong, for the return of a disservice or assault will be repaid. Therefore, feed your enemy and give them water if they are thirsty. By remunerating good for evil, you place overflowing coals of destructive burning on their heads (Rom. 12:19–21).

The unbeliever's salvation encouraged by you as a believer when you show them that you still have prolonged joy even when treated unfair and unjust. You are to be watchfully and vigilantly ready for spiritual armed conflicts. Also you must be cautious not to slip into the deception of the enemy, who will bring false implications your way and encourage you to take wrong actions, which you will later regret. Listen to your heart—the heart of Christ. All believers must offer an unbeliever unconditional love and unwavering mercy; by doing so you have carried out the law (13:8).

## A ROBBER OF JOY

Pashur, the son of Immer the priest, was the chief governor who was in charge of punishing the troublemakers and for deciding their punishment. He heard that Jeremiah was prophesying judgment and sentencing on Judah. Pashur took Jeremiah into custody into the stock, which was by the tabernacle of the Lord. He imprisoned Jeremiah falsely and accused him of being a troublesome nuisance for speaking the legal truth. Pashur wanted to put fear into him to stopping preaching the gospel. He released Jeremiah at daybreak, but God gave Pashur a new name for to falsely imprisoning and accusing His prophet for speaking the truth. Maggormissbib was Pashur's new name meaning "terror on every side" (20:1–3).

God was telling Judah that He was going to give them over to their enemies the Babylonians for their uprising and actions taken against His prophet. God wanted all of them to know that they would not have a kingdom for long nor would they be kings where they were going. Pashur pretended to be a prophet and he brought damnation upon his kindred, who were going into captivity in Babylon. He would die and be buried there with all his friends to whom he prophesied lies (v. 6).

My friends do not think that God will not deal with your enemies the same way He dealt with Jeremiah's enemies. Jesus is intervening in your business; I have been in the same place many times thinking that I will never have any joy in this life because every time I made an ally only to find out later they were really my foe. There may be people who don't like that you are a faithful believer or follower of Christ and daily try to take away your joy by commencing conflict and strive in your life. You are called to be courageous and fearless soldiers for the army of the Lord. This story displays a great lesson how to love your enemies and good to those hate you. You will have to keep praying and loving them without any grudges or antagonism.

How do you think Jeremiah felt that no one believed in him? He was alone fighting his clan with no one on his side but God. He could not give up the fight, for it was his indication to the world of how God was victorious and strong power. The world was taking away his joy. He had no friends or family on his side. He thought that if anyone would stick up for him for being truthful, it should be his loved ones. He was at his wits end. He was wondering if he might as well give it all up since he gave it a try and no one would listen to him.

Do any of these excuses or complaints sound like you? Yes, to them all. Regardless of how you may feel about the flight that is ahead, learn how to soar above all the cares, worries, concerns, and regrets on this planet. Jeremiah became weary on the journey and wanted to permanently rest from preaching the gospel, but he couldn't because God's words were in his heart as a burning fire, fastened securely in his substances (v. 9).

Jeremiah was befriended by King Zedekiah who was unmindful and vacillating. He relied and sought Jeremiah's advice, but meanwhile permitted his enemies to mistreat and imprison him. The same is true today, people will befriend you, yet allow the enemy to try to destabilize or despoil your commission. Jesus will be your true friend when you are friendless. During Zedekiah's leadership, Jeremiah entered into a reciprocal agreement with him to divulge God's will to him in exchange for his own isolated safety while under house arrest. The Lord God would conqueror decisively all the inhabitants of this city, and inflict both man and animal with a great contagious or infectious disease, very adverse and even fatal. King Nebuchadnezzar defeated Zedekiah and imprisoned him. After the defeat, the Lord handed over Zedekiah king of Judah, his servants, those that requested their life, and all the people left in the city after the pestilence, wrath of God, and famine into the hands of Nebuchadnezzar king of Babylon, their enemy. The sword of retribution came and no man was spared with pity or mercy (21:4–7).

Jeremiah's message to Judah's kings was viewed as harassment and hostile criticism because of their antipathetic ways toward the people of God. The kings became very cross with Jeremiah and kept him imprisoned until they went into captivity. Today people who don't want to hear or receive sound doctrine will withdraw from or ostracize those who speak the truth. Judah was selfish and despondent in their ways of thinking and they would not repent. Their heart persisted to be unconsecrated and uncircumcised.

## AN EVIL LIFESTYLE WILL DESTROY YOUR JOY

The kings of Judah would not take responsibility for their ungodly leadership over God's elected people. God's official expression of strong deprecation would be handed out to the shepherds that led the people of Judah astray and dispersed them all around. This was just like the clergymen who have not provided spiritual nourishment to the people, permitting the scattering of church members from under the arch of safety or place of safe retreat. The Lord God will visit you for your deviation from His general rule (23:1–2). God wanted rulers that would chase after His heart and rely on His guidance; those that were aware that their joy didn't come from the world, but from the Lord. Although Judah's sins and the sins of their leaders had caused them to be driven away into expatriation, the Lord primarily directed the motion and results for His people's repeated violations. The absence of a concerned shepherd invites attacks by the wild animals and derails the people from the covenant commitments. Still a remnant of His people would be responded to after the deliberation by which everyone was seeking a remedy against their rigid taskmaster to receive an appeal of restoration. God's court of law will propose order for every person to be productive and thrive. God would set up shepherds over them who will feed them and not condemn them or persecute them, and they would not lack anything from the Lord (23:3–4).

God was already looking for a Savior for His people: One who would lead them out of ungodly living by being a living example of God's uprightness. The Savior would be called Jesus the Messiah, the ideal King. He would add up to be the finest quality of the best rulers, and infinitely more.

The supreme King shall reign and prosper, while executing

sound and reasonable judgment and justice in the earth. During his reign, "Judah shall be saved, and Israel shall dwell safely: and this is his name whereby he shall be called, THE LORD OUR RIGHTEOUSNESS" (vv. 5–6). Jesus, the Messiah, would resuscitate God's people and bring them back to Him so that they could receive the promise of God's blessings. In the meantime, the false prophets uninterruptedly misled and misinformed their hearers, even in Babylon, encouraging the people not to turn from their repelling, inveterate conduct and detestable habits (v. 22).

The Lord wanted Judah to know that the day of inquisition was fast approaching and summoned for a public inquest. The public defendant would carry out an examination or investigation with regard to all the aberrant facts from the plaintiff. The plaintiff, the false prophet, would speak statements that are known to be false, utterly displeasing and harassing, and connivances against the intangible objects of God. They would be found inculpate of perjury with deceit in their hearts, that which caused the people to intentionally pretermit their God. Their dreams were about imaginary and illusionary visions that were lulling and soothing to their neighbors. They turned from servitude to God as their fathers to willfully serving Baal, a false god, for a pleasurable feeling and sensual satisfaction (vv. 26–27).

Jeremiah was repetitious in his inducements and earnestly warned them to repent and return to God with a circumcised heart. God was soon to write a new covenant with Israel in which He would write His law on their inward parts—to be consecrated to service. God's strong sensitive and sympathetic nature and personality attributes would adjoin a spiritual union with Judah. The union would connect the two with absolute coherence for their mutual desire. God's desire was for them to be delivered, and Judah's desire was to be freed from sin. The holy marriage is prompt, informal, hasty, and arbitrary when people return unto Him with genuineness and straightforwardness (24:7).

The king of Judah, Zedekiah, imprisoned Jeremiah because He was giving them prevision that they didn't want to receive. His words to them were to repent and turn from their profane and deplete management. Jeremiah was under judgment by his enemies for giving them the true and authentic Word of God. They were fatigued of hearing him every time he saw them, telling them what was going to take place with their mortal soul if they didn't repent.

Today many believers, as well as unbelievers, will discharge you because they see you talking about the Lord or telling others about the goodness of Jesus, singing lyrics of adoration and veneration in time of despair, and building others up with words of comfort and console. Some will take pleasure and delight to see some evil or bad, unfortunate consequence fixed by the captor handicap your specific duty or function for which you were sent to achieve.

Jeremiah faced the same accusations from the priests and false prophets. They told the male monarchs and all the townspeople that Jeremiah deserved a death sentence for speaking condemnation and inevitable destruction upon the city. They probably called him to several town meetings and publicly asked him what would was going to happen to them. He gave the prediction of the Lord (26:11–16).

Man would rather live a lie than confess to or acknowledge the truth. God desires to have amity between Himself and His children; there is reprieve, but there is also punitive retribution. The Lord is longsuffering, merciful, pardoning iniquity and transgressions, clearing the guilty or perjurers. But, He will visit the iniquity of the fathers upon the children to the third or fourth generations. All the earth shall be filled with the glory of the Lord.

## A Remnant of Joy

God's heart desire was to forgive and cleanse the people from the breaching of God's law and sound justice. He is going to give them a new day filled with His promises and covenants. God wanted Judah to realize that He had not forsaken them, but merely temporarily denied them. It is imperative for you not to lose your joy when the cares of the world try to overtake or overload your mind, as they come disjoin and dismount you from the relationship you have with the Lord. The prayers of the righteous maybe paused when you choose to harbor ill feelings and enmity toward others. You must repent and rise above those who transgress against you. In spite of Judah's insubordination and reckless qualities, the Lord would to no degree be unable to remember His people.

He has, for all future time, expectations of freedom for public disturbances to abate, with a lightsome and unpresuming finality. The Lord is waiting for you to evoke His presence in prayer, and He is listening carefully. If you are searching for Him with an endearing and straightforwardness innermost nature, He will not be difficult to access concerning your subsistence. The Lord will not turn a deaf ear to those who are in need and in distress. Regardless of how deeply they are in sin, He is able to bring about retribution for the wandering and bashful who departed from the sheepfold. (See Jeremiah 29:11–13.) God cannot be discovered by chance, for everything about Him is a mystery to man.

God's heart's desire is that His children understand that He wants them to have joy while remaining in readiness or anticipation for Him to rescue them from this pitiless world. God wants you to have the heart of Jesus so that you can receive God's instruction and guidance with a receptive and open communication of understanding of His binding promises. He wants the best for everyone that is willing and ready to come into His place of rest and receive healing and restoration. There is no place of rest in this universe like the embracing arms of the Lord.

God gave Israel a fair opportunity to make a new covenant with Him; one which would exist forever. He's going to perform open-heart surgery upon His people and implant a pacemaker to stimulate and synchronize His wishes with the one pulsation, or full contraction and dilation of the heart. These hearts will fear and reverence God's holy and enshrined commandments and laws, which keep them on the erect and heedful path of uprightness. They will no longer succumb to foolish enticements to do sinuous deeds, from this day forward and throughout all generations after them. This heart will impel apprehension and deep respect in their innermost parts and at no time will it turn aside from the living God (Jer. 32:38–40).

God's love for you is far greater than you could ever imagine, and He wants you to have gratifying joy in your heart, which will grant you absolute gladness. God is not like the world; He will never lead you into the hands of a disgruntled adversary. He will punish you so that you will turn from the inaccuracy of your ways but God takes pleasure in giving blessings and supplying your every need, not imposing corporal discipline. He doesn't want to hold any good thing from those He loves who have a simple and chastened heart.

He going to reestablish Israel in the land ensured to those with an undoubting heart and unquestionable soul. This will be the deserved compensation for all extended ominous and ill fortune concentrated upon them and also the redemption of the preceding promissory words (v. 41).

Sickness and illness will possibly injure your body and trials can bring unreceptive and undeserving pain, disarranging incidents, and congenital distress to address or confront you, but maintain expressive and extraordinary joy through it all. In due time, the Lord will adjure un-defective vitality and preservation of strength. He can replete exemption from explicit illness to everyone at the same time, unmasking His most sufficient supply or quantity of proportionate arrangement and quality of being in agreement with reality or facts. The time would come when He would release Judah and Israel from the imprisonment of their oppressor and rebuild their homestead (33:6–7).

If you are going through testing and trying, believe that God will not place more on you than you can endure. God aspires to give you a reestablished occupancy in life, first by way of cleansing your temple and psyche from all unrighteousness acts and forgiving all breach of laws and duties of the past. The basis of the institution of the reformed covenant was to purge every person from all lack of fairness and revoke all offenses or faults that infringed the sacred precepts. This new fringe benefit would bring them back to the subliminal joy through God's holy name. Praise and honor will be restored before all the nations on the earth. The entire earth shall consent to the fullest possible generosity that He will give a portion to the chosen nation. Every man, woman, boy, and girl ought to feel reverence or awe with powerful fear for the abundant goodness and flourishing manner God can procure (33:8–9).

There is no worry or concern under God's procurement—protection and security from trenches of life. Press on and walk in the joy of the Lord while keeping the Word hidden deep in your soul. Jeremiah kept God's solemn pledge stored in his heart; it ignited a Pentecostal breakthrough. This experience can be yours for the asking. Receive the empowerment of the Holy Ghost and not incommodious onus, debts, or irresolute cares of this morally vitiated temporal sketch. It's not too late for the Lord to throw you a life jacket if you have fallen over the ship. This life jacket or vest is a life preserver to help bring you into safety from wiles of the enemy. If you are deeply sunken in the abyss of this world's entrapment or abandoned, there is a lifeboat that will conduct you back to safety. Jesus is an incredible lifeguard, an expert swimmer who is watching over all of God's children to bar them from drowning or being submerged under treacherous waters. Regardless of circumstances being mixed together with adverse effects, the servants of the Lord are capable of living together harmoniously with others and working well together with a spirit of compatibility for the sake of the ministry.

## A SERVANT'S JOY

Jeremiah was a great prophet who was imprisoned many times for speaking and preaching God's word in a time when people were living indecent and perverted lives. Today you see people are living the same, like there is still time to get their life together before Jesus returns. But the scripture tells you that no man knows the hour when the Savior or Master will return. You are a chosen priesthood and royal generation who does not go along after the ways of mere men Therefore, the traps of deception and schemes will not be able to grow vigorously or prosperously in you. Many believe that they have all the time in world and should sow their wild oats and get everything out of their system before coming to the Lord. The night is early or young, but the prince of death can call for you at anytime. You can drive your car around the corner and get into a deadly hazard that can take a life. You can be walking along the street and be killed by gunfire. You cannot know when your life will be done, but you can find out what is your purpose for being here and begin to work on your life's destiny. Life is not all about having good times and looking out for number one. You should know some things that you go through can be omitted if you pass the test the first time and don't have to learn from repeated experiences. Practice does make perfect, but that is when you are learning from life's experiences and tests. As children of God, we should never want to see someone else go through persecution, ridicule, isolations, and torture. The love of Jesus will cover a multitude of sins.

In the Old Testament, Jeremiah had the love of Jesus in his heart. He retained that joy even when he was imprisoned, talked about, and lied about. Jeremiah said on many occasions that he wanted God to ruin his enemies, but I don't think that he truly meant that because he was always praying and interceding for God to have mercy on them. You can ask God to punish your enemies, but never quit praying for them. Keep in mind that one day you may want someone to have mercy on you when you become overtaken by temptation or a fall. Sometimes the only way to receive everlasting joy is to take flight and leave everything else behind. Keep in mind that God's ways are not your ways, neither are His thoughts as yours. There must be a severing of association from anything or anyone that will uninterruptedly instill agitation, inquietude, or incredulity, when family, friends or loved ones bring conflict against your destiny.

## THE MYSTERY OF JOY

You have to ask the Lord to come into your heart and remove all senseless and fatuous pride and supersede it with a heart like Jesus. Then when trouble comes, you will know how to call on the Holy Spirit. Judah could not comprehend that they had done many noisome things before their God. The wicked kings wanted them to believe it was Jeremiah's fault that they were in captivity and not their own. The kings of Judah were not willing to accept responsibility for their misfeasance and were making a scapegoat out of Jeremiah because of their unbridled pride and obdurate hearts getting in the way. God was losing His patience with them because they would not repent. Zedekiah was twenty-one years old when he reigned over Jerusalem for eleven years. His mother was Hamutal the daughter of Jeremiah of Libnah, and he did pestiferous things in the eyes of the Lord, incorporated from King Jehoiakim before him. Due to Jerusalem's failure to show a feeling of slight regret or guilt, the Chaldean army was allowed to overtake the king and disperse his army. They took the Zedekiah and carried him to the king of Babylon in the city of Riblah in the region of Hamath, where sentencing was given by the Babylonian king. Babylon's king intemperately killed his sons and all the royal men of Judah right before his eyes in the city of Riblah. They pulled out of the eyes of Zedekiah, shackled him in chains, and later carried him away to Babylon; there he was imprisoned until he died (Jer. 52:1–11).

When everything was said and done, whose joy remained? Jeremiah had on-going joy in the Lord. Later he was emancipated from prison and sent on his way. Jeremiah was left with the joy of the Lord in his heart, not the joy that Zedekiah had. Zedekiah's wretched joy brought him destruction and devastation since he was only concerned about pleasing man rather than God. Jeremiah was found in the end to be a faithful trustee, a dependable and honest steward of the Lord, first condemned and later pardoned and granted special privileges.

Our wondrous Pardoner died for all the world's iniquity and transgressions to be expunged and forgiven. Jesus rose from the grave so that the world could receive parole and freedom any future sentencing, on the merits of remission. This immutable gift of joy is God's ultimate source of contentment.

Jesus is the superior profit, if you are looking for everlasting and unchanging joy. The world didn't give you His joy, and the world can't take it away from you. The Lord Our God, He is faithful and will sustain His covenant and enduring mercy to all those who love Him and keep His biblical truths.

# 9

# I WANT EVERLASTING JOY

*Looking for unto Jesus the author and finisher of my faith; who
for the joy that was set before him endured the cross, despising the
shame, and is set down at the right hand of the throne of God.*

—Hebrews 12:2

THE HOLY SPIRIT PRODUCES Christian attributes, disposition, and moral fiber. Also, one fruit that comes off the production assembly line is joy. The Holy Spirit is capable of sustaining burdens and creating joy in your spiritual vintage if you are willing to mandate your will under subjection to Him.

The instruction and guidance come from the Father, who refers to Jesus as the faithful, loyal, and authenticated vine that grows and coils around the Father. He is the cultivator or farmer who watches over, protects, and equips His livestock for ministry assignment. In the book of John there is an illustration where Jesus represents Himself as the true vine. *Webster's Dictionary* defines *vine* as a plant that has a flexible stem requiring some kind of support. In the supernatural realm this is a parallel regarding this parable by Jesus. Jesus is the foundation, the underlying base or support for the institution of

God, with the tools for advancing the Kingdom and uprooting all barren and lifeless insensitive matters. The Holy Ghost is the comforter and custodian, responsible for helping maintain conducive and productive qualities. God is the husbandman, the Provider for church. The assemblage or gathering is the branch with the extensions rooting from the trunk or main limb of tree or shrub (Jesus). The division of a family, however, is a separately located unit of an organism or any living thing in its complexity of structure or function. The organism must offer itself for inspection of productive fruit or the vinedresser will uproot it. The units that yield fruit will be purged or pruned to bring forth more fruit (John 15:1–3). The purging cleanses all of the uncommon constituent materials that might be pollutants or cause undesirable dissipation. The pruning produces fruitfulness, the product of a godly life, virtues, or character.

The production of joy will come from the warehouse or storehouse of Jesus, who ramifies the Word by dividing or spreading out into branches or branch-like divisions upon the members so that all good fruit is coming directly from the manufacturer, God the Father. The true believer has no fruitfulness apart from his union and fellowship with Christ. A branch out of contact with the vine is listless; in essence, the branch is ramified into intertwining divisions not beyond the family cycle. The main stems cannot diverge or go off in different directions from a common point or from each other without the aid of the vine, Jesus. The branches have to abide or make emphasis of acknowledging and accepting the union between Jesus and the believer; without Christ nothing is possible (vv. 4–6).

As believers we must not forget that the world will not receive us as they did not receive our Lord and risen Savior. The Word of God gives us evidence to adduce the truth of a life of fruitfulness through genuine salvation. We should never be dismayed or worn out, for God's desire is for all His children to have joy for all future time. This joy will never cast us out of the presence of the Lord as the Holy Spirit upholds us when all things seem to be dissipating. God will never take His intense and sufficient affection from us, but He will install an unsoiled heart to house His spirit of perpetual joy.

You are weak and useless if you do not stay linked with Jesus, who is the lifeline that allows unity and fellowship with the Father. You are barred from the Father, except by going through the vine, Jesus; you are despondent apart from Him. Salvation is evident proof that you are connected with the vine (Jesus), even when you think that your prayers are useless and in worthless repetition. You must call on the name of Jesus to reconnect or stay connected to the vine. Jesus is the stem or branch of the vine that grows from the Father, who is the root or base of the tree of life. God is the source or cause of all action, quality, state, and condition of the core supplement.

This core subsidiary comes to the body of Christ to furnish nourishment and development of the good and ample result or action. Natural food for the stomach will not ruin man's spirit, but God has power to spoil completely the physical and spiritual being. God's sacred temple is not for fornication, for the two have become one. The foods that one eats have no spiritual bearing, but the physical actions do affect one's spiritual life (1 Cor. 6:13). God is glorified when you are bearing (good fruit) product and doing the work of Providence. When you have skeptical, fearful, or suspicious thoughts in the Lord, He can give an unequivocal revelation to free your mind from a disturbed feeling of fear, doubt, or apprehension.

Christians are required to have strong utterance of praise that prepares them to be fertile, through having a closer, intimate, and personal relationship with the magnificent One. The ramification branch or offset process's derived effect, consequence or result, will be withered away if not conjoined to I AM, Jesus. He heeds the listeners to take note, each group or interval offspring which the Heavenly Father has not set in place firmly, shall be plucked up by its roots. The Word of God says, be circumspect, note the things sown among the thorns which institute obsession, vexation, and irritation causing you not to receive the good news. Also deceitfulness of prosperity tends to give a mendacious sense of self-sufficiency, security, and well-being. These delusional and misleading desires will choke out the truth and spring up to be unfruitful. Seeds sown on efficient ground that merrily perceives and receives the word will establish much fruit and a promise of joy—thirty, sixty, or hundred times more fruit of joy (Mark 4:18–20).

## The Promise of Joy

Joseph is an expository example of someone who was born with a promise of exceptional joy. Joseph was the eleventh of the twelve sons of Jacob. He was Jacob's favorite son. Joseph helped his older brothers tend the flocks in the fields. One day, when he was seventeen, he was given a beautiful coat by his father. The coat was a sign that Joseph had a greater purpose than being a sheepherder like his brothers, and they became envious and jealous of Joseph (Gen. 37:1–4). Their jealousy grew into hatred when Joseph told them about two dreams he had. The dreams were visions of his future power as a great leader. He did not know what the dreams really meant. In his first dream, he dreamed that he was binding wheat in a field with his brothers. Suddenly his sheaf, a bunch of cut stalks of grain bound together, stood upright while the sheaves of his brothers, which were bundle, together bowed down to him. In his second dream, the self-luminous sun and the reflective moon (his parents) and the stars (his eleven brothers) bowed before him (vv. 5–10). These dreams were prophecies of the time to come when he would reign over them as a ruler.

Many people may feel the same way about you, that God cannot raise you above your circumstances and situations, such as if you have not been on the job long enough to be promoted so quickly. You have not gone through as much as they have to have a new house. How did you get a new car before they did? Why are you walking in divine auspicious of God and not them? The answer to all the above questions and statements is that the Bible says that God will bless whom He pleases. Moreover, the reason why many people are not walking in the blessings of the Lord is because of their disobedience and fractious spirit. The Lord is not inclined to favor one person or party over another or show prejudice. I believe that favor and partiality comes because of compliance and submission to the Word of God and relinquishing to a holistic and purified lifestyle.

They want the blessings but they don't want to turn away from sin. They have not yielded or submitted their lives to the Lord. They choose to harbor hatred and jealousy, like Joseph's brothers. From afar they saw him coming to them, but before he came near unto them, they conspired to kill him. They began to mock him and call him a foolish dreamer (vv. 17–20).

Some are continuously setting up evasive devices, schemes, and tactics to destroy another's name, reputation, and character, if permitted to do so. They will imitate or mimic your mission and purpose, since they are unaware of their mission and have failed to consult God for their purpose. They have chosen not to ask the Lord what is their mission since they are not willing to die to the flesh. They may be wandering in the spirit of ignorance, taking for granted how to go to God in prayer and make all their requests known until the Him. They may lack education from spiritual leaders by not being properly educated, equipped, or rooted in the Word on how to go to God in the spirit of truth and holiness, while not having a personal experience or developing a genuine relationship with God that teaches prayer and submission. Some may enjoy living in sin, since it allows them to be free of obstacles, accountability, or responsibility to anyone or anything other than themselves.

The day when the brothers saw Joseph coming toward the field, they finally agreed to not kill him, but to put him into a deep pit. They concocted a story to tell their father that a wild beast devoured him. They thought that would put an end to Joseph's dreams. Joseph's dreams made them not only irritable, but also envious.

The reason why some want to deactivate spiritual thinkers and disengage those who have unusual foresight and imagination is because of their own insecurity or lack of confidence. Oftentimes these individuals are not morally sound or industrious in the things of God. Many are undependable, unreliable, or untrustworthy because they are filled with anxiety, doubt, and fear. Their insecurities are kindled from not being sure of their purpose or heart intentions, having low self-esteem or self-confidence. They are threatened by anyone who is exhibiting, displaying, or showing apparent signs of spiritual growth or maturity. Some are still waiting for a leader or spiritual advisor to validate their calling or purpose; without that validation they feel empty, incomplete, or void. In other words, they are still seeking man's approval. Their viciousness enables them to harm and provoke others that are assured, certain, and positive as flourishing and thriving overcomers in Christ Jesus.

Judah and some of the other brothers decided to take Joseph out of the pit and sell him for twenty pieces of silver as a slave to a group of sojourning Midianites (vv. 25–28). When, friends and family forsake or seclude themselves from you and leave you in a pit of dejection, isolation, and loneliness, some may wish something awful would happen to them. Nevertheless, you are to pardon and love them in spite of their malicious words and deeds. Again, you are dealing with individuals who are being used by the villainous one to hinder you from walking in the vocational call that has been placed upon you by the Lord. Many will not accept you as being authentic after transformation has taken place in you due to the light now reflecting or transpiring from your disposition. Disregard the pessimistic comments, remarks, or suggestions which are coming from within their inner man.

Joseph's brothers were reluctant to give assent to his mission, because they would rather see him far away from them, even if it meant him being sold into slavery. There will be many people that come down your path of life who will not receive your calling constructively or positively; but that is fine, for "greater is he that is in you, than he that is in the world" (1 John 4:4). God will set a table before you in the presence of your enemies, and they will have no choice but to see or watch as God begins to move and use you in your prospected vocation.

Then the brothers killed a goat, tore the beautiful multicolored coat that Joseph was wearing, stained it with the goat's blood, and took it to their father, Jacob. They told their father that a wild beast had devoured Joseph and all that was left was his robe torn into pieces (Gen. 37:31–33). While you are going through your various trials, these types of people will pretend not to be aware of or observing that you are in need of prayer and consolation. This is the very time to take advantage of a dead-end situation; as they begin to count you out of the game because you choose to remain silent while you are waiting for further instructions from the Lord, by no means identify that you are just resting for the next round of ordeals and tribulations. The world will try to desecrate you with deceitful comments and thoughts while sending harmful gestures and remarks to reopen unhealed wounds. In addition some will begin to pay close attention to and scrutinize your reactions, waiting for you to cave in or collapse back into a previous profligate nature.

Joseph was resold by the Ishmaelites to an Egyptian officer, Potiphar, who was captain of the guards of Pharaoh. The Lord stayed with him throughout his cloudy days and stormy season. Joseph served Potiphar faithfully, later becoming the overseer of the other servants and maintaining Potiphar's household affairs. After a while Potiphar's wife made a pass at Joseph and attempted to proposition him for sexual encounter. Joseph rejected her, being a man of integrity, loyalty, and valor, knowing that this would displease the Lord and his master, Potiphar, if he were to submit himself to such a moral act or offense (39:1–9).

He refused her proposal and quickly ran from the house, but she would not take no for a reply or response. She became enraged and furious and conjured up a story, stating that Joseph tried to take advantage of her. She yelled out with a brazen scream to the men of her house and said that Joseph tried to sleep with her. She was so ferocious that she demanded that her husband put him into prison for bringing embarrassment, humiliation, and shame on her in front of their servants and others watching. Potiphar, at the request of his wife, wrongfully imprisoned Joseph (vv. 7–20). Joseph was unjustly incarcerated for a crime he not only never committed but never even thought of committing. There will be times in your life when you will falsely accused of committing acts or deeds that you would never even imagine committing, The enemy will use all kinds of schemes to coerce, influence, manipulate, or persuade others into believing hoping to kill, steal, and destroy your purpose. Nevertheless, Joseph was not alone, for the Spirit of the Lord was with him through all the adverse time of quandary and ill-favored cycles or series of events.

Though Joseph's crisis changed more dramatically every time he began to do well, evil was always present; but God's love and commitment to him never changed. God's undeserved favor remained with Joseph everywhere he went, even in the prison cell. Joseph soon obtained favor with the jailer and was place in charge of all the other prisoners (vv. 21–23). No matter how low you may get in life, there is still room for God to give you favor even with your foes. God will give you the same favor from man, who may have put limitations, regulations, or restrictions on your ministry or missionary assignment regardless of your educational background, social upbringing, or theological training. God will never fail you; He will give you favor to get everything back that the culprit has taken from you and give you a two-fold blessing as well. In spite of one's emotional burdens or oppression, financial problems or perplexities, ideological issues or inactivity, physical infirmities or spiritual deficiencies, the Great I Am is able; He is a deliverer, healer, and keeper of those whose minds remains on Him.

Although Joseph's natural body was shackled in the prison, he maintained a spirit of trusting joy as he put others concerns or needs before his own. The greatest opportunity for giving someone the perfect gift of joy is by: (1) sowing a seed into another's ministry, (2) investing into another's spiritual enterprise, (3) helping someone get out of debt, (4) doing something as simple as purchasing someone's groceries or buying someone a meal after Sunday service, (5) assisting someone in reaching their dream. The realistic essence of joy is aiding, helping, or supporting others in their state of danger or desperate need.

## Joy, the Perfect Gift to Have When Helping Others

Two years later, Pharaoh had two disturbing dreams which required an experienced interpreter. The chief butler spoke up and told Pharaoh that he knew a man that could construe his dreams, for he had interpreted a dream for him as well. He told Pharaoh that the man's name was Joseph and he was being held in the dungeon. Pharaoh sent for Joseph, one who was a mental image explainer or expounder, also translating impractical and practical sequences of sensations, images, or thoughts. He told Joseph that he needed him to interpret his dream, and Joseph stated that his gift came from the God of the Jews. Joseph informed Pharaoh that he had no power to do this without God's help, and that any peace of mind would come from Him (41:9–16).

Pharaoh's first dream was of seven fat cows that were grazing in the reeds near the river, and then seven lean cows came and devoured the fat cows. The second dream was of seven good ears of grain which sprang up, but then seven thin ones ate them. Joseph said that the two dreams meant the same thing; there would be seven year of plethora in Egypt, followed by seven years of famine. He advised Pharaoh to choose a judicious man to compile and manage the remnant or residual food among the people during the times of plenty, so there would not be any regret in times of general mass shortage, which could leave the land laid bare by inadequacy and insufficiency. Pharaoh turned to his servants and asked if there was a man as discreet and wise as Joseph, who had the Spirit of God. Even Pharaoh was keen enough to notice that Joseph had favor with God and he wanted a man like him working in his palace (vv. 17–40).

We have the reassurance of knowing that we have endless favor evoked with heroic deeds, economic well-being, and favorable outcomes while being kept in the hands of the Lord. Jesus says that His sheep know His voice and a stranger they will not follow. He gave this splendid gift to humankind, which is the sureness of being safely tucked in His hands from the abominating one and the demonic preponderate of this world system. This guarantee gives us the insurance coverage against anything or anyone that hampers us by way of inferiority manipulation—in other words, against those who desire to have power over the physically disadvantaged or those with sub-average intellectual ability, by using dominated subjective reaction forces to influence others' thoughts or feeding on the spiritual immature or handicap. God's ceaseless or perpetual state of felicity helps us stand against the ensnarement and misfortunes of this world system.

## ETERNAL JOY

Pharaoh took Joseph's godly advice and realized he would be the worthiest man for the job of being the governor and overseer over all of Egypt. He removed his signet ring, containing a small seal used in making legal decrees or documents as official, from his finger and placed in on Joseph's hand. Then he clothed him in fine linen clothing and put a gold chain around his neck to represent leadership and royal authority. Pharaoh made a public decree in front of all his servant and leaders that Joseph would be second in command in all of Egypt and he would also ride on the second chariot (vv. 40–43).

As you submit yourself to the will of God, He will permit your foes to watch you being raised above your unpretentious beginnings and embarrassing circumstances of the past and present, to be elevate to the future. Your undergoing analyses, evaluations, or examinations are the measuring tools used to determine your qualifications, progressions, or limitations during the probation period. They are stepping stones of life to aid you to move more rapidly from the mole hill, to valley, to the mountaintop. When you walk into your new destiny, the hardship, trouble, and suffering will be a passing wind, now that you are a survivor and can do all things in Christ who gives you strength. What was revealed to Joseph in his dream bloomed into a profitable composite. Likewise, God will give you a new outlook and new attitude on life when you receive this gift of eternal joy. Even your close friends, family, and loved one will not recognize who are, just like Joseph received a new name and calling when he reached his place in the palace (v. 45). This does not meant that the preliminary tests of faith, patience, or stamina through being subject to suffering or temptation will cease; only that you will have a brand new point of view on matters of concern.

Unlike Joseph's brothers, Pharaoh saw that he was divinely elected, had a notable gift from God, and was going to use that gift for the intent of saving him and his people. Moreover, Pharaoh was greatly appreciative to Joseph for selfish reasons, in that his insightful astuteness and range of understanding would save Egypt from starvation, beside a financial gain they would receive from all of this.

But for Israel, who was not prepared, the day of extreme scarcity of food came and no grain had been saved or stored in Canaan. Henceforth, Jacob and his family soon were in need of nutriment. Could it be that this was the perfect opportunity that God was going to use to bring restoration back to Israel and Joseph as well? Jacob sent his ten sons into Egypt to buy food. They did not recognize Joseph as their brother when they arrived in the city. Nonetheless, Joseph recognized them and he summoned for them to be brought to his house stating that they were spies. He asked them were they had come from, and they told him Canaan. Joseph was only a teenager when he was sold into slavery, and now he was wearing Egyptian garments that made it virtually impossible for them to perceive who he was. Also he spoke through an interpreter for he did not want it disclose his identity. He told them that before they could leave the city they would have to bring their younger brother to him. Their cowardice came to surface as they realized they were going to reap what they sowed, for rejecting selling their brother into slavery. Joseph attempted to see if they were now remorseful for their earlier actions. One of the brothers would be required to stay behind while the others were free to go back home to retrieve the younger brother. And he promised that when they returned with the younger brother, he would allow them to leave the city and spare their lives (42:1–21).

Now it was going to cost them another brother or their own lives for their sin of the past. Reuben told the other brothers that blood would be required for the wrongdoing that they committed against Joseph. Although Joseph was using an interpreter, he understood everything that they said (vv. 22–24). The same is true today; your offender will begin to wonder why does nothing seem to eviscerate your joy? Why do the schemes and snares seem not to overtake you in a fall? They heard all about your past or present struggle or bold resistance, how you continue to make great efforts to give God the utmost glory for persecutions, sufferings, and tribulations. Then when trials come their way, they are not able to handle or withstand them with strength and trust in the Lord. They begin to blame others for what they have brought upon themselves, from their sinful deeds and actions. Some people are unaware that the authentic portrait of their existence is observed by their ungodly or wicked lifestyle, only to come back to haunt them, so there are going to be some difficult days ahead for their crafty plotting against ethical believers.

The brothers returned to Canaan and told their father that Simeon had been imprisoned in Egypt and that they had to bring Benjamin before the ruler before they could get Simeon out of jail. After time and a heart-wrenching decision, Benjamin finally returned to Egypt with his brothers. When Joseph saw him he was moved with compassion and wanted to embrace his brother. He went into another room and began to weep with tears of joy. Benjamin was his only brother from his mother, Rachel, while the others where all half-brothers. Joseph tested their temperance before he told him who he was (43:13–30).

Joseph made himself known to them, and the brothers were so ashamed that they could not look at him. Also they became very remorseful of their deed of offering him for sale and making an untrue statement with the intent to deceive their father, stating that a wild animal killed him. He granted forgiveness for their pernicious behavior, after their affectionate and repentant reunion. The trouble that the enemy meant for evil, God worked out for His benefit He put Joseph in his place in Egypt to be a blessing for his family and the people of God. Joseph never tolerated letting the enemy dislodge the adoration, conviction, and expectation he maintained in the Lord being victorious (45:1–8).

He told them to make haste and bring his father to him so that he could be in the land of plentitude during the great time of famine. Joseph looked forward to spending his future with his extended family besides his wife and sons. He wanted to see Jacob before his father died so he could see what he had accomplished in the Lord. At last he was going to experience the trueness of family and sharing the richness of God's blessings with them. As the brothers shared with Jacob that Joseph was still alive and living in Egypt, Jacob's heart was faint in disbelief (45:9–28).

Finally Joseph was going to see his supernatural manifestations occur. He told them to bring their father and families to Egypt where they would obtain sufficient edible provision. God came and spoke to Jacob (Israel) in a dream reaffirming His earlier covenant made to him and his family (46:2–4). You most certainly will ascend above all opponents' mean and reprehensible ill treatment in order to enter into the land of plentitude and receive great entailed inheritance. God wants you to be like Joseph, sustaining your jubilation when perpetrators begin administer physiological competition, confrontation, challenges, and disputes. You must keep them in your prayers and make supplication for their moral debacles, extending grace and mercy. Do not return evil for evil; neither take revenge in your own hands. Jacob could not believe that Joseph was alive, and even the second ruler in charge of all Egypt, but when he saw the chariots sent to carry his family into their new residence, he knew that Joseph his son was truly alive and highly favored. Pharaoh gave Joseph permission for his family to settle anywhere he wanted them to. They had the best of all things (47:7–11).

You should deposit an impression of a sweet-smelling spirit in any atmosphere by transmitting a sunrise aroma of encouragement, enthusiasm, or stimulation with an exceptional and extraordinary fragrance to inhabit every area, locality, or neighborhood with apt bliss and felicity. Joseph realized that his father's days were ending, and he was glad that he had found him before he died, so that his father could see the many blessings that God bestowed upon him after endurance, long-suffering, and patience. After their pleasant reunion, Jacob laid hands on Joseph's two sons, Ephraim and Manasseh, and well blessed them (48:1–20).

You will be captivated by infinite and keen enjoyment despite violations of confidence, physical ill treatment, or victimization. There will come a day when the Lord will divulge to others who you are in Him. God knows you have been a benevolent servant or steward; He will compensate you openly for the extensive and tolerant fortitude you show during your preliminary examination. God knows the difficult tasks you had to succeed in even during the days of persistent distress or noxious stimulation. You are urgently mandated to demonstrate warm affection for and forfeit resentment toward antagonistic individuals. In spite of mischief-makers who cause offensive and repulsive behavior, the Lord will work things out for your good (50:20).

It is good to be a living epistle and outward expression or sign for observance of those who will never willingly go inside a church building, prayer meeting, men's or women's conference, or a church revival. Also, by being an energetic and vigorous demonstration in addition to a public declaration of faith, others can bear witness or have affirming evidence that your God is real. Your testimony will out weigh anything or anyone by showing your enemies how you can have joy in the midst of adversity and that no one take your joy without a fight. Subsequent to everything that Joseph had achieved or accomplished in Egypt, one thing Pharaoh, Potiphar, the butler, fellow servants, and prisoners knew was that Joseph's God was real. Since Joseph was walking in the spirit of joy throughout every situation or tribulation, His joy was evidence of absolute faith. One thing we can learn from the lesson of Joseph is not to lash out against human opponents as if they are actual and vivid enemies, assuming that this supernatural battle can be fought with natural or superficial human resources.

We must understand that human efforts are inadequate but God's power is invincible. We have to become individual soldiers withstanding assault from massive invasion or invading forces. Only the breastplate of righteousness can protect us from the principalities, powers, rulers of darkness of this world, and against spiritual wickedness in high places (Eph. 6:10–18). Even during Joseph's state of oppression, God never ceased to guide or make provision for Him. Children of the Most High God, in spite of your depressive, regressive, repressive, or obsessive condition, the Lord is able to sustain you in the midst of the grievous influx, sudden disturbance, or violent commotion.

## JOY, A FRUIT OF THE SPIRIT

Joy is one of the most exceeding and prevailing ways to war against evil rivals. Joy is one of the most needed distinctive, individual, and unique qualities that will be shaped by moral excellence, discreet temperance, and generous thoughtfulness. It is one of the most accepted Christian virtues in the believer's life. Joy cultivates supernatural attitude of cheerfulness, contentment, and wholeheartedness that later manufactures spiritual oneness with love and peace.

What is fruit? *Webster's Dictionary* defines *fruit* as a succulent plant part, a product of fertilization in a plant with its modified natural enclosing or projecting component, the part of the pinnacle plant that contains the plant's seeds. The word comes from the Latin word, *frui* meaning "enjoy." There are many miscellaneous types or kinds of fruit, which include cultured, distinguished, or enlightened outgrowth. One must be cautious of the prevalent fruit that could be outrageous or scandalous byproducts that people may tend to misstate as fertile and prolific refreshments. Many fruits are nutritious as well as appetizing; for example providing large sums of Vitamin C. Most fruits have high sugar content and offer quick invigorating refreshment to the body. Fruits alone cannot compose a balanced diet, because the majority of them supply little protein.

The same is true in your spiritual life; it is required that you bear fruit, whether it is implies positive contribution that benefits the foundation or institution of the mental, physical, or spiritual body. It can be noxious fruit, which is physically harmful or destructive to one's godly lifestyle, constituting a harmful influence on mind or behavior, as well as being morally corruptible. Will you select to bear the fruit that provides growth, maturity, and stamina to one's physical body in addition to the spiritual being? This fruit should supply spiritual balance accompanied by appropriate nourishment for psychological and sociological growth. These nutrients will come under the direction, guidance, and leadership of the Holy Spirit, who will help protect you from some of the attacks of the aggressor such as depression, suicide, gender confusion, habitual obsessions, or various physical or mental diseases.

The Holy Spirit uses precautionary measures when incorporating the Vitamin C supplement along with the fruit of the Spirit to rid all extrinsic matters from defeating the chosen vessel of God. Living by the promoting power of the Spirit is the key to downsizing and overcoming the perceptual desires or offenses of the flesh. This form of deep-rooted conduct will strive for moral excellence, freedom from dubious character flaws, and promote reassurance from disturbance or unrest.

The free-flowing gift from the nine virtues of the fruit of the Spirit, love, joy, peace, longsuffering, gentleness, goodness, faith, meekness, and temperance allows one to walk under the guidelines of these optimistic and positive characteristics. The spirit of love is good will towards others and a deep affection for, attachment or devotion to someone, or the expression of inspired enthusiasm. The spirit of peace is freedom from opposition, uproar, commotion, or quarrelsome or litigious behavior from one who would breach public or private matters openly. The spirit of longsuffering has a bearable and tolerable fortitude along with a non-exasperating will or endurance; one who does not give an indication or significant sign even during ill treatment or harassment. The spirit of gentleness is a suitable but mild and polite mutual consort, a refined persona with a courteous demeanor, or someone that has a noble and chivalrous disposition and is not intemperate or abrupt toward others. The spirit of goodness is a discreet personage, unselfish and gracious with ethnical virtue and exclusive merit; someone with a remarkable visage of being dutiful and conforming to authority. The spirit of faith is dependable, reliable, and bold in upholding to one's unquestioning or non-disputing state of believing God for all things. The spirit of temperance is not easily displaced or offset and shows innermost self-discipline, self-restraint, and self-control; it may appear eccentric or peculiar to others because one does not deviate from their directional aim, effort, intention, or purpose, but can adapt or adjust to abnormal environmental conditions or factors. (See Galatians 5:22–23.)

Those that belong to Christ realize that the flesh must be crucified; so carnal affections, desires, and lusts for things from this world system are daily being nailed to the cross. The indwelling of the Holy Spirit produces Christian virtues in the believer's life, even though justification by faith does not result in full civil liberties. Christian character is produce from the

Spirit of God, who provides us with exceptional attributes, features, individuality, personality, and ethical traits.

If we were not overlaid with grace, the works of the flesh would resume to public visual sensations such as sexual misconduct, sporadic intervals of inactivity, internal and virtual impurities, and indulgence for temporal pleasure, immoderate attachment to material entities as gods, or the use of power gained from the assistance or control of evil spirits (vv. 19–22). Other characteristics are holding discriminatory hostility toward others, discrepancies, having ambitious or envious rivalries, upholding strong vengeful anger and indignation, having bitter and violent conflict resulting in dissension, aggravation or insurrection against authority, deviation from biblical truth, being habitually excessive with intoxicating drink, overindulging in beverages or food, or taking part in wrongdoings. Such shameful actions, demeanor, or tendencies will utterly pulverize your hopeful determination, certain intention, or future resolution in life; they are like a septic tank, full of bacteria and infectious waste. On a daily basis, they will set loose micro-organisms, familiar and outlandish agents that will conceive the spread of putrefying corrosion into the essential core of reasoning. This nature will constantly keep you from running the race with a more cheerful or exuberant drive, strive or thrive.

Everyone can easily see if there is a spirit of joy residing inside, for this keeps the correspondence, harmony, and order within any group setting. The person whose mind is undisturbed by concentrated proceeds, has residual serenity and focus to take on the task. They know when to speak and when to be sedate with a tranquil dispensation in an ungodly conversation. There is no boasting in preaching or teaching the gospel, rather to be a loyal and steadfast steward unto others. Everyone's spiritual growth or development happens differently based on escalating of self-realization, fulfillment of oneself and one's capabilities, or segments of sympatric, deep, or consecutive steps or stages of further itinerary or lessons.

You must never measure your ordination chart by the criteria of others by trying to be an "ideal Christian" based on someone else's implications or insinuations. They may be creating a false or misleading impression as an irresponsible and insensitive source. The best thing for you to do is let God place the measuring chart and thermostat to regulate peremptory challenges and oppositional contradictions. He will tell you where improvement is needed and what is pleasing or displeasing. The best results are produced from reasonable and sensible stewardship. Your service must be capable of stating rational grounds and motives by providing explanation or logical defense against repetition of tribulations. Endowed astuteness, awareness, and perception can produce this seedling of truth, which can verify the difference between the Lord's will and self-will. For light by natural or superficial disinterment reveals what is obscure or illuminate. (See Ephesians 5:9–11.)

Like anything that needs to be cultivated or tilled in order to thrive or survive in this universe, there is a necessary need to nurture or foster new babes and converts. Proper cultivation is needful for a breakthrough in the soil from cares and problems encircled around the seedling. This cultivation is essential to aerate it and grind out the weeds in which are the vilifying annoyances. The joy that Jesus gives is going to take sometime to produce maturity; conflicts and distractions will fight to remain connected as deterrents and hindrances. Christians must first learn how to be overcomers themselves before trying to manufacture realistic joy into another's life. We must rely on the Holy Spirit to point out how to master or prevail over stinky mindsets and opinionated remarks, which surmount from our emotions that rise from the lust of the flesh, lust of the eyes, and pride of life. If you never learn how to diminish the flesh and yield to the true Spirit, there will be no delight in missionary work. Meanwhile your oppressor will use cunning and skillful thoughts to overpower and overwhelm you.

Plants and fruits are cultivated in the same manner and with similar amount of care; they are grown from seeds that vary in many ways from harvest to harvest. However, growers struggle to generate plants that will bear fruits of homogeneous category, composure, and quality. Such fruit brings the maximum value or worth when marketed because of their peculiarity, rarity, and scarcity. A distinct, eminent, and reputable planter produces descendants or offspring of quality if developed, grown, or nurtured properly. The subsidiary division assimilates advancement, expansion, and progression of new structural materials and parts that are identical to those of the parent plant.

The fruit that is produced in a Christian life should reflect the farmer so that everyone will know who is responsible for personal, private, as well as public cultivation. Now you may be recovering from some form of compulsive, habitual, or obsessive transgression, yet years down the road, God can generate or invent an inspirational teacher, enthusiastic advocate, proclamation speaker, or successful missionary of all who are wholesome kingdom builders. At one point, you were following the things of the world, but now you are following the standards of Jesus, keeping in mind that *rejection brings direction*. Therefore, if the world never rejected your indefinite or uniform conception or opinions, then you would not have been able to accept and obtain clear and precise direction from God. First, some individuals are put in your life as derailers and distractions against your aims, goals, or intentions by circumventing, averse, and reluctant forces of evil. Although pessimism may encroach you with enmity, obstinacy will prevent you from being overtaken by the craftiness or ingenuity of your adversaries. Second, some individuals are put in your life as a test from God, to see if you will choose things of man over Him. The joy in your life will help you to not give up nor give in while under the influence of the world or man; also you need to hold onto God's unmoving hand, and He will take care of you. There are three ways fruit plants are engaged in nutritive growth functions as contrasted with reproductive functions: (1) by transference or grafting–by redirection of feelings and desires especially those unconsciously retained from childhood memories, (2) from penetrating cutting–by actual establishment of discernment or influence, and (3) by forming specialized structures–concentrating one's cognizant exertion of power toward a exceptional activity, field, or practice.

Grafting or transference, which reproduces most fruit plants or trees, is a shoot or bud inserted into the stem or trunk of another for subsistent growth as a permanent part, destroying past deficiencies or inadequacies. As stewards of God, you too have been grafted into His family through the blood of Jesus, Jesus came to save the lost and provide abundant life to the church so that one might have eternal life through the tree of life. Some fruit plants are produced from cuttings (penetration) or from specialized structures. All stewards of the Lord will have to go through some cutting away or pruning of things that are not pleasing or satisfying to the will of the Father. All conversion or contrivance that does not encompass the characteristic or personality of Christ has to eliminate the presence of defilement or superfluous elements in order for total righteousness to take root and produce holiness.

Specialized patterns of organization called runners are long and slender shoots that mature plants and spread out along the ground. A long ravel will be placed in soil to develop a new plant. You are the runner who is not afraid of spreading the gospel everywhere you go and living a godly lifestyle that bring others to Christ. In caring for the crop, the fruit, most growers use special machinery to fertilize, cultivate, and otherwise care for their crops. Fruit crops must be fertilized at least once a year. Many fruit growers cultivate their soil around young fruit plants periodically; the majority of fruit crops which grow in extremely dry regions must be irrigated. Farmers use miscellaneous methods, such as ditches or sprinklers, to distribute irrigation water.

When new converts come into the body of Christ, they are all different, coming from diverse up-bringing, ethical backgrounds, moral standards, and social environment. Many have strong, deep-rooted, and serious shortcomings and have committed moral offenses or transgressions against God's law. For someone who is trying to move his or her membership from one church to another, there will come a time when God will place a credulous need of sound and remedial spiritual direction in one's heart. It may come through a little tough love, yet never be the culprit who is responsible for chasing the unlearned away from the household of faith. Communicate and talk about wholesome and healthy things of God. "Be not deceived: evil communication corrupt good manners" (1 Cor. 15:33).

Often, when someone has been wounded, they began to communicate their emotions, feelings, and thoughts with others. They are unable to see that many are not spiritually acute or mentally prepared to advise others who have been hurt by the church because of their own self or inner issues. It is very important for a believer to understanding the cultivation, growth, and reproduction of a fruit plant or tree, because the same is true in the body of Christ. Even a little sin has corrupting and polluting factors of influence in the life of the saved or the lost. From the world paradigm view or philosophical framework, the literal principles of examples can be seen through animals such as:

1. A donkey for its stubbornness (Job 11:12)
2. A bear for its cruelty (Dan. 7:5)
3. A dog for its uncleanness (Prov. 26:11)
4. A fox for its cunning (Luke 13:32)
5. A leopard for its fierceness (Dan. 7:6)
6. A moth for its appetite (Job 27:18)
7. A sheep for its stupidity (Isa. 53:6)
8. A spider's web for its flimsiness (Isa. 59:5)
9. A pig for its filthiness (Luke 15:16)
10. A greyhound for its speed (Eccles. 9:11)
11. A sloth for its laziness (Prov. 18:9)
12. A turtle for its endurance (Heb 12:1)

In addition, from man's theological view, his sin is compared to a snake, a treacherous or worthless individual, an "adder or "viper" known for its venom or poisonous substance abstracted or secreted from its mouth. There are also those who have the capacity for spontaneous movement and rapid motor skills to stimulate negative or positive responses.

But all still must take time out to sleep and slumber, many times without giving any real thought about tomorrow (Prov. 27:1–2). God wants us to have this same confidence, reliance, and trust in Him. There is no room or time for kingdom builders to believe that they can serve two masters with loyalty and sincerity of heart, for total loyalty to God cannot be divided between Him and one's material belongings or possessions. Jesus warns those with few or least assets and goods not to be anxious about things that are out of ones control, for this is an equally dangerous tendency. Anxious concern or doubt is direct opposite of faith, therefore, even the underprivileged are not to agonize needlessly about what they should eat, drink, or wear (Matt. 6:24–34).

## THE PARABLE OF THE SOWER

> And he spake many things unto them in parables, saying, Behold, a sower went forth to sow; And when he sowed, some seeds feel by the wayside, and the fowls came and devoured them up: Some fell upon stony places, where they had not much earth: and forthwith they sprung up, because they had no deepness of earth: And when the sun was up, they were scorched; and because they had no root, they withered away. And some fell among thorns; and the thorns sprung up, and choked them: But other fell into good ground, and brought forth fruit, some a hundredfold, some sixtyfold, some thirtyfold. Who hath ears to hear, let him hear.

—MATTHEW 13:3–9

This parable is set in an agricultural context. Jesus gives an example of the sower, who received various responses and result from his harvest. The sower used the same fertilizer each time, but got a different solution or unusual consummation. The young seed all received the same education and instruction, but the development was varied. Jesus interprets the parable and makes comparisons. The reference to the seed represents the Word of God, and the sower is the good news messenger or evangelist. The first category is the wayside, which is compressed or trampled on, viewed as being inflexible, rigid, and stiff. The seed could find no place to take root so the fowls (the wicked ones or demons) snatched it away. The second category is called stony places or rocky ledge beneath a thin and shallow or superficial layer of soil. This thin crust would warm quickly causing the seed to sprout instantly, but without adequate depth for rooting or moisture, the sun would scorch the crop and it would gradually wither away. The third group of seeds fell among thorns. These thorns or wild growth choked out the crop. The fourth category, called the good ground, was well-plowed and prepared soil capable of producing a large crop. This ground represents the hearts of those who have accepted and obtained the message beyond their physical hearing and are able to collect and convey it with an inner spiritual reception for the truth.

If you are in audible range of adequate teaching and sound doctrine, then you are held answerable for artistic production, exercise of creative talent, expenditure of creative effort, or execution of workmanship, regardless of what others may be investing their time toward. Christian liberty does not permit the implementation of total independence without being held under obligation, which may contribute to criminal or illegal waywardness. There must be conformity to spiritual obedience and submission. This should happen by upholding a praiseworthy and reputable lifestyle, which is inevitable if the fundamental source is manufactured by the fruit of the Spirit. This conduct will certainly and evidently reproduce peace and joy (Rom. 14:16–17).

The true joy of Jesus will take root in your heart and mind when you have yielded or surrendered them over to Him by provision of the Holy Spirit. As fellow laborers of God who graduated from the carnal state to the spiritual arena, be ready to go the next supernatural procedure by putting down the milk bottle and quitting all the whining and disputing. Now as free moral agents, our hearts should be free from all unrighteousness, such as malice, strife, dissociation, and invidiousness. This is the only way the Lord will be able to speak to you when you have moved from sensual to supernatural. Also prepare for solid food from the Word of God, whether through correction or direction. As you move from carnality into spirituality, be ready to obtain a summary or synopsis of the true gospel of Jesus Christ, not choking on the things that are not pleasing to the old man or nature. This is why it is vital to be rooted in the Word of God, no longer holding grudges due to past disappointments or being constantly suspicious of others intents due to disloyalty of family members, loved ones, or associates.

Your sufficiency and adequacy in Christ is in the variation or variety of sharing His immeasurable joy and peace.

## VARIETY OF JOY

Some fruit will be bruised easily, so they must be harvested with greater care. This is what Jesus wants you to learn to do. Believers must acquire tasteful speech, graceful social communication, informal conversation, and companionship with their encircling or surrounding party of believers as well as unbelievers.

Everyone is different. Some people do not approve of people making jokes of them while others have learned to have selective hearing. They choose to only hear things that are pleasing and about the matters of kingdom business. These people have learned how to cope or use the "water off the duck's back" analogy. They do not even concern themselves with petty, small, or trivial consequences, details, matters, or things. This kind of posture is coherent with an action or mood that comes with practice and with having profound endurance, patience, and tolerance. Endurance is the ability to withstand adversity or hardship with the capability of sustaining in prolonged, stressful conditions, events, or outcomes.

Patience is having the capacity to put up or deal with others' shortcomings, also realizing that you were once in the same position or stage of immaturity–lost and deep in sin. Tolerance is having the capability of becoming less responsive to insults and being immutable against unfavorable elemental factors.

God created everyone with the power to comprehend, inter, or think because there are demonic influences or forces that are rising up to sabotage the commission of the church. God is your Creator. He did not create another creature like you; no two people are alike in organizational aspirations, in spite of how identical they might be at birth. Their individual commission is different. Even in marriage, the husband and the wife are different. Each will have a unique approach in communicating, correcting, or disciplining the children, yet they both reach the same outcome. On the other hand, one may be a planner and the other may be a procrastinator. Although dissimilar, they are free from conflict, fighting, or turmoil having freedom in their executive abilities. They are not lacking enthusiasm or interest, but celebrate and recognize that the diversity in their marriage is an asset, not a liability.

In James 1:3–4 speaks about the trials of life that bring forth good fruit. There are various testings, whether from the world system, Satan, or God, which come against the godly to produce specific fruit. The Scripture explains that negative experiences are to be acknowledged with great delight so that the positive working of God can be consummated through assessment, inspection, or tribulation. The preliminary testing of faith is expected to construct phenomenal ripeness. Unfortunately, sometimes they do not; oftentimes the testings make believers *bitter* instead of *better*. It is not one's present condition or state in such trials, but one's victory over them that brings forth supernatural growth and maturity. Those believers who God can use the most are those who God has bruised the most. Patience is the first thing that comes forth. One must learn how to outride the testing, tolerate others' affronts in performance, and maintain composure and posture simultaneously.

There are things that try one's faith, James says. One's endurance in and victory over trials brings God' blessings. Therefore, believers are not instructed to seek avenues of escape; rather we must mature in the situation rather than move from it (v. 12). On the other hand, God does promise to provide an escape if the testing becomes unbearable (1 Cor. 10:13). James acknowledges that every good and unlimited gift comes from God, since God is immutable. There is no altering and shifting with God; He does not deviate in His ways nor has apparitional plans for life's reason (James 1:17–18). God's expectation for your life is to do what the disciples started by using all physical or mental exertion to reach the masses and bring others into the family of life.

He wanted the Christians to know that if they remained in His will, they would not have to worry about irrational schizophrenic behavior, since they were relying on the direction of the Holy Spirit. The Word of God teaches all men how to have unemotional reactions to things in the world. Trials require silence and patience, because talk inflames anger and anger inflames negative talk and distracts you from listening for the voice of God. The voice of God is what gives us divine instruction. This takes us back to the earlier discussion about the four different soils, which represented the implanted Word of God. Through this parable, Christ was trying to get the believer to understand the importance of hearing and receiving God's Word, for the Word has the ability to preserve and mature a Christians' life through various trials. Christians are to obey the law of the land, as well as carry out the orders of Jesus Christ. He wants us to live a holy and undefiled life, resisting the undesirable elements which assault us from inferior forces of evil (vv. 19–25).

Both Christ and James deal with the proper hearing of the Word of God. The doer and hearer who leave the inner life unchanged are unprepared for ministry duty. There most be some change within the spirit man to be able to bridle one's tongue and realize how deceiving the feelings are. In other words, we must learn how to control our speech, provide altruistic service, and separate ourselves from the world (vv. 26–27). Today many Christians continue to do God's business making partial decisions, exhibiting inconsistency in their demeanor, and making errors in opinions, which may provoke God's judgment. Nevertheless, you have to learn that the best medicine for those who are operating under prejudicial or injurious misguidance is to kill them with kindness. After awhile they will get tired of being used by enemy forces, desiring to be set free and to allow God's saving power to infiltrate their grievous, miserable, and wretched lives.

James says the reason why the church has so much inconsistency and confrontation is because they need heart transplant; otherwise, the old heart will halt from functioning properly. The new heart will pump out humility and meekness that produces joy and peace. We must reach a place where we are longer able to murder with words and deeds of malice or premeditated, miscreant schemes, which bring deterioration into church association with other members. Through these you are controlling the body of Christ with your selfish actions and manipulating tactics. You are still warring against each other while being fooled by the adversary; the problem is not with individuals but with the principalities and rulers of darkness. The child of God must come from under the influence of the offended; seek God in prayer instead of striving and wrestling against one another. These manners are produced from discontented, unfulfilled, and unselfish wishes of the believers; therefore, all ungodly parts have to be buried along with all the other offensiveness, repulsiveness, and spitefulness.

If you choose to omit God in your plans, it not merely bad planning but sinful. The Holy Spirit is the only one that can give you the timeless joy that comes from Jesus. No one can lay a hand on you so you can receive through deposit or impartation, blow on you to catch it, or prophesy until it becomes a reality. Only by way of prayer can this occur. This joy is produced by the non-varying aid, force, or power of God, who alone manufactures Christian character. And, to get the true fruit of joy, you must learn to delight yourself in the Lord all the days of your life.

## 10

## THE REMEDY OF JOY

*Now the God of hope fill you with all joy and peace in believing,*
*that ye may abound in hope, through the power of the Holy Spirit.*

—ROMANS 15:13

THE REMEDY FOR JOY comes when you receive true salvation and the Holy Spirit. The *Webster's Dictionary* defines *remedy* as any medication or treatment that cures, heals, relieves a disease, or tends to restore. In addition, it is the protective application or material that corrects or counteracts. On a spiritual level, it is something that brings purification or rectification to an evil or wrong by using repeated distillation. Also, it corrects by removing ignorant or imprudent ethics, restoring someone who has deviated from accuracy or truth.

The Holy Spirit is the One that can give you the wondrous remedy of joy. Peace, joy, and love have to operate as one in order for someone to be truly flowing in the anointing of God. Peace is the added remedy to aid you to walk in the freedom with a serene and tranquil mind, free from any artificial or synthetic substances or prescribed medication. These are joyous heavenly resources. Joy is the invoked impression of well-being and contentment, not impulsively or obsessively driven by outside influence.

Love is strong affection for another arising out of kinship or personal ties as well as warm attachment, enthusiasm, or devotion. When you put these three together, you get to walk in the absolute freedom while erecting good will toward others with a delightful spirit in the name of Jesus. The Father, the Son, and the Holy Spirit are One; producing blissful anticipation and delightful expectation. They are the curative formula for humankind, since the divine resource, Jesus Christ, came to restore to health to the spiritually and morally unsound and corrupt, as well as the contemptible. The word *remedy* means any medicine or treatment that cures, heals, or relieves disease or sickness and tends to revitalize general well-being. It is something that is a corrigible counterpart to evil or wrongdoing, relief, or a legal means by which a violation of a right is prevented or compensated. The Spirit of God has all power to rearrange or set any atmosphere with the aroma of optimism.

## CORRIGIBLE COUNTERPART

The remedy of joy revokes all unclean spirits that may come from any inner child controversy, disputation, or violent endeavor within one's inner or external elements. It deals with some of the disputes or spars that may need to be repealed or solved by specific cases determining the right or wrong in conditional surroundings or by applying general principles of ethics to disclose the truth.

These may have subtle, but misleading or false, reasoning, especially concerning one's moral issues of joy: First, *rejection*—refusing to take, concur to, use, or believe; to discard or debar as without merit or worth; to pass over; to negate love or acceptance. Second, *anger*—a strong feeling of displeasure and hostility that usually turns into antagonism resulting from injury, or mistreatment. Anger has different levels, such as: (1) *rage*—loss of self-control; (2) *fury*—overmastering destructive rage that can verge on madness; (3) *indignation*–stressing righteous anger regarding what one personally considers unfair, mean, or shameful, and (4) *wrath*—suggesting a desire or intent to seek revenge or punishment. Third, *rebellion*—resisting one who has authority or dominance; engaged in armed, bold, or open (usually unsuccessful) resistance or defiance against an established government. This counterpart brings on characteristic flaws due to: rebellion, revolution, uprising, or mutiny. Oftentimes individuals with these unresolved issues are difficult to treat or handle. Fourth, *shame*—the painful emotion caused by consciousness of guilt, shortcoming, or impropriety oftentimes bringing censure or reproach. Fifth, *failure*—the abrupt act of failing one's normal functioning, falling short of individual aim or goal, losing one's inner strength, or breaking down due to lack of self-confidence.

These are things that become barriers or hindrances, which usually create dysfunctional interactions, or fellowship with others, due to preexisting issues from childhood aversion. For instance, a person dealing with rejection may think that no one will accept their ideas or thoughts since their mother, father, or siblings rejected their opinions—even going as far as seeking others to validate their distinct notions. A person suffering from suppressed antagonism may impose callous and pessimistic feelings on others, habitually, randomly, or subconsciously. A person with a rebellious or insubordinate spirit does not take constructive criticism very well and refuses to give way to those in authoritative positions. Lastly, a person with failure issues believes that he or she is forever missing the mark, always coming up short, and dissatisfied with personal outcomes or results.

Believers must not be intimidated or manipulated by churchgoers that use bullying tactics to persuade your personal decision. These are only trying or attempting to keep you a prisoner of emotional and spiritual bondage by browbeating those who appear non-influential in title or weaker in faith. They do not display any emotional or intellectual harmony within the body of Christ; never once will they consider the needs of others. They also distribute gossip, lies, or slander that will keep many prisoners to fear and suspicion of other co-laborers. Remember, a prisoner of fear is full of panic, agitation, or anxiety when facing danger; there is no peace in these individuals' lives. First John 4:18 states, "There is no fear in love; but perfect love casteth out fear; because fear hath torment. He that feareth is not made perfect in love."

Henceforth, reverential fear of God is based on dread of punishment, but God's love for us renders protection and safety. Reverential fear is still part of the Christian walk in reference to exhibiting insightful and profound reverence to the magnificent One, with the unwillingness to violate His predetermined expectations. The world's suspicion brings about convulsive strife or agony, lacking God's perfect and unconditional love. A prisoner who concedes reluctantly will easily take revenge toward a person that has hurt or aggrieved them in the past, while transferring the incident onto an innocent or unsuspecting individual. A prisoner of confusion has no spiritualistic order, and is tormented with strife due to twining fluster that housed within the inner man. If you are feeling spiritually inferior to others for no apparent reason, then look into yourself before striking out at others. Do not be misled; many will mistake your kindness for weakness. However, you must not let false leaders and teachers direct you down a pathway of destruction, causing you to miss your purpose in life.

There is a broad and spacious walkway that leads one to unhelpful or unfriendly conclusion; many will acquire this pathway (Matt. 7:13). You need the Holy Spirit to assist you on this path of life, since it is difficult to stand firm against the enemy's forces alone. Do not become deceived by others into thinking that the only way you will have joy in this life is if you follow the majority's way of doing things; don't worry, this world is not your home and it will cause you nothing but anguish, pain, and trouble. In Matthew 7:14, it states that the right way is a narrow, upright, and permanent roadway, a structure with limited point of views which has the shortest deviation route. There are few who will find or take this channel along the highway. Do not comprise to the enemy's tactics or schemes. Anyone who is created by God should be accepted for his or her uniqueness. You must have the heart of Jesus so that you can stand firm against the skillful methods of Satan's cunning and crafty maneuvers. Joy is the healing medicine for the mental, physical, and spiritual body—the part that rests on the seat of consciousness. Although the flesh will oppose the spirit and create discomfort, keep in mind what the Word of God says, "a merry heart does good, like medicine, But a broken spirit dries the bones" (Prov. 17:22, NKJV).

## THE RECIPE FOR JOY

Ingredients:
  3 cups of love
  Pinch of mercy
  1 cup of peace
  Pinch of grace
  1 cup of gentleness

1 tbsp. of humility
1 cup of goodness
Dash of rejoicing
1 cup of meekness
Dash of praise and worship
3 cups of righteousness

Combine love, peace, gentleness, goodness, and meekness into a large crock pot. Mix together righteousness, mercy, grace, and humility in a large melting pot. Allow the mixture to simmer until ready to add together and allow transformation to take place. Stir humility and rejoicing into the melting pot. Bring to a boil. Add praise and worship. After 5 minutes add the ingredients from the 10" skillet. Stir everything together; wait for the Holy Ghost timer to go off. The end result is a recipe for cheerfulness, gladness, and contentment.

Servings: Infinite

**CAUTION:** Will not remain if not properly maintained.

## JOY IS HEALING MEDICINE

Some of your strongholds in life will keep you from having refreshing joy. The word *stronghold* means a place of having strong defenses; a fortified place; a place where a group having certain views and attitudes is concentrated. A stronghold can be the sphere of your mind where darkness resides. A stronghold's existence is a hidden cloud behind an area of a lie within one's way of thinking. A stronghold begins to take root in the thought patterns that are detached or foreign to the Word of

God; in other words, the region which reprobates the truth, assembling itself in unforgiving territory and state of mind. This becomes the home where demonic spirits dispense bothersome effects and have stations or situated control units within the residing walls. It is capable of creating illusion and bringing false apperception to distract the reception or intake of the Word. This stronghold keeps individuals from adapting or containing true character or the Spirit of Jesus Christ. It teaches you how to negate the truth. There are many invaders that will cause a major shut off to the access that directly connects to the healing medicine of joy.

The first stronghold is bitterness, which causes pompous hurt, pain, and sorrow to others due to feeling odium of resentment to others. Bitterness can come in when you feel that you are being overlooked for recognition or honor. Bitterness can take residence in your spirit and takes root as a mental hurdle that connects stimulating intention to egocentric and prideful ambitions. A person overcome with bitterness is entrapped by a stronghold that prohibits believing enacted facts, in a state of transference that everyone is treating them unfair. In order to be delivered from a stronghold of unpleasantness, one must become diminutive and permit God to have total control and range over his or her life. Joy will cause you to repent and forgive those who have hurt or caused severity in your life. God is the preponderant force who is indispensable, desirable, and tolerable to fix the brokenhearted who are crushed by plaintive complaints, grief, and disappointment and viewed as inconsolable. He will allow you to recover and revamp from disappointments and give you self-confidence for a brighter tomorrow. He will bring godly counsel and comfort to the fainthearted.

The second stronghold is depression, which presses down or

lowers one's hopes, making you moody, and causing you to be low in spirit or despondent to warm affection. Depression is the root cause of physical vibrant activity to decrease. Individuals suffering from depression, feeling dejected and unworthy become effete inside. Depression is a precarious and pernicious state for anyone to be in, especially of the open practice and very unconventional conformity against the acceptable principles of God. This turns them from the way of truth and living according to the doctrine of Christian faith. Any believer that has permitted this captor permission to camouflage the truth, has been tricked them into having false hopes, beliefs, and faith. This false hope causes a feeling that what they want will not happen and there is no reason to trust God, because they have come to believe that they have put their trust and confidence in an illusive God. This false faith in the illusive God seems relevant in their lives, since nothing has ever gone their way. The reason someone can so easily be overtaken with the spirit of depression is because they refuse of are unwilling to yield their flesh under the subjection of the Holy Spirit. They are trying to have all the solutions or answers to their unresolved problems. Once you ask God to fill you with the presence of the Holy Spirit, joy will come in and arrest the spirit of depression and replace it with the spirit of surpassing joy. This joy will bring much happiness and serenity into your soul, giving you a loving heart with zeal to go on.

The third stronghold is lying, which is to make a statement that one knows to be false, especially with the intent to lead into wrongdoing; also, to give or make a false impression and have lack of accuracy or truth. Individuals with a lying spirit are desensitized from all stages of reality and rationality. Their recreant demeanor tends to cause them to deprive and denounce themselves from the truth. The stronghold of lying causes individuals to not be loyal or faithful. Lying is a stronghold that brings falsity into a relationship. The stronghold of lying will authorize other unclean spirits to take residence within your inner man such as: (1) *cheating*—to defraud or swindle others to meet one's selfish gain or wants; professionals at deception by making fools out of naïve unaware individuals; through sly or surreptitious means, to gain for self-serving urges, or (2) *killing*—to cause or bring spiritualistic death to others, which will permeate any form of godliness from others and incorporate a killjoy spirit that will lessen others' enjoyment in life. The stronghold principle of lying must be neutralized before it causes more harm to the House of Prayer; and the only way to do this is that everyone must receive a new heart—a heart like Christ. Your new heart will bring all things back to remembrance that Jesus taught about uncondi- tional love and illimitable peace, which will escort the spirit of joy into the inner man to take root in one's heart. Joy will bring in the spirit of truth, which will give you a reason to gain spiri- tual knowledge and understanding in reference to the nature of your true heart. The true heart will instruct you on how to be faithful, loyal, honest, and sincere, not only to God, but also to His creation.

## JOY OF THE LORD

One remedy of joy is praise, a beautiful way of expressing one's love for the Father of all creation. Praise is to commend the worth of God's love and forgiveness, which is granted and bestowed upon His children. Praise is the articulation of total admira- tion and approving delight in song; by lauding and making a mirthful noise unto the Lord. Praise gives acknowledgment to God through worshipful adoration with great passion and affec- tion. Zion was very zealous and delighted that God kept them from being their enemy's captivity. There is a city where there is a safe retreat for God's people and on the elevation of holiness. It resides on a beautiful location full of joy for the entire world to see (Ps. 48:1–2). The place where unshakeable and firm faith in His Word was created in the hearts of men—coming down from heaven. The Lord saturated them with propitiate in the midst of controversial or debatable opposition. God never left them nor forsook them. He gave them a cause to celebrate the security they have in Him.

Psalm 30 is a captivating description of David singing and giving God praise for returning the ark of Covenant back to his people. In this psalm we see David clearly making a pledge to God, exhibiting commendable and honorable praise. The same is true for you; give God the glory and honor in for whatever may come your way. Whether being bestowed with blessings or being imposed by unsteady and unstable deportment over life's cares, take control with conventional or regulated choices and decisions. There must be a midnight experience in order to appreciate the days of radiance. The word of the Lord says weeping, crying, or wailing may last for a night, but joy will come in the daybreak when the light appears.

Psalms 30:5 tells us, "Weeping may endure for a night, but joy cometh in the morning." This is where you shout your hallelujah, in spite of the pain your body, mind, and soul experienced. God is rejoicing on His throne, and He will give peace in the midst of your adversity. God will wipe away all your tears, remove all your fears, and impart a ray of glee that is capable of completely erasing tears of hopelessness, and engage you with unrestricted love and unfailing happiness. If you feel the desire to be in a state of weeping because of what has taken place in your past, your enemies will take pleasure in seeing you fall by the wayside. But don't be dismayed or lose your joy, for the Lord is on our side. He will put you back in the game when He feels that you are ready and fully equipped to complete the task. The Lord will vindicate us in due season. You may feel that your joy has come to an end or discontinued to bring delight into your life, but you can't refrain from praising and worshiping the Lord. Keep on rejoicing in the Lord in times of sorrow and be vigilant—He will turn grieving into singing, laughter, dancing, and shouting.

David and Jeremiah were both chosen as youth journeying on God's designated pathway. They gave glory and devotion in the prevailing altercations. David vowed to the Lord to have prolonged glorification forevermore and dance with the spirit of joy to supplant his wailing and sackcloth, with songs of gladness solemn affirming never to be silent (v. 11). Jeremiah exhorts the people to delight in the Lord; both young and old in unity, for God will turn deep sorrow into great joy. It will bring calmness and peacefulness to the sorrowful and grieved heart (Jer. 31:13).

Lastly is the firsthand joy that comes from Jesus, who is primary in time and in the order of all primitive existences. Jesus came to give life. This gives confidence to take possession of joy when our opponent comes in the middle of the day or night to rob us. If you have diplomacy and total activity of your mind and the ability to regulate specific faculty or powers—formerly thought of as composing one's mind, will, and reason, therewith, be vigorous and lively in joy of the Lord; it causes no hurt or harm. His joy will make you prosperous and useful to the kingdom of God.

Whatever you must do, get this antidote today. This remedy is able to counteract against all works of evil or malicious elements that try to take residence in His creation. Magnificent and admirable joy must stand fast in the Father and Son, while the Holy Spirit intertwines us into one synchronized body of believers.

## Joy Is Intertwined to One

Daniel, chapter 3 tells of Shadrach, Meshach, and Abednego, three Hebrew boys who were put into the flaming furnace. Their Babylonian names were Hananiah, which means "the Lord shows grace," Mishael, which means "who is what God is?" and Azariah, which means "the Lord helps."

They, like Daniel, obeyed the Word of God above the word of the King Nebuchadnezzar. And the Chaldeans who had been watching them determined to mark the three Hebrew men for not obeying the king's order. They decided that they were going to tell Nebuchadnezzar that Shadrach, Meshach, and Abednego were showing dishonor to the king's decree. Some Babylonians went to the king and accused the three Hebrew boys of not respecting the king and disobeying the law. They reminded the king of his decree of putting those into the furnace who did not bow down and worship his golden image (vv. 8–11).

They told the king that he had leaders in the kingdom who were daring to go against his official order, and they gave the king their names. The king called for the Hebrew men and asked them was it so, that they refused to worship his statue as the others did. They told the king that they would always respect his predominance and rulership, but they could not worship any other god except the God of their fathers. The king became enraged with fury and told them he was going to put them into the fiery furnace because they would not bow to his golden image. The furnace fire was turned up seven times greater its normal heat capacity. The king commanded that they be restrained and put into the fire without hesitation. They were bound with their overcoats, socks, head coverings, and other garments and were cast into the central part of the seething inflamed furnace. The heat was so intense that the guards that took them to the furnace were charred to death. However, Shadrach, Meshach, and Abednego showed no fear. They told the king that their God was able to deliver them from the burning furnace, but if he didn't, they would still be at peace (Dan. 3:12–21).

Every believer must have joy in the midst of the glaring furnace just like the three Hebrew boys. Now the king was astonished as he rose with haste to find the men still alive. He questioned his counselor in reference to how many men were put into the consuming fire. He was informed that three men were placed into the midst of the rampantly cruel heat. But appeared to the king as though there were four (vv. 24–25).

The Spirit of the Lord came down and walked in the middle of the fire with them, sent the predominant God of the Israelites. When Shadrach, Meshach, and Abednego came out of the fire, they were unharmed and unburned. The king was astonished with great surprise and sudden wonder that the men's bodies were the same as when he put them into the fiery kiln. Their clothing was intact, not even one hair was burned, and they had no scent of fire on their person. The king gave deference and respect to their living God. He changed his decree, permitting Shadrach, Meshach, and Abednego to worship and serve their own God (vv. 26–28).

The king changed his royal orders, stating that no one would ever be allowed to speak against the Hebrews' freedom to worship to their God without being imposed for a penalty or offense. The punishment would cost them and their family. Then the king helped them forward in their position in the kingdom (vv. 29–30). When God is on your side, no man will cause you to lose your blessings. God will deliver you from your enemies when the time is right.

Child of God, there is a duration and season for all things. The same is true with God, nothing before its time. The Lord may have you in a season of uncertainty before preparation or restoration. God knows when to bring you back to your former condition or position, but maybe He wants to give you a promotion. He knows when to restore the things that the adversary has taken away from you, and when it is time for your harvest. The remedy of joy will bring promotion and prosperity into your life, since you have become totally dependable on the Lord as your provider, He is Jehovah Jireh. Joy will cause you to grow in your spiritual and natural possessions. The joy of the Lord will give you the key to your blessings and inheritance since there is no entitlement in God. Joy can bring good health and wealth in knowledge, which is conducive to success and brings overwhelming goodness of unmerited and granted privileges from the north, south, east, and west.

Effective and specific duty is warranted valid for the desired agents that all things are working together for the benefit of them that love God and who are selected according to His proclaimed declaration (Rom. 8:28). Nebuchadnezzar reached his conclusion to leave the Hebrew men alone, in view of the fact that their God was too powerful for him to combat. Special virtue was bestowed upon the Hebrew men when God rescued them out of an extremely hot furnace; it was the remedy that they were seeking God's protection throughout their tragic ordeal.

## Joy Is Restoring Medicine

The loss of joy will cause unwholesome relationships with others, by transferring animosity and anger onto innocent bystanders that are trying to help and encourage you. Sometimes being a spectator or onlooker can bring unwanted tribulation.

Joy can birth a vivid picture created out of faith and hope from God, something that was given to you in a dreamlike vision or pleasant reverie. God will show you a mental image or picture of a blessing that is on the way or give you a desire to have something that you have been praying for. God will give you a sneak preview of your prospective condition, which can result in increasing faithful allegiance to the will of God. This will prevent you from returning back to prior occurrences due to lack of confidence or trust.

First, acknowledge what is true, then be transformed by the renewing of your mind so you can be in receipt of God's joy. If you don't do this, then you will remain psychologically and spiritually deranged, and will relapse back into emotional regret. This kind of turmoil will bring you to a life of a roller-coaster ride full of horrifying torment.

Second, the remedy for joy comes after experiencing true salvation and deliverance. Ask the Lord to rescue you from the consciousness of sin and give you complete joy regardless of circumstances. The Lord will preserve and free you from the wiles of the enemy, or endangering agents. The Lord can deliver you from a sinful lifestyle and remove His wrathful judgment and punishment.

Lastly, do not repress your emotions or feelings from the Lord. Don't force painful ideas, harmful impulses, or unnatural behavior into your regenerated mindset that stores memories, thoughts, or feelings; later to prevent unperceived stored data or information from becoming a conscious reality. If you are tired of being subject to the strongholds that subdue your natural and supernatural contentment, take them to the Lord with supplication and expressed concern. Then you can receive your glorious therapy for supernatural joy. This joy is not an over-the-counter prescription, but everyone can receive this physician's order. All you have to do is ask the universal doctor, Jesus. Dr. Jesus will spend some time with you and find out what you need. Once you have devoted yourself to His will for your life, He can prescribe or make adjustments for the error of your ways, after the Holy Spirit has come into your heart to be your comfort and security. This cure can be shared with other believers. It has no side effects and will not cause drowsiness or sleepiness; however, you can take it any time of the day. It will drive or motivate you to reach small or large destinies; it is best to use while around others, especially unsaved and unbelievers, and it is recommended that you tell others.

## THE WORD IS A REMEDY FOR JOY

God used Abram to carry the first remedy of joy through His word when He made a covenant with His people, bringing restoration and new life back into the world. Abraham was the first patriarch and ancestor of the Jewish people. He was born in the city of Ur, in ancient Mesopotamia, which is now Iraq. The people of Ur were worshipers of many gods. However, Abram believed in God. God first spoke to Abram when he was in Mesopotamia and told him to leave his home and kindred. At God's command, Abram left Ur and made a journey westward with his wife, Sara; his nephew Lot and other members of his household (Gen. 11:31). Abram was sent on a pilgrimage into a new land, to be the beginning of a new generation of people. God wanted His people to be nurtured in a more spiritual and wholesome environment, away from the post-Babel people.

The Lord gave Abram a seven-part infrastructure. He promised to: (1) make him a distinguished nation, (2) bless his household, (3) make his name eminent, (4) make him a lender and not a borrower, (5) bless those that endowed him, (6) imprecate those that execrate you, (7) destine blessing to all families of the earth through him. God's fundamental blessing on the entire human race would be restored and fulfilled through Abram and his offspring. These degrees and promises were reaffirmed to Abram in enumerated ways (12:1–3).

After they reached a land called Canaan, God told him that the land would be for him and his family. God chose Abram to become a father of special people coming from his ancestral background. God's covenant promise was that Abram would be a father to many children in the land of Canaan, if he remained faithful to God and His Word. The Lord frequently appeared visibly to Abram, but never in all His glory. Wherever Abram had memorable spiritual events, he built an altar. Canaan was a dear and spectacular land dedicated to the Lord. Canaan was the Promised Land between the River Jordan and the Mediterranean Sea. (See Genesis 12–24.)

Melchizedek released a blessing to Abram for his obedience of bringing him a peace offering and tithes from his firstfruit (laboring). Melchizedek name means "King of righteousness." This oblation brought a blessing to the children of Israel and for nations to come. Melchizedek was the king of Salem, a shortened form of Jerusalem and kindred to the Hebrew word for "peace." Although Canaanite gods were sometimes accredited with names they didn't deserve, the highest God, possessor of heaven and earth, is the only true Lord of heaven and Creator of earth. Jerusalem was in central Canaan. Melchizedek was king-priest, and through Abram's response to his blessing he indicated that they served the only true God. Abram offered the king a tenth of his spoils in honor of the most High God, and Melchizedek blessed him with God's efficient speed and victory over all his enemies (14:18–20).

Abram lost his hope and faith in God's provision of an heir through Sarah and slept with his wife, Sarai's, handmaid, Hagar, who bore him a son. The same is true for us; never lose sight of what God has promised, even if it may take some years to come to pass. God sent an angel to reaffirm to Abram that God was going to give him a great heritage, regardless of his age. Even though your dreams and hopes may appear to be bleak at the present time, at no time forget the promise or pledge of the Lord. He will provide a sign that gives reason to expect a successful and propitious outcome to all fond hopes or aspirations. The Word of God is a promissory note, a written promise to yield a certain recompense of wealth and health to a chosen people or bearer on demand or on specified date, given preference by Him (16:10).

The covenant is God's; He calls it "My covenant." He will initiate, verify, and establish it with His chosen people. The covenant was to make Israel a nation of multiplicity and to greatly exceed in all things. The previous covenant was to richly bless the land; now He broadened His vow to include the offspring of Abram to be endowed. Abram means "exalted father" and Abraham means "father of many." Abraham's new name was his testimony—that he was chosen and called by God to do His work. God changed his name from Abram; His close friend now called Abraham.

God spoke and verified to Abraham that He would receive his promise. The earth would be filled with the presence of the Lord again, if Abraham maintained his focus until the end. Abraham had compassion to bring God's people into better place to worship and serve the Lord. Later came the promise, which was the remedy of joy for the children of Israel. The pledge came also to Sarai his wife of proliferation of Abraham's offspring, which would someday become many nations and pervade over the earth (17:6–7).

God blessed Sarai and changer her name to Sarah, which means "princess." Her new name emphasized that she would be the mother of many nations and kings who would serve the Lord's purpose. The original vow made to Sarah was reaffirmed—to give a child from the seed of Abraham, who was one hundred years old. When Abraham told his wife, Sarah, that the lord was going to bless them with a child together, Sarah laughed with disbelief, since she was then ninety years old. God gave His pledge and told them to name the child Isaac (vv. 15–17).

As the Lord tells or gives visual picture of what will come to pass, don't get faint and weary, but trust in the credible Lord. Also, ignore the opinions or words from others that laugh at your dreams and visions. They create conflict and turn aside your hope and sight of spiritual reality.

The Spirit of God visited Sarah. Sarah became pregnant at the ripe old age of ninety. She later gave birth to the promised son, Isaac. Sarah doubted and was uncertain of the pledge of God because of her age (21:1–7). Some of your dreams and visions are long overdue. Have confidence and belief in the Lord, the true dream maker, the One who can make an ideal, transitory, or unreal vision come to life as a realistic and practical business enterprise or venture. God is able to bring your mental images and thoughts to actual fact. You will leap from having visions to being a visionary in things of the Lord.

The Lord may test to see if the promise means more to you than Him. Your love for the Lord means more to Him, than you having all the wealth and success you needs or wants. He is a jealous God and will allow no other God before Him. Sometimes your promise can become more valuable or precious to you than your covenant relationship with God. The Lord spoke to Abraham and instructed him to take Isaac to the land of Moriah and offer him as a burnt oblation upon the mountaintop. Isaac was his son of the promise, and now he was asked to sacrifice him. Burnt offerings represented a voluntary act of worship, atonement for unintentional sin, expression of devotion, commitment, and complete dedication to God. God wants to see if you will give up that ideal career, car, home, family member, or friend who has come between you and Him. He wants to see which will be your choice, God or the promise. For many of us the choice would be difficult. Abraham was man of uprightness and honor and obeyed the voice of the Lord. He rose early, saddled his donkey, and took two of his young men along with Isaac, his son. He cut the wood for the burnt offering and went to the place where God had instructed him (22:2–3).

Abraham, unlike many of us, believed and trusted God at His faithful word. God told him that He would make him father of many nations, therefore he believed that the Lord wouldn't take his promised gift away. God is not a covenant breaker; He is a covenant maker. At the very moment of greatest testing, Abraham lifted up his eyes and saw behind him a ram caught in an underbrush or small shrub by his horns. Abraham went and took the ram and offered him up for a commitment offering instead of Isaac (v. 13).

About nine years ago, the Lord gave me an ideal job that could have eventually become a career. I had been dreaming about having my own office and separate workspace, then came the ideal job—working with the general public and helping those who were viewed as unfavorable, inferior, or were in discriminating conditions. My task was to assist with receiving funds for repairs on small projects such as replacing roofs, restoring fixtures, and providing painting to the interiors and exteriors of dwelling units. As well as providing monthly My Home training classes, professionals come in to train recipients on how to maintain their homes after the rehabilitation service has been completed.

Meanwhile the Lord was speaking to my husband and telling him it was time for me to leave this wonderful career. When my husband came to me and told me what the Lord had told him, my immediate response was that it was the enemy trying to destroy my passion to help others. I believed in my heart that this job was the perfect career for me. And, there would be no way God will give me something and tell me to give it up. What I didn't realize at the time was that the Lord had a greater and more purposeful design for my life. Eventually, I did resign from my career, because the Lord spoke directly to my heart and brought conviction, but not without a fight.

I received the word in my heart, but had a common hang-up; I dissented with the platitude of not working and having someone else take care of me. Then one day the Lord spoke to my spirit and said, "Either you obey My word or you will not be here for your family." I knew that word was confirmation of what was happening in my life, multiple attacks occurring within my home. After that I began to take steps, and eventually within fourteen months, I totally deferred and relinquished my will over to the authority and submission of the Lord. It was neither an easy battle nor an intricate contentment, yet it was an understanding of who God is the same—yesterday, today, and tomorrow—the righteous and living God. The first year I was to learn how to be subservient and obedient, yielding the old nature or man under the total authority of the Holy Ghost. The second year I was to experience humility and the removal of pride, no longer with an over high conjecture of my self-accomplishments or achievements. The third year brought me character transformation and a heart transplant (change of heart condition), operating in spirituality rather than the carnality. The fourth year, I became steadfast and bold in the things of the Lord, shunned evil, and stood up for righteous sake. The fifth year, I was delivered from fear of people and loving my enemies as myself—this was the year of revelation and jubilee. Today I am entering into the sixth year of restoration and breakthrough, praying for my family to be saved, delivered, and restored back into fellowship with the Father.

Now, as a result of obeying God, I have witnessed many blessings come into my home starting with my husband and filtering down to my children. If I was given another chance to do things over again, I would not give up this opportunity of serving the Lord full-time. I would rather be employed by the Lord, for His benefit package and unchanging incentive plan, than anyone else. His rewards excel any Fortune 500 corporation or major industry.

One day in His courts is better than a thousand before kings, presidents, or rulers of this life. I will cherish being a doorkeeper, guarding the entrance of God's house in prayer and supplication, rather than dwelling in the tents of underhanded plots and schemes of impish men and women. The Lord God is a brilliant warmth and safety screen; He provides beauty and charm arrayed with splendor and grandeur. There are no enjoyable things withheld from them that walk respectable and honorable with the King. The Lord of Host shall make those sacred or holy who move along uprightly and trust in Him with their heart, body, and soul.

*I thank you, Lord, for Your grace and mercy as well as unmerited favor.*

The blessings of the Lord will be upon you as long as you stay in His will. Now an aged and well-stricken man in his stage of life, the Lord had hallowed Abraham in all things (24:1). As a child of God, never forget where the Lord has brought you from, for it is the key to unlock the door into your future. Trials, tribulation, and persecution will give you a heart to keep quarreling and not realize that God has already vanquished the oppressor.

Abraham rekindled God's procreation oath of continuation of his lineage through Isaac, and reconfirmed his promise. The culprit will try to evade your mind into believing that you need a surrogate provider (the devil) to receive or have real joy in this life. Joy will execute passion, which is needed to help others birth out ardent and fervent ambitions.

Make certain that you are on the straight and narrow path of the Lord in every area of your life. If the Lord told you to do something, then go for it. I never thought God would lead me to write a book to help others seek His riches and miraculous promises. But six years ago, the Lord told me He was going to bless me for my longsuffering and endurance. And He will do the same for you. God can use your trials to be testimonies for others that need an entrance pass into the Kingdom of Heaven. The Lord will validate His promise to His children, just as He declared to Abraham that all his children would be blessed. The blood of Jesus seals the adoption process, and makes you a chosen child in a covenant relationship with God and all your siblings.

The seed of Abraham is a part of your new patrimony, as an heir or heiress to his belongings and property. First, you must be seeking God in and for everything and then all His richness will be escalated in quantity. Therefore, take no power of reasoning in defense of tomorrow, since the day after today will undertake attention for the affairs of itself. Sufficiently resourceful is the day of depravity and disaster (Matt. 6:33–34). Second, you must pray for everyone in love, including your enemies. Prayer is one of the feasible ways love is put into action. Jesus denotes to all descendants to love their foes and bestow favor to those that cause severity and misery in their lives, while doing good to those that robustly despises you. Pray earnestly for all that despitefully maltreat you and are unvarying nuisances who try to stimulate conflict and strife. Displaying love toward one's enemy is what makes us sons and daughters of the heavenly Father, now known as heirs and heiresses. The love of the world will not profit man anything, for if you only express love to them which love you where does the compensation protrude or spring from (5:44–46)?

Jesus was heedful and observant that the two principles would be the most difficult tasks to accomplish, especially if one has not received a circumcised heart. When you receive a regenerated heart, all selfish potentialities and gain will be buried with the old man. You have become a true heir or heiress ready to receive your bequest. If you yearn or seek after God first, then all things are done with the right motive, by loving everyone. You will not use grace as a license to hurt or harm others. All that is the Lord is yours for the asking. We must be well informed about the reward of the inheritance for serving Christ in the mood of gladness and consideration (Col. 3:24). The most differentiate and eminent recommendation as a suitable and noble servant to the Lord is to receive a forever legacy. After making acclamation as a rightful joint-heir to the Kingdom of Heaven, it is time to advance into your season of faithful joy.

## TIME FOR JOY

The book of Ecclesiastes states that for everything there is a fitting or convenient time under the sun (Eccles. 2:1). Its name comes from a Greek word meaning "a gather" or "speaker" at assemblies. The author describes himself as "son of David, king in Jerusalem" (1:1). The writer, Solomon, is called the preacher of wisdom. The book is a collection of essays and thoughts on life. Its author questions many accepted beliefs of his time. Solomon declares that all of this life is unfounded, hollow, futile, and unoccupied if not rightly related to God's plans. He also states that age has no effect on one's spiritual maturity, while the appearance of God's wisdom and knowledge does.

The true believer's heart's desire should be God's heart's desire—to develop the kingdom of God. Your incumbency is to work in the vineyard and not to let your work be done devoid of physical exertion. Anything or anyone gathered in the harvest that does not look like Jesus should be put back on the Potter's wheel. Attempting to succeed in this life will bring acute sorrow and failure without God leading the way. Any work or deeds done without putting God first will not have longevity. All human physical or mental exertion will present itself to be without benefit or purpose, if done profanely. All frantic efforts will reach a saturation point, the point at which the maximum amount of something has been absorbed and incorporated into one's thinking or limitation beyond which nothing can be waived or adjourned. A designating solitude stage in the succession of descent, contrasted with the next production, will pass away and another generation comes; but the earth stands conscientious and dedicated forever (vv. 3–4).

The believer must see life as full of meaning, significance, and having purpose to achieve his individual destiny in the

319

Lord. Your ministry work should be serviceable, helpful, and can be used to build the kingdom of God. Your spiritual life must be filled with God's impartation of Himself as united and infringed. There should be nothing in your life that is of no avail, hopeless, and baseless when talking to others about Jesus, for He is our keeper. You can tell the world that if they are trying to access temporal wealth and riches, it will not bring them happiness. Man cannot gain any prestige, reputation, or impression if his labor is not from God's heart but is full of malefaction or malfeasance. Most of his days of toiling under the center of the planetary system are numbered. Your lifestyle should not be so fickle, frivolous, or irresponsible that you cannot witness or give a testimony to the ungodly. Your character is to be genuine, significant, and effectual to the body of Christ.

But, when God gives you treasure-trove of joy, intact with multitudes of blessings, take pleasure in sharing it with others. Without Him, life has no meaning, true pleasures, unquenchable thirst for pureness, or hunger for trustworthiness. But with Him, you can find satisfaction and gratification. True pleasure comes when we acknowledge and revere God for supplying and providing for our wellbeing. Each man will be merited according to his work and heart condition. The believer will be blessed with the desires of his heart that will bring him profound joy. The unbeliever will never be satisfied with what he or she has obtained in this life, for his or her heart will never be content. Man should take more pride in godly enhancements that bring admission to the Savior. God gives enlightenment, unprejudiced, and blissfulness to every man who does well in His sight. On the other hand, He gives the sinner intense pain, as what he accumulates and piles in a mass goes to the unspoiled. This measure of compensation is unsound and nagging to the spirit (2:22–26).

Solomon's emphasis to the reader is not to excessively flaunt one's possessions, since it is all of no avail in the sight of the Lord. The believer must stay focused on the will of God in his life, to enable God to give the increase based on his permissive and free decision. A diplomatic man leaves an heirloom to descendants, while the wealth of the heinous is laid up for the well-founded. The principle is workable rather than visionary, and often occurs to a villainous man's possession. The unrealistic man sees abnormal insight, impractical ideas, or daydreams. Their insight is subliminal, below the threshold of consciousness, involving stimuli intended to take effect subconsciously through repetition. It's almost like being haunted by dreams, sequence of sensations, images, or thoughts that recur repeatedly and don't cease until the dreamer reacts or processes the information into the logical apprehension.

The duration of things happening in the past, present, and future, which cause joy, will accompany you into your divine role in life. God will give you amenity, obliging agreement, and attractive or desirable features to add to your tranquil and convenient life. To everything, there is a portion of time, and a time to every purpose under the sun, the amenities of cordial social gratification (3:1–8).

God speaks revelations and gives provision arrayed with seasonable joy, giving you clear instructions on how to walk with your head looking to the hills from which comes all your comfort and help. It is time for you to walk into your moment of joy, contentment, and peace. Nothing that has not come from God will be able to fill the vacancy or emptiness in anyone's life. Do not let treacherous culprits have you walking around aimless and purposeless. Everyone is confined to a system of measuring the passing hours and undergoing variation over which there is little or no regulation. Contrasted to this status is God's eternity and sovereignty. God's dominion predetermines all of life's activities and is divinely appointed. There will be no profit or reason for one to work and labor all his days, never taking into consideration it's for the ministry of God (vv. 9–10).

This world is not your home, and cannot offer you anything but grief-stricken and severe distressed outcomes. The world system is too saucy for you to accomplish everything, too trifling to offer you savoring joy. A self-made individual, who is successful and rich through one's own eyes, is also self-opinionated, stubborn, and conceited with regard to his or her own formal knowledge and will never comprehend true joy. They will never find out the mysteries of God from beginning to end. Since He made mankind for the eternal preservation, His tangible objects of time cannot fully or indefinitely satisfy one's peculiar disposition. God's breath-taking creation is to be tantalizing but is not boastful, yet the inheritance settlement is considerate of all (v. 11).

God can give you a carefree heart as you rejoice in His munificent glory. God's charisma is benign and very beneficial. He is a generous benefactor rewarding happiness, generosity, and merited favor. God wants you to take advantage of His benediction that is requital, free from any cost to the patron. God's patrons find meaning in life when they blithely accept it from the hand of the Master; all amazing things come from heaven above.

It is an incline or dive and imbued talent, a specific quality of leadership that inspires great popular allegiance. There is enjoyment for labor when accomplishing details that are pleasing to God (vv. 12–13).

Children of God, count your suffering for the Lord as a

blessing to the world. When the last days come, take pleasure in rejoicing and praising the Lord for your prevailing attitude of joy and quality of life. All your work, efforts, achievements, success, and accomplishments will be squandered away and only a dim memory will remain in your honor. If you want to leave a landmark or legacy, do everything and all things to the glory of God, making a concise statement or summary of your existence (v. 22).

You should look at your life of servitude as a blessing not only to others, but also to yourself. It is all right to enjoy life with your family and friends. Good health is a blessing; enjoy it and live life to its greatest and fullest extent. Those who know you the best can measure the quality of your life and your accredited character made to advance the kingdom of righteousness. So leave a personal testimony by helping and serving those who are in need and ministering to the lost (unsaved). You will have a more optimistic and benevolent life if you live according to God's word and will. Genuine virtuousness and a judicious plan of action will not necessarily prevent erroneousness infiltration or careless sabotage due to one's misleading legalism of others to the faith. God uses both prosperity and adversity to succeed in doing His purpose; no one knows the future whether it will hold conductive wealth or poverty and trouble. Man cannot change what God determines, but living according to the Master's plan will assure you an easier roadway.

Solomon was a great example of someone who knew the secret to the remedy of joy—God's ending joy. God bestowed upon him great wisdom, wealth, and mental strength; he had victory over all his enemies; and what he did along the way separated him from the sovereignty of God. Solomon composed writings about natural history and practical philosophy. He states that all his success and prosperity led to pride and self-indulgence.

He states in all man's vanity of attaining and gaining, superficial prosperity will not bring glory to the Lord, it's counted as void and worthless. God doesn't look at what you have in front or behind your name, but is your name written in the Lamb's Book of Life.

Solomon urges the believer to find joy in life that is anchored with God. All the spirals of life's goals are "vanity of vanities" (12:8). All this life can offer you are futile and ineffectual promises and vows. The most important things in this existence are fruitless, without eternal salvation through God's redeeming power.

Do not be led by a factitious move of one's natural feelings or impulse without constraint. You only live once in this life; live it to the fullest with richness of the Spirit of joy. Schisms and cliques that are unmanageable operate and motivate the joy of the world; they desire and want to control all existences while dictating how and what others may do or feel. The function of a schism is to split any unified group or loving fellowship, especially a church, because of dissimilarities of opinion of doctrine and ethics. They transfer offenses like a cancer, causing separation and division within the congregation. A clique is a small and exclusive inner circle of people who hold to an inherited, established, or customary way of thought, behavior, or interests.

True believers know that faith comes by hearing and hearing by the Word of God, therefore obey the Word of God. The belief in God is a faith treatment and united remedy to any bodily disorder or personal shortcomings.

## THE REMEDY FOR JOY: GOD'S HEALING MEDICINE

Rejoice evermore. Pray without ceasing. In every thing give thanks: for this is the will of God in Christ Jesus concerning you. Quench not the Spirit. Despise not prophesyings. Prove all things; hold fast that which is good. Abstain from all appearance of evil.

—1 THESSALONIANS 5:16–22

Walk in wisdom toward them that are without, redeeming the time. Let your speech be always with grace, seasoned with salt, that you may know how ye ought to answer every man.

—COLOSSIANS 4:5–6

Now unto him that is able to keep you from falling, and to present you faultless before the presence of his glory with exceeding joy, To the only wise God our Saviour, be glory and majesty, dominion and power, both now and ever. Amen.

—JUDE 24–25

# 11

# SALVATION BRINGS REASSURING
# JOY AND PEACE

*Therefore do not let your good be spoken of as evil; for
the kingdom of God is not eating and drinking, but righteousness and peace and joy in the Holy Spirit.*

—ROMANS 14:16–17

THROUGHOUT THE BIBLE THERE are key references to
salvation bringing joy and peace. We have discussed joy
in every chapter, but only touched the surface of how
peace has to be a counterpart in order to bring one complete
contentment and enjoyment in this life of ups and downs.

Joy cannot be sustained unless there is a state of calmness
that enters the confused and disrupted individual mind-set,
and overtakes all outside pollutants such as elemental disturbances, environmental distractions, or external disagreements.
Peace does not necessarily mean total harmony among people,
communities, or nations. Even during times of peace, individuals take part in some forms of conflict such as civil lawsuits,
open forum debates, and political badgering. The world has
seldom had a long period of unbroken peace. *The World Book
Encyclopedia* gives five types of assuring peace:

(1) diplomacy also known as negotiations or discussions, (2) international organizations that are working for the peaceful settlement between nations, (3) disbarment in which involves the control, reduction or elimination of armed forces and weapons, (4) collective security is the balance of structured power system using combined strength of the group to discourage the enemy attacks, and, (5) improvement of international communication and trade that increases understanding among nations by reducing the danger of war by covering the cultural and economic barriers that divide countries. In knowing this, one can never hope to have peace in this world henceforth; the only peace will come from divine intervention. As for the believer, one must never allow present condition or location to cease God's comforting peace.[1]

Salvation is God's motive in providing a magnificent rescue operation for those who are in desperate need of redeeming quality. You are the elect. In the Greek verbal tense, *elect* means "to pick out or choose for oneself." This is God's sovereign plan to deliver such wretched and undeserving people from the bondage of sin. He was under no obligation to elect anyone and since the recipients are very unworthy, it is an act of grace. The Father has several motives for His salvation that offers peace and joy: The first motive is to satisfy His infinite love for the lost. The second motive is to deliver those who believe from condemnation and give them eternal life. The third motive is to secure good works from the saved. The fourth motive is to show the exceeding riches of His grace and kindness toward mankind (Eph. 2:7). And His last motive is so that His glory might be praised for all eternity.

Salvation refers to delivering a person or group of people from distress, danger, or some restricted condition out of which they are unable to help themselves. In other words, to move from distress to safety requires some form of deliverance; generally deliverance must come from somewhere outside of the party oppressed. (See Exodus 14:30.) In the New Testament, the verb *sozo* (to save) and the nouns *soter* (Savior) and *soteria* (salvation) parallel the Hebrew word and its derivatives. However, the Greek *soteria*, which translates the Hebrew *salom* (peace or wholeness), broadens the idea of rescue or deliverance to include recovery, safety, and preservation.

There are three progressive concepts: (1) rescue from imminent and life-threatening danger, (2) a place of safety and security and, (3) a position of wholeness and soundness. In the physical concept, the words *save* and *salvation* refer to physical not spiritual deliverance, which occurrences suggest not only rescue but also remedy and recovery. The spiritual concept reaches the depths of one's needs and lifts us to the highest grandeur imaginable to mankind. Spiritual salvation involves three tenses—past, present, and future. Doctrinally these are expressed as justification, sanctification, and glorification but each one is part of the broad scope of salvation.

| Salvation Plan[2] | | |
|---|---|---|
| Past | Penalty of Sin | Justification |
| Present | Power of Sin | Sanctification |
| Future | Presence of Sin | Glorification |

Salvation is necessary work, for the human race is a unit, all are somehow involved in Adam's sin (Gen. 2:7 and 3:19) therefore everyone is under sin (Rom. 3: 9). Release from being "under the bloodline curse" or "power of sin" comes only by salvation that is being spiritually rescued and place into a new position or right standing with the Father. One must never forget that providing salvation to mankind was a far greater task for God than creating the universe, for He had to see His Son become some-thing that He was not created to be that was "sin" for a dying generation of people. Whatever God starts He always finishes.[3]

Repentance and salvation go hand and hand, like joy and peace, for the condition of eternal salvation can only come after one has repented. There are two requisites of repentance, (1) to turn from evil (sin) and (2) to turn to good (God). From this saving grace power, peace and joy are poured out. Turn from the sinful nature, renouncing all detestable practices, vile ways, and malicious lifestyles. You must abandon evil intentions and evil deeds; both motive and conduct are to be radically changed. One may detect the two sides to this turning or converting: the free sovereign act of God's mercy and making a conscious decision to turn to God (a turning that goes beyond remorse or sorrow, but comes from godly sorrow). Confession of sins is both commanded and needed in order to receive atonement and forgiveness, henceforth, confession belongs to repentance and is needed for divine forgiveness to take place. Without these actions, there can be no place for joy and peace in the heart of a believer.

The two chief forms of repentance in the Old Testament were cultic and ritual; they were expressed in public ceremonies, fasting, various displays of sorrow, liturgies, or days of repentance. The New Testament repentance came in the form of stressing a change in relation to God and His creation. To repent and to convert involve obedience to God's revealed will, placing trust in Him, and turning away from all evil and ungodliness. Repentance leads to salvation; salvation seals ones faith in the life to come.

Those who are in the right relationship with God have the joy, peace, and responsibility of public acknowledgement or declaration of one's personal relationship and belief. Confessing Christ has become the hallmark of genuine Christianity. Since the church has become more exposed to alien influences and false doctrinal beliefs, it is necessary to make a public announcement regarding one's stand for the gospel of Christ. God is sacred, and no one can come into His presence without a circumcised heart, clean hands, and illustrious soul. If strongholds continue to keep you bound to sin, they will cause problems with turning or deferring mind, body, and soul over to the Lord. You are going to have a difficult time walking in the richness of joyousness and tranquility without God's love that is free from imperfection and sinful contamination.

While on the other hand, you must not let your liberty bring reproach on your personal testimony or witness, especially to the unsaved. Life under God's rule is identified by righteousness, which is expressed in fairness to a brother or sister who differs from you, in peace which results from fairness and consideration for each other, and from the joy that comes from responding to the Holy Spirit who should be the guide for conduct. Because your stewardship to Christ is rooted in *righteousness, peace,* and *joy,* the traits that are derived from the fruit of the Spirit are given by the Holy One to help you productively grow stronger as a believer in faith and holiness.

Any actions that you may take that permit you to compromise your spiritual walk come from self-consciousness and the sinful nature within. There are three blessings that come out of a seed of salvation with joy and peace: (1) if you do not condemn yourself by injuring another with your foolish conduct or mannerism, (2) if your conscience does not trouble you over nonessentials in life and, (3) if you do not do what others allow when your own consciousness cannot approve of malicious behavior. For any action that violates one's Christian conscience is a sin. Don't let your conscience allow you to do something that might cause a weaker brother or sister in Christ to sin. You are not to please yourself at the expense of another, and you are to help strengthen your neighbor spiritually. Christ is out example of self-denying love being willing to endure the curse of sin rather than to please Himself.

Although, we may not agree with each other in all state of affairs, we still must determine in our hearts to strive for unity that will surpass our menial and petty differences. Therefore, the transformation made by God in the spirit of the believer must be shown in the daily life. The center of physical activity must be renewed by the moral guidelines. The transformed Christian has an attitude of resistance to the values, goals, and activities of the world, which would pressure us into its own shape of existing. You are continually being molded from within by the power of God.

In the spirit of humility we must use God-given spiritual gifts to strengthen one another in the spirit of unity and love; this is done not by mere emotions but by actions resulting from the heart. The heart is the center of hidden emotional, intellectual, and moral activity, Jesus says that the heart's secrets are betrayed by the mouth, even as a tree's fruit discloses its nature (Matt. 12:33–34). Solomon says that a wise man's heart guides his mouth (Prov. 16:23). Samuel says, "Man looks at the outward appearance, but the LORD looks at the heart" (1 Sam. 16:7, NKJV). Jeremiah quote, "I the LORD search the heart" (Jer. 17:10). In 1 Corinthians 4:5 it tells us that in the time of judgment God will expose the hidden counsels of the heart.

The emotional state of the heart affects the rest of a person. "A merry heart makes cheerful countenance, But by sorrow of the heart the spirit is broken" (Prov. 15:13, NKJV) and, "A merry heart does good, like medicine, But a broken spirit dries the bones" (17:22, NKJV).

The heart thinks, considers, reflects, and meditates, because the heart functions as the conscience therefore your understanding cannot be separated from biblical principles. It is the inner forum where decisions are made after discussion or consideration.

In order to walk in the absolution of joy and peace, there must be a rebirth of the spirit man. There must be a regeneration or transformation, the changing from having the appearance of this world and taking on the form of Christ. Now you can possess the spiritual character, heart condition, and true function of Christ Jesus. Humanity has the opportunity to own the virtuous soul, the Spirit of God, by taking off the spirit of sin. Man must learn to walk in the spirit of love and forgiveness while operating in the active mode of worship and praise. Sons and daughters of God must be subservient to the authority of God and while maintaining His commissioned mandate. The church must walk in the spirit of unity with all brethren and exalting the Lord in sincere praise and worship.

In the previous chapters, God gave us exemplary men and women who lived their lives as honorable stewards. Many lost family and friends while making numerous enemies along their perilous exploration of servitude. These noble-minded forerunners were esteemed as worthy imitators of Christ and also making an admirable contribution to the hall of faith and body of Christ. Thank God for the distinguished leaders who came before you and me, to show us how to tolerate insult, endure pain, and overcome tribulations patiently while pursuing hopefulness and peacefulness. (See Hebrews 11.)

## Joy and Peace Are the
## Fruit of One's Labor

God desires that you display the human disposition that fuels acts of kindness and mercy just like Christ; this is the true fruit of one's labor that comes out of compassion. Compassion is a form of love that dispenses joy and peace to a dying generation that is looking or seeking answers for internal conflict and external turmoil. As believers, your duty is to display zealous thanksgiving when facing pessimistic or optimistic situations.

Natural compassion that comes from joy and peace cannot produce any action to alleviate the suffering due to geographical remoteness or lack of means, which oftentimes prevent someone from acting upon their compassionate feelings. Godly sympathy constitutes God's very being, since kind-hearted acts flow from kind people. By imitating God and Christ, you can learn how to have an exemplary life overflowing with joy and peace.

True fellowship comes when you make loving and encouraging comments or remarks, not uttering fabricated fables, inventive stories, or spreading hearsay or rumors, when encountering other believers. The believer should spend more time praising and worshiping the Lord than talking about things of this world that will perish away. Greet or address the brother or sister in Christ with joyous praise or a warm smile, not fault-finding or making sarcastic or negative references. The peculiar people of God can tell if someone is really a fellow believer by the forthcoming expressions, body language, and gestures. Anyone who is always speaking of mundane or trivial matters should cause you to begin to wonder whether they are putting their trust in man or God. Your journey is very crucial, so don't sacrifice your testimony or witness before an unbeliever by the comments that are made regarding another believer, pastor, or ministry.

Christ is the head of the church and the center of everyone's joy and peace, so put away all the stinky, ungodly thoughts and feelings. Jesus discloses an eschatological power that reveals His messianic goal for all. In him, the reign of God is personified, for He is our anointed agent, and one by one, prisoners who once belonged to Satan's workforce are redeemed daily. The evangelism mission is to suffer while proclaiming the message to those whom God is calling into His family. Your participation as a believer in the sufferings and glory of Christ bring reconciliation that builds the family of God; since Christ has fulfilled the Old Testament requirement. The foundation of everything that Jesus said and did was in line with His personal conviction that was granted, the Heavenly Father God, the Creator of heaven and earth, knew what He was doing and was involved in all human affairs.

By the renewing grace of God, one enters the kingdom after being converted, born again, or made new—from which the whole new life begins. The newness of life is not an option, but required so; being in the kingdom means accepting the mandate preordained from the beginning of time. If there were no newness in your life, then you would look like the tree, without any evidence of reproduction of fruit, so Christ cursed the fig tree (Matt. 21:19–21). A good tree produces good fruit, but a bad tree produces bad fruit therefore the fruit of joy and peace should be transferred from your life onto others when they come in direct or immediate contact with you on a daily basis.

In prior chapters we discuss the process of cultivation, but now let's talk about God demanding the land to produce vegetation: seed-bearing plants and trees on the land to bear fruit and with seed in it to replenish the earth, according to their various kinds (Gen. 1:11). You are the special fruit of God's creation as explained in John 15:1–8. From the beginning God created man and woman, endowing them with moral, intellectual, and spiritual power to procreate or reproduce, be fruitful and increase in number and to fill the earth and subdue it (Gen. 1:28). This implies that Adam and Eve's descendants were not only to be physical fruit of the pair but also to be endowed with moral, intellectual, and spiritual power as they were created in the image of God (Gen. 1:27). The offspring of the human pair were called the "fruit of [the] womb" (Deut. 7:13), "the fruit of [the] body" (Ps. 132:11), or the "the fruit of [the] loins" (Acts 2:30).

The good fruit or tree is the repentant individual who will not produce bad fruit because the life has been transformed. The unfruitful trees are individuals filled with wickedness coming from bad fruit (an unrepentant heart) who cannot produce good fruit because their heart has not been changed. In retrospect, the good fruit or tree is represents a life that is manufacturing godly works, with their humanity in cooperation with the Spirit of God.

It is important to note that natural and metaphorical fruit of the Spirit have similar characteristics. Natural fruit cannot be produced without any effort, just like the fruit of the Spirit does not come into being automatically without any preparation. Spiritual fruit comes from an obedient steward heeding to the demands of the Scriptures and in cooperation with the Holy Spirit. There must be a balance of demands in daily and biblical accountabilities, obligations, and responsibilities. The declarations of the individual mood are to be balanced with all of the exhortations of the imperative mood.

All of the fruit of the Spirit are expected to carry out God's mandates. For example, the fruit of the Spirit described as love helps a believer to love God with all their heart and to love their neighbors as themselves. Another fruit of the Spirit known as joy enables the individual believer to persist while rejoicing in all circumstances. The identification of the fruit of peace is characterized by one who rejoices in all sorts of conditions, exhibits peacefulness and serenity of character and peacemaking among mankind, as well as has the ability to keep composed and under control while facing some adverse situations. This fruit of the Spirit called peace instructs cohorts on how to guard their peace through life's tedious journey. Also followers of Christ are expected to continue living in peace with all citizens and to seek reconciliation with those who consider themselves foes. In other words, the Scripture clarifies that you are to diligently attempt or endeavor to make peace and maintain the other fruits of the Spirit as integral parts of your own individual existence. Keep in mind that you will never move into spiritual maturity or excellence without submitting or yielding to the Spirit's leading through the Bible, which can at times result in a real battle. In actuality, the Christian life will always be a combination of efforts by the Spirit of God to combat the original fruit of self along with the cooperation of the will of the individual. When the time of judgment comes, those who have lead unfruitful lives or did not show good deeds that are the fruit of repentance will be judged.

As wise laborers and stewards of the Most High God, we must be wary of false prophets or teachers who may look as innocent as sheep, using religious language and sounding spiritual, but whose lives do not bear the good fruit of obedience to Jesus' teaching. These are false guides. You should remove their influence from your lives as radically as an orchard owner would cut down a fruitless tree (Matt. 7:15–20). In Matthew

12:33–37, Jesus rebuked the Pharisees because they hypocritically claimed to be good when the fruit of their lives was bad. He instructs believers to keep our attitudes, actions, and words consistently good, because wicked words and sinful actions are to be considered the overflow of a deceitful heart that full wickedness, profane, and unholy words and unrighteous deeds. The heart overflowing with the fruit of the Spirit is running over with the spirit of excellence, integrity, valor, and virtue. Now, you are ready to aid others in their walk of life.

To aid believers in the walk before the Lord, God-given wisdom is far better than any earthly riches. Even before the beginning of creation, wisdom was with God. Therefore, His ways, the ways of wisdom which instruct believer's paths, are written into the very fabric of the world.

Christ has laid the foundation of ultimate conception, discernment, and perception. The Old Testament teaches us that wisdom is at the heart of good government; Solomon was the prime example of the role of a good governor and judge using this wisdom over Israel and royal leaders. It is the paradigm of the Old Testament established under the law and through prophecy and the New Testament through practical advice for sacred living. The true manifestation of wisdom was from Jesus Christ, who ultimately revealed wisdom as: aptitude, discretion, insight, perception, responsiveness, and understanding.

The Holy Spirit develops within the steward the fruit of the Spirit. Thus, with the enablement of the Holy One, the believer can flourish like a tree planted by streams of water (Ps. 1:3). Consequently, it is important not only to know what the fruit of the Spirit is but also diligently attempt to make it an integral part of one's own personal life. No one drifts into spiritual maturity or excellence; it demands a life yielded to the Spirit's leading

(Rom. 8:14; Gal. 5:18). The Bible is the foundational textbook by which we must evaluate this leading.

This fruit is the evidence of the Spirit-filled and sanctified life. The fruit of the Spirit was left by Christ to complete His bride.

## GRACE BRINGS JOY

The fortitude of peace will host resourceful measure of grace that hosts forgiveness, repentance, regeneration, and salvation. Grace goes as broad as relating the activity and entirety of God's will toward man or as narrow as describing one subdivision of that movement. The first occurrence of *grace* is in Genesis 6:8 when "Noah found grace in the eyes of the LORD." The Lord was grieved at how great man's wickedness on the earth had become. This statement about the Lord's antipathy toward man is followed by His promise that He will wipe humankind from the face of the earth because of His anger for their condition (Gen. 6:5–7). Noah is illustrated as having found favor in the eyes of the Lord. Election, salvation, mercy, and forgiveness are all linked in this first illustration of grace in the Old Testament.

The themes of judgment and salvation, through which the vast majority of humankind are condemned to destruction while God finds favor on a few, occurs often in connection with the idea of grace. Moses was another who found favor in the sight of the Lord. He led God's people out of bondage in Egypt. Moses made one of the most remarkable requests of God ever made in Scripture by asking God, "Please, show me Your glory" (Exod. 33:18). Moses found favor with the Lord many times as recorded throughout the books of Exodus though Deuteronomy.

Gideon received unmerited favor from God as a servant

to lead Israel against the Midianites (Judg. 6:17). As God was with Moses so was He with Gideon telling him that He would be with him to strike down all the Midianites together (6:16). Also, Samuel found favor in the sight of the Lord (1 Sam. 2:26). As a boy he grew in stature and favor not only with the Lord, but also with men. David was another servant of the Lord who found favor with God and man (1 Sam. 16:22; 20:3, 29). Another prominent example of grace in the Old Testament is found in the book of Esther. She found unmerited grace in the eyes of the Lord and the king and was later rewarded with the freedom of her people.

In the New Testament, the prodigal son is the most obvious example of one who has no basis upon which to be shown grace other than the fact that he had asked in humility and repentance. The concept of grace is most prominently found in the New Testament in the epistle of Paul. Many times Paul points out that the gift of grace from God accompanies human responsibility and that the notion of grace is connected to the Spirit of God. The Lord will supply grace to cover everything with enriching love, to bring about inclusive wisdom and guidance.

The virtue of peace is a peculiar and precise way to dispense favor from the Triune Being, which goes beyond comparison. Elementary biological function and acceptable behavior is changed into invigorating and enlivened celebration by administrating the virtue of peace upon the earthly realm.

## THE VIRTUE OF PEACE

The virtuous woman is a great paragon of someone having general moral rarity, goodness of character, and chastity of peace while serving others. (See Proverbs 31.) The sacred writings begin by prompting a question to the reader, "who can find a virtuous woman?" (v. 10). She is distinguished woman who is a dependable, professional, and efficacious worker, one is responsible and having full control of one's actions, affairs, and feelings.

She is a cherished jewel, crowned with priceless and endless wisdom far above anything of value and worth in this global region. Her goals and social standards are impeccable. She is an amenable and positive helpmate to her husband—maintaining a household enriched with peace. She is helpful and useful to her husband, children, and community by interceding and intervening for those who are in emotionally, physically, or spiritually needy. Her husband holds her with high esteem, regard, and respect, for it is not a burden to be a protector or provider for his family since his virtuous wife works alongside of him. The heart of her husband trusts her. All her needs and wants are met because she lives according to the Word of God.

She is a positive feature, not a liability. She transmits cheerfulness, enjoyment, and satisfaction without reservation. She does not convey ridiculous discord or feeble discrepancy into the marriage or home. She will not hinder her husband's ambitions, aspirations, or visions, for she does him good and not evil. She finds optimistic topics to discuss in the home, for she has no time for idle, busybody, or tale bearing affairs. She offers constructive observations and positive explanations. She has a productive meditative and contemplative life, as there is no room in her day for foolish or virulent small talk or chatter.

She has a business and enterprising mind that is ready to take on new ventures given by the Lord. She is a wise consumer and buyer gaining profitable knowledge from her adventurous travels and surroundings.

She begins her day with preparing the family breakfast, then having devotion, meditation, and prayer before leaving her home. She is not slothful or sluggish, rather having exquisite energy—even as she presses on to the mark of the higher calling in Christ Jesus. She is very motivated as she puts on her garment of peace and crown of righteousness before exiting through the door. She uses unknown data given by the Holy Spirit to help plan and schedule her daily appointments and errands. She has awesome people skills, using them to compare and make sound decisions throughout the day for her family's future investments. She is a fabulous and talented investor, who does not spend time or money imprudently without consulting the Spirit of God. She is fully aware that investing in stocks, bonds, and mutual funds without sowing seed offering into the kingdom of God first is pointless, useless, and ill advised.

She is healthy and sound, preserving and careful in governing her home. She does not give up easily and does not procrastinate, taking full authority when necessary. She is enlightened with ethical and intellectual character that is girded with grace and wisdom from God. She stands behind her work with integrity, sincerity, and veracity. Her work is substantial and essential as she pursues the path that the Lord has mapped out for purpose. She never tarries in her toil for the advancement of the kingdom of God. She perceives that her merchandise is good. She never lets her light go out before her work is finished to satisfaction. She is always working on something new and initiative, focusing on leaving a legacy or landmark for others to follow.

She is energized and enthusiastic when visiting the sick, hospitals, homeless shelters, and volunteer work within her microcosm of community and church. She sometimes takes flowers and bouquets to uplift other's spirits and also distributes clothing to those who are deprived or underprivileged. She never judges others' present situations but realizes that only by the grace of God is she able to help those who suffer from personal deficiency or lack. She extends and makes time for others.

She goes out in all kinds of weather to help uphold her family and husband when in need. She puts her home and its affairs above herself. Her husband is brave and has great courage. He has high standards and moral character. Her husband is known within his distinct social circle of influence for his spirit of integrity and valor.

She is prosperous within her organized setting, renowned for her accomplishments and achievements through the grace of God. She creates and prepares superior quality cloth or fibers to sell and her work is immaculate and without impurities.

She distributes her ware and merchandise in an expeditious manner. Her good work brings in earnings and revenues for her family because of the profound craftsmanship. She is arrayed with creativity while restraining a legendary reputation, credibility, and purity throughout the neighborhood and house of faith. She refuses to be worried or display anxiety or fear regarding her future, for she realizes that she is in the hands of the Lord. All she does, she does voluntarily as a free moral agent.

She has a word of encouragement, edification, and exaltation for those she come in contact with, speaking no discourtesy or foul language. She affiliates herself with good and ethical company. She is amicable, generous, and sympathetic. She does not pervade gossip, lies, and rumors or tell others secrets, bring detriment to another's reputation, or mix into others' private affairs. She does not construct arguments, disagreements, or dissension, for her words are humble, kind, and temperate, those of a discreet, sensible, and hospitable counselor.

She is a mark of true professional, career-minded woman

of God, who toils without hopeless, meaningless, or needless efforts, never giving into inactive, inoperative service or time. Her children announce to others that their mother is committed and devoted to the stewardship of the Lord. Her husband has overwhelming optimism and harmony; she is the joy and pride of him and her children as well as those who is surrounded by her grace and love for humanity. She is endowed with divine favor from God.

She is an openhearted person that customarily gives her time, money, and talent. Other women come to her for affiliation, guidance, and recommendations, in addition to special privileges. She puts great effort into her ministry and missionary work in the spirit of distinction and grace.

She candidly and frankly acknowledges that all she has is because of the unwarranted acts of kindness and leniency of God. She gives God deference and awe, for He is in her life; she is not quavering and unsteady in her praise. She fears the Lord in spirit and truth. She admits all her beauty and charm one day will be dispersed; therefore, she puts all her trust and hope in the Lord.

The Lord has blessed her with privileges and good health for industrious laboring with attentiveness and thoroughness. She gives the Lord admiration and reverence for He executes undying peace in her life. God will reveal to the world that she is a true and fruitful asset to the kingdom, for grace will bring peace in the midst of every storm.

## Grace Will Bring Peace

God's peace is the absence of civil, emotional, physical, or spiritual disturbances or hostilities. It brings a personality free from internal and external strife. It means the victory over one's enemies or absence of war. The biblical concept of peace is larger than that and rests heavily on the Hebrew word *salom*. God is the absolute source of peace, for he is Yahweh Shalom. True peace can never be achieved apart from the righteousness and justice of God. Harmony will never happen until man has a right relationship with Yahweh.

Grace is God's unmerited love and favor toward His children. God's goodwill toward men was why He sent His son, Jesus to save a conceited, egotistical, and prideful world from being eradicated. Grace is the key substance of peace mixed with love and virtue. Grace will execute a proper standard of living in your spiritual life that permits you to be suitable and not ill-considered for the work of the ministry: a living epistle to testify and give witness to the best part of Jesus' character—integrity and love. A lightsome demonstration of peace was God's gift of amnesty toward those who confessed obsessive indulgences, deplorable transgressions, and repulsive wrongdoings against the rules of God.

A believer with grace has apt and modest integrated posture with devout morale accompanied by the moral and mental conditionings of confidence, courage, discipline, and enthusiasm. This unmerited resource of favor compels or drives you to offer prayers for others to have abundant peace and contentment. Grace and peace bring expression of benevolence, consideration, and appreciation to co-laborers, with a willingness to offer exoneration and make immediate reconciliation. While you are going through tough trials, trust that grace and peace are coming alongside to guard your emotional well-being. By imploring and making supplication for others, the Lord will supply your prerequisite or sustenance.

Grace and peace are a beautiful and whimsical team that will last throughout eternity, if you allow them to remain under the authority of the Spirit of God. No one can extract them from your inner core. Grace reveals all egregious hidden deliberation, impulsive ideas, or secret notions, which the mature or seasoned steward should be ready to exterminate. Grace will not let you feast on counterfeit teachings, infallible truth, or unauthentic doctrine. Grace will give you supernatural ability to perceive sounds and make perceptive observation. Grace does not make injurious, poisonous, or venomous comments to cause harm or pain to anyone.

God wants to see the fruit of the Spirit in your life, the byproduct that will bring improvement and progression in the kingdom of God. Since only what you do for God will last forever, the Lord desired that you share His beauty through His miraculous healing and deliverance. The acts of kindness and good deeds can come from God and man. Wise stewards should not be congested with arrogance, conceit, and egotism by taking God's grace for granted.

In the sixth book of Romans, Paul tells us that sin has no legal or moral right to enforce disobedience in our life and cause us to sin, for grace came to wash away all sin by the saving blood of Jesus. The first step toward overcoming the obstacles of sin in believer's life is to boldly oppose and openly defy the enticements of lustful obsessions. Not to succumb as sinful instruments or tools, but yield ourselves unto the authority of God. The insightful and lively constituents are implements utilized and adorned before Him, for iniquity no longer has dominion power. We are no longer under its jurisdiction influence but subjected to God's vindicated support (Rom. 6:14). Sin has been extinguished from your present life-style, and by faith the light of truth shines within and begins to radiate outside.

The second step is refuse to let sin have pervasive rulership, for all have sinned and come short of the glory of God, justified by this new found grace through the redemptive covering from Christ Jesus (3:23–24), Today, you can say that you are not available to do the things that you use to do.

The third step is to offer oneself to the Lord as a sincere contribution or sacrifice for worship. No one else has saving grandeur or power but God who is ready and willing to release the promises. Although there will be traps and snares set up or against you to delay your progress, remember the spoken Word has gone beforehand to direct your path if you continue to stay on the "straight and narrow" pathway. You must maintain a carefree attitude while finishing your course, which was established while you were in the womb.

The magnificent source of the grace shields you from the consequences of sin or feelings of guilt and shame that are subjective acknowledgements of an objective spiritual reality. Guilt is juridical in character, but shame is relational, although connected shame highlights sin's effect on self-identity. Sinful human beings are traumatized before a holy God, exposed for failure to live up to God's glorious moral purpose. They become guilt-ridden and unable to face Him, like Adam and Eve who hide in the Garden of Eden (Gen. 3:7–8). Shame is a godly motivator, because a virtuous life shames the ungodly, which provides an opportunity for evangelism.

The spirit of grace is able to destroy disappointments, frustrations, and regrets. Therefore, believers must be diligent to renounce shameful behavior, even though it is tempting not to since it is a hidden character unknown to many. The suffering of Christ is identification that one cannot be ashamed of the gospel because it is the only antidote for humanity's future. Suffering comes to help you oppose carnal indulgences, resist hideous misdemeanors, and to constitute or institute holistic values. God's grace is sufficient for everyone, for it requires no labor on the recipient's behalf; it conveys no physical pain or mental distress.

The Lord supplies redeeming value to extract the consequences of the flawed nature of creation, to help one overcome the consequences of sin, and in addition to cope with collective and individual suffering. Grace and mercy may not be able to rescue one from disappointments or grievance; it will give leniency when one does miss the mark in pursuing the things of the Lord. Unearned and unwarranted kindnesses can increase one's eagerness, fervor, and zeal while dealing with sorrow and harassment from the world system. The grace of God will usher joy into one's lifeless situations or mundane dilemmas. The Lord's gracious gift of affluence and influence is contingent according to individual's willingness to abandon malicious proposals and iniquitous activities. There is an inheritance of joy and peace for those who surmount with grace, aiming to prevail and survive the experiments of living.

## THE INHERITANCE AND ENTITLEMENT OF PEACE

Joshua was a lieutenant of Moses that guided Israel in the conquest from Palestine after Moses' death. Joshua was Moses' faithful warrior, successor leader of the Israelites; his responsibility was to lead them into the Promise Land in Canaan. His name means, "The Lord has delivered."

The place of inheritance was first told to Moses in Exodus, and reaffirmed several more times the remainder of Pentateuch. Moses gave the instructions to Joshua to carry on and direct the children of Israel into their inheritance, specified by the correspondence and contract modulated by the Lord. The general line of the southern border is from the Dead Sea and through the Wilderness of Zin to Kadesh Barnea. The Bible describes the land as "a land flowing with milk and honey" (Exod. 3:8), which implies as a bountiful territory. The image can be denoted as a lush and attractive green climate that produces an abundant and fruitful harvest. The spies observed that cattle and goats produced much milk in areas rich with forage, copious with vegetation. Honey, in the biblical references, usually is associated with nonagricultural areas that were covered with wild vegetation, plants. The Lord was giving this land to His people as a heritage and ancestral allocation. It was to be passed on from generation to generation as a means of preserving the wealth and health of the family, integrating livelihood, and faith of each new generation.

The Lord revealed to them the military action that would be required to conquer and defeat each area's regime. They needed to use psychological and spiritual warfare, as He would equip them with required instruments, missiles, and utensils to create collision and bewilderment counterattacks.

When Israel entered the land of Canaan, the hill country was uninhabited and covered with natural forests and thickets. The place was called the Promised Land. Every year the Jordan River, which produced ample and constant supply of water to irrigate the area fields, would overflow its banks with rich alluvial soil. The border of the land of Israel would cause one to demonstrate an important principle of faith therefore God instructed them not to engage in foreign trade or adopt expansionist policies beyond its borders.

God is a jealous God, who desires exclusive rights and allegiances to His chosen generation, royal priesthood, holy nation, and peculiar people. Consequently, you should show or exhibit praises unto the true Deliverer who called you out of darkness into His awesome and marvelous light (1 Pet. 2:9). Although you once were children of obscurity, now you are recipients of enlightenment, who are hedged under God's tender and benevolent fondness. The object of one's inheritance is the kingdom of God; there is only one way of constituting legal rights to gain this entitlement. All believers have an entitlement blessing that offers us designate benefits and specific privileges. The Scriptures states that the concept of the believer's inheritance and entitlement highlights the dignity of the family relationship of the believer in Christ. There is no higher position or greater wealth we can acquire or obtain than to become an heir of God through faith in Christ.

Today you can have triumph peace by possessing salvation, eternal and joyful inheritance through the family bloodlines of the resurrected Savior.

## Sin Consumes Peace

History reveals many with impenitence multifarious offenses, oftentimes amplifying their sins by superficial repentance or compounding their transgression by rejecting and persecuting the prophets who pressed God's covenantal claims. The first place from where peace was taken was in the Garden of Eden, with the tragic fall of Adam and Eve from their high original status of humankind, created in the image of God. Satan introduced doubts about God's authority and goodness to Eve, while inviting her to consider how the fruit from the tree of knowledge was good substance for food and knowledge. The tendency of sin began with a subtle appeal to something attractive and good in itself. This first sin, which was doubt, disclosed the essence of later sins. Sin involves the refusal of civilization to accept its God-given arrangement between the Creator and lower creation. It flows from decisions to rejects God's way and to steal, curse, and lie simply because that seems more attractive or reasonable. The apparent trait of sinful nature came through to the seeds of Adam and Eve. Because of sin, man was sited into accountability or upheld responsible for making personal choice. The slaughter of Abel by his brother Cain quickly escalated into an early stage marked by a rapid misconduct, severe illegal behavior, deadly course of intractable consequences, and unlawful activity, representative of when Satan prompted Adam and Eve to sin. Man is an active free moral agent capable of making self-decisions; therefore God could not talk Cain out of slaying his brother but held him accountable for his act. The sacrifices and rituals for cleansing listed in the Pentateuch remind one of the gravity of sin and transgressions are more than mistakes.

Oftentimes sin will spring up spontaneously from within; it is an uncultivated power that is trying to master one's subliminal will with hopes to devour. Sin becomes more motivated and provoked with premeditated intentions. It can take a hold in midst of praise and worship, with the purpose of directly accusing and harming a brethren. Periodically, after one has committed offenses against God and the brethren, there is manifesting form of guilt or remorse. Many will not confess to any misdeeds and refuse to repent for any wrongdoings, thus they do not see a need for reprimand and punishment from the Father. (See Genesis 4:5–14.)

Genesis 4–11 traces the development of sin. Though proud and deliberate, the line of Cain, sinners still fulfilled the mandate to fill and subdue the earth. Sin had permeated the earth to the point that every inclination of thoughts from the human heart was evil all the time (Gen. 6:5; 8:21). Even after the Flood, sin threatened to reassert itself in both direction of disobedience and idolatry. God revealed His new objective to restrain sin by confusing human language at Babel, resulting in divisions so that humanity could no longer stand together in rebellious state against God.

Genesis 15–20 demonstrates that sin brought plagues to the affiliates of the covenant family by manipulation, betrayal, and dialoguing underhandedly to deceive one another. The history of Moses narrates that punishment will naturally follow such built up iniquity. Sin had brought on the penalty of adversity, captivity, deprivation, persecution, starvation, and torment.

Sin is indefinable, intangible, mysterious, obscure, subtle, and unspeakable. It has no substance of independent existence. It cannot even exist in the sense that joy, love, and peace do; and it survives only as a parasite to consume good or good things. Sin delivers or generates nothing, for it neglects, perverts, spoils, and destroys the wholesome matters God has made. The presence of sin and temptation persist to demand the considerable and desirable good of mankind. For example, sin boasts, seeks self-honor, breaks promises or vows between people, community, countries, and nations, and offers false hope of release from hardship. The world system offers a persuasive defense for almost every pervasive offense. In the eyes of a believer, sin should be observed as insignificant, senseless, and unimpressive. Despite all its miserable qualities, sin make one donation to the body of faith—to move God to redeem humanity from its alluring factors and seducing elements. Sin has been the incentive for God to demonstrate joy, grace, love, patience, and peace.

Jesus give numerous biblical examples citing that sin arises from the heart, "bad trees bear bad fruit, blasphemous words spring from hearts filled with evil, and wicked men demand signs even when they have already seen enough to warrant faith (Matt. 7:17–20; 12:33–39). Christ explains that evildoing is not simply a matter of choice; rather, a person is a slave to sin, for

He came not to illuminate but to pardon and remove the presence of sin. The Son of God had to bear the cross to accomplish and emancipate the enormity, severity, and solemnity of sin. Christ's rising from the dead demonstrated that sin has been defeated. After the Resurrection, Christ sent the disciples out to proclaim the victory or triumph of forgiveness of sin through His name. Keep in mind, failure to believe or unbelief is the root of sin.

Today you have triumphant victory over sin through the resurrected Savior, Jesus Christ—Lord of lords, Prince of Peace, and King of kings—providing you with peace that surpasses all understanding.

## Triumphant Victory of Peace

The Lord takes delight in His children's praise and worship, but He requires a spirit of prayer. This is the only thing that can consume or destroy extreme impiety that is integrated from reprehensible principalities and rulers of darkness, a vex world system, and wickedness in high places. Sin infects a person's life from the split second of conception until the day of one's death; whoever gives self over to sin is a fool. Sin includes a failure to do what is decent and moral; it insults others sincerity, it disburses aggression, cruelty, and hostility, it exhibits selfishness toward others, and, eventually, it brings rebellion against God. Throughout the Bible, almost every sin reaches for things with some intrinsic value, such as security, knowledge, peace, pleasure, or a good name. Meanwhile, behind the impressive application of good, sin ultimately involves an unprocessed consensus between obedience and rebellion.

There can be no victory or triumphant peace when one is unwilling to allow the superstructure of God's intervention plan to have an undoubted formative influence. The believer's life is a result of a continuous response to God's will, for this provides clarity and direction. The will of God must be done by believers if they are genuine Christians. But for this to occur two things are required: First, it must be taught and understood. Paul was chosen by God to know His will (Acts 22:14), and Paul endeavored to make all of God's will known to others. His prayer was that the believer would be filled with the knowledge of God's will (Col. 1:9), and he challenged the unbelievers to attain an understanding of God's will as their chief aim in life (Eph. 5:17). Second, God must equip the believer to be able to execute the divine will in appropriate behavior because human inability continues to coexist alongside divine sovereignty. In other words, God must give enlightenment necessary for the believer to perceive what the will of God is for their personal and ministry life.

The will of God and His guidance brings triumphant peace when one elects to allow the His will to direct matters of life's decisions. A great deal of the biblical teaching about His will pertains to behavior and His plan of salvation, learning what God's Word says about aspects of our response to Him and in concert with the church, and determining how that teaching is to be applied in new historical and cultural contexts. The there is a mystical element, looking or seeking God's direct guidance in time of need, in which one is to search for God with your questions about vocation, wisdom and leadership instruction. Prayer is the means to reach God's counsel and receive wise assessment applications.

The concept of victory or triumph signifies more than just a military conquest; ultimately victory comes from the Lord, and it is the Lord who carries on the fight. The vast terminology within the biblical context suggests that sin has three aspects: (1) disobedience to or breach of law, (2) violation of relationship with people and, (3) rebellion against God. While these are taking place, there will be no room for victory. Therefore, one must learn to stand firm in the presence of evil because obscurity opposes illumination and weakness opposes strength. The Bible provides several examples of conquering and successful battles won by God's people under His direction and oftentimes they were not peaceful events. It tells us in Judges chapter 4 how during the reign of Jabin, king of Canaan, the children of Israel did offensive and salacious things in the sight of the Lord. They were overthrown by the Canaanite captain, Sisera, who resided in Harosheth the land of the Gentiles. The Lord permitted the Canaanites to take them as slaves, due to their disbelief and obedience. While they were imprisoned, the Israelites cried out to the Lord to deliver them from their state of oppression. Deborah was one of the early judges and a prophetess to the nation of Israel. She was the wife of Lapidoth. They lived on a hill outside of the village in the country of Ephraim under a palm tree between Ramah and Bethel. The children of Israel came to her for inspired knowledge, progressive opinions, and spiritual verdicts. Deborah was the fourth judge of Israel; the children of Israel were captured during a time when they were living according to their excessiveness, independence, self-government, and unreasonableness; so they were without joy and peace because of non-compliance to the law of the living God.

They were a group of insincere and deceptive people, who were not willing to submit to God's delegated majesty. Deborah was a courageous and fearless woman of God. She was the only woman to hold the office of judge. She had extensive knowledge and wisdom outside of man's normal experience or the known law of nature. All Israel was under her administration, jurisdiction, and range of governmental rule. She was responsible for administering and distributing justice from under the palm tree located outside of the city limits. She gave a prediction before the war began that the nation of Israel would be delivered from their enemy and King Sisera, but due to the lack of faith, the warriors had callous confidence in defeating their foes. Barak name means "thunderbolt," something that stuns or acts with abrupt push or mayhem. God called Barak to lead the children of Israel out of their state of oppression and bondage, by killing their enemy. The Lord allowed them to set a trap for Sisera's army; they encamped all around them so they would have no room to escape. They did as Barak instructed them, based on Deborah's presentiment. Like any other leader who is facing a challenging charge, Barack was filled with anxiety and fear from an unknown circumstance.

Barak was like many, having problems accepting the call for duty due to diffidence or wariness. This is one dismaying reason why several have become aggravated and discouraged in the body of faith because they are seeking validation and declaration from illogical and impractical individuals. They are providing manipulative and unsound spectators, opening access or entrance to their minds, not submitting to consecrated authority. The only time some will attend an extracurricular activity or program at the church is when it bring them self-gratification or pleasure. A steward of God must remain confident enough to know the only way to have the sufficiency of joy and peace is to walk in the authority of God, according to one's calling or elect purpose. The church of Christ must understand it does not matter to God who will successfully lead His people to victory, just that someone will be willing to obey His commands and instructions on how to get there. He disregards gender, the color of one's skin, or physical stature. The Lord is strong and mighty, and is looking for some credible and vigorous warriors to enlist and take the assignment. The Lord did turn Sisera over into the hands of a woman, Deborah, because of her compliance and persevering spirit. She arose to the occasion and went with Barak to the city of Kedesh (Judg. 4:7–9).

Sometimes fright will cause us to forfeit or lose the professed blessings of the Lord. It is our duty to go, say, and do whatever the Lord has assigned us to do, so triumphant victory may be won through endurance, stamina, and temperance. God is not responsible for releasing the spirit of fear; it is the devil who ushers in this disintegrate unpleasantness and dreadful calamity to shock your spiritual foundation. You must be willing to fight and not allow anyone to come in abduct any blessings or promises that the Lord has loosed into your life. If you abdicate your responsibility, the Lord will find someone else who is eager, enthusiastic, and ready to go through the agony and pain while enduring the tedious examination, irritating experiments, and overwhelming ordeals. I do not know about you, but I would not want to go through all these excruciating and unbearable trials, only to later forfeit or lose everything because of lack of faith—to get near a breakthrough, only to jeopardize it due to lack of dependence in the omnipotent One. Nobody has any persuasive power over God's decision in selecting earthly management.

Even though the Canaanites were uniformed with impetuous forces, it was too late for them to cork what God had already put into motion. There is no harness that can contain or hold God back. The enemy will recruit earthly allies in his attacks on your life, but do not be heart-stricken, he will never be able to overpower or overthrow God's anointed one who is kept in His arms of safety. For the Lord will baffle, bewilder, or confuse the assault boundaries of the enemy. His hand is not shorted that he cannot reach the sinner, nor is His ear to heavy that will not hear cry of the inexperienced and immature.

Deborah joined Barak tin the battlefield and gave order unto the mighty men of valor, the warriors of the Lord to assail. The Lord had already set up their counterattacks and strategies the conquest; all they needed to do was show up with faith and prayer. The war was already won in the heavenly realm before they got there; but the Lord needed them to be there in the earthly realm. The Lord brought in the spirit of diversion and discomfort so that Sisera was sluggish in the craft to maintain focus on the combat. The presence of God came and made an inattentive and disturbance against the troops. Sisera, the captain of the army, became so overcome with fright that he left his chariot and fled away on foot.

He did not know his fate. He ran into village were a woman invited him to take refuge. She felt obligated to help the Israel-ites destroy Sisera. She perceived that she could not let him go with impunity. Jael invited him in and offered him shelter. Then she covered him with a cloak to keep him warm and hide him. She was very hospitable, giving him water and goat's milk for his thirst. She invited him into her tent for refuge and safety, only to trap him later. Jael did not breach the covenant that was made between her country and Israel in their early alliance. She placed something over him, so that he would feel at ease and peace. She waited until he fell asleep and murdered him with a nail through his skull as he slept. Deborah prophesied that a woman would murder Sisera. Deborah was one of several women named in the Bible who were given a prophetic gift of being able to feel the heartbeat of God.

She did more than a give a word of prophecy. She aided and sustained the nation from its state of hopelessness and misery.

After Sisera was killed, the Canaanites could no longer cause harm or punishment upon the children of Israel. The Lord blessed them and they prevailed against King Jabin and over the Canaanites. The king was eventually consumed (vv. 14–24).

Deborah had become a mother to all of Israel; God gave her an official incentive for compassionately caring for His people in a time of sorrow, suffering, and turmoil. This reward would bring her ultimate joy and overwhelming peace. Her great leadership skills gave the children of Israel exultation and jubilation over their triumphant victory, as they moved into the celebration of a victorious defeat. Her obedience allowed the Lord to pour out the spirit of foresight, so God gave the glory and honor to a woman with aid of another woman, who was in covenant relationship with Israel, Jael. Now that Sisera was dead, the kingdom of Jabin was no longer a threat to the children of Israel. The land that the Lord promised, filled with milk and honey, would be theirs, thanks to two fearless women of God, Deborah the "mother or queen bee" and Jael the "mountain goat."

Deborah was one of several persons in the Old Testament who were endued by God with the anointing of the Holy Spirit for certain tasks. As a judge in Israel, she was given special knowledge and wisdom to defeat the enemy. On the day of Pentecost, God poured out the Holy Spirit, filling the people with power and giving them spiritual gifts. The Comforter and Spirit of Truth, which Jesus promised them had come to do His work, and will remain until Jesus returns.

The church of God needs more Deborahs and Jaels—women who are not afraid to stand up for righteous sake. So many are standing by the door of the safe haven, which is apparently unmanned, allowing the opponent to come and take undeveloped and untrained members into spiritual bondage. They will not give appropriate guidance or proper instructions on how to fight spiritual battles. The measure of one's spiritual impartation from God has to do with your calling; consequently the gifting is not for self, but rather for the edification (teaching) of the body of believers. You are prepared for service when you listen to the audible and tranquil voice of God telling you what battles are to be fought and what battles are to be declined.

## PEACEFUL IN THE MIDST OF THE STORM

You are involved in a spiritual battle daily. No matter what your personal talent, gifting, or anointing, Satan's (the god of this world) goal is to try to blind your eyes to his existence, as well as keep you from knowing that salvation and deliverance come from the Lord Jesus Christ. The arch-enemy uses three ways come against you: (1) a tempter, (2) a deceiver, or (3) an accuser. The first time he came to mankind was as a tempter in the form of a serpent. He tempted Eve and then also Jesus in the wilderness. Paul acknowledges the role of Satan in 1 Thessalonians 3:5: "For this reason, when I could no longer endure it, I sent to know your faith, lest by some means the tempter had tempted you, and our labor might be in vain" (NKJV). The second time he came was to cause harm as the deceiver, which is a more subtle tactic than temptation. Paul referred to this attack in 2 Corinthians 11:14–15: "And no wonder! For Satan himself transforms himself into an angel of light. Therefore it is no great thing if his ministers also transform themselves into ministers of righteousness, whose end will be according to their works" (NKJV). The third and strongest form of attack is that of an accuser, one who opposes honesty, integrity, and morality. In Revelation 12:10 the apostle John tells us: "Then I heard a loud voice saying in heaven, 'Now salvation, and strength, and the kingdom of our God, and the power of His Christ have come, for the accuser of our brethren, who accused them before our God day and night, has been cast down" (NKJV). On the other hand, we must understand that God sometimes permits Satan to tempt, to deceive, and to accuse just to test our faith. The house of prayer is engaged in spiritual battle, as Satan tries to convince the believers that the there is no triumphant victory. But the Father has provided protection and weapons for the children of the Most High God, it is up to us to pick them up and use them.

## SPIRITUAL BATTLEGROUNDS

### Bodily

Not all disease, infirmity, and sickness are attacks of Satan, although a number of them are.

### Morally

Satan will tempt you to break God's ethical and righteous laws, when you refuse to follow the gospel of Christ. Then he will delude you into justifying your actions and wrongdoings, and blind you to your need for repentance.

### Viewpoint

He sends seducing spirits, doctrines of demons, and false prophets to attach our assurance, confidence, reliance, and stamina.

### Offspring

Children that move out from the covering of believing parents will become susceptible and vulnerable to assaults of Satan.

## Places and Effects

Due to alliance and involvement with the occult and super-natural demonic activity or influence, some buildings and artifacts have been imparted with satanic curses, spirits, and strongholds.

The Word of God offers us defense, fortification, guarding, safety, and security during supernatural warfare. This warfare requires the girdle of truth, the breastplate of righteousness, the gospel sandals of peace, the shield of faith, the helmet of salvation, and the sword of the Spirit (Eph. 6:10–18). Stewards of the Lord have various arms to employ during spiritual combat: (1) the sword of the Spirit, the Word of God (Heb. 4:12), (2) the blood of the Lamb and the word of their testimony (Rev. 12:11), (3) singing and praises to the Lord (2 Chron. 20:22), (4) praying in the Spirit (Eph. 6:18), (5) Spiritual gifts (1 Cor. 12:8–10), (6) the name of Jesus (Acts 5:40–41), (7) fasting (Isa. 58:6), (8) binding and loosing (Matt. 16:19), (8) resisting evil forces by faith (1 Pet. 5:8–9), (9) drawing near to the power of God (James 4:7–8), and (10) abiding in Christ and prayer (Rom. 8:26–27).[4]

God shall receive all praise and thanksgiving for your meager victories, as well as your exceptional ones. The Lord is not listless; He can overturn any antagonism of the enemy. He is your banner, *Jehovah Nissi*, held high in every conversation and the strong tower who will shield you from criticism, grievance, or peril. You have the jurisdictional rights and power to reclaim your possessions in the name of Jesus Christ. The Lord will protect and defend your good name, returning joy and peace. Under the Lord's rule, in the creation there is decency, order, and dependability having a radiant or resplendent quality or state of non-violence. There is celebration for security against the iniquitous and pestilent mouths, hearts, and hands united in the pursuit of injustice. Trust the Lord while under the siege by a hostile intrusion by prominent weapons of the aggressor's tongue or vicious comments. The false and malicious statements are pestiferous and pernicious, meant to hurt others' reputation and leaving scars on their name. This is the time for prayer and supplication with thanksgiving. In spite of the current situation, there is a peace, thanksgiving, and blessings on the horizon.

Deborah used her spiritual insight to facilitate and assist Barak when it came to waging war against their persecutors. Barak is proof that anyone with determination can do all things with the help of the Lord. Deborah is a prime example of someone making a difference or impact in others lives. She took on her God-given obligation with self-assurance and self-possession, refusing to let any devil rob or steal what the God had promised her and His people.

## PEACE THAT SURPASSES ALL UNDERSTANDING

There may be days, weeks, or months at a time when you feel sad and hopeless. Sometimes you become extremely irritable with thoughts racing a mile a minute, or you just feel on the edge. Only the Spirit of peace can cancel such extreme mood swings, episodes of ups (mania) and downs (depression). Does this sound like a commercial? If so, then the Spirit of God has your attention! If this sounds anything like what you are experiencing on your roller coaster ride there is an effective treatment available for you today. There is no prescribed medication necessary or over the counter dosage recommendation, only improvement in your overall standard or quality of life, gratification of peace, satisfaction with everyday activities, and optimistic relationships with friends and family. All this can occur after the Spirit of God takes residency in your body, mind, and soul.

It is clinically proven that there are three forms of chemical disorders, mood swings, or chronic episodes that one can suffer from without the habitation of the Spirit of truth: (1) mania, (2) depression, and (3) mixed. Common symptoms of a manic episode are from feeling extremely happy at one moment to being very irritable and anxious the next, talking too fast and too much, and having more energy and needing less sleep than usual. Common symptoms of a depressive episode include feeling overwhelming sadness or emptiness, low energy, trouble concentrating, changes in appetite or sleep patterns, loss of interest, and contemplative thoughts of dying or suicide. A mixed episode includes symptoms that are unrelated and varied with both depression and manic temperaments. The Scriptures teach that the Spirit of God cannot dwell in a tabernacle that is unclean, henceforth in order to be released from such false impressions or misapprehensions coming from vex entities, there must be a transformation.

Oftentimes, the absence or being void of the presence of the Holy Spirit can be the reason why you are experiencing adulterated feelings, contaminated thoughts, and impure motives. It is said that these disorders are illness caused by an imbalance of brain chemicals; but the Word of God tells us in Ephesians 6:12, "For we do not wrestle against flesh and blood, but against principalities, against powers, against the rulers of the darkness of this age, against spiritual wickedness in the heavenly places."

These forces come against unsound or unstable intellectuals, creating contemptible insinuation, counterfeit impersonation, or creative images dispensing from their powerful and unseen world system source. This leaves room for a massive invasion or takeover from the sphere of malevolence. It is vital that you become a skilled and trained soldier, prepared to withstand assaults from vile counterparts or wicked spirits that have invaded your mentality or mind set. The helmet of salvation is here to protect your mind, for all of Satan's work has been cancelled and destroyed at the Cross.

Today the Lord is repositioning His church to line up with the heavenly kingdom, as ambassadors of Christ. You are called to represent His rule as:

- A set apart nation
- A people consecrated for God's possession
- A purchased people
- An acquired generation
- A government of positive influence

God has chosen, acquired, consecrated, and set you apart as His nation in order to move His purpose forward and put His plan in action, to bring the Word of Truth to a dying generation.

The peace of God is the only object that can productively set in motion revelation and transformation. As Christ's legislative body, you are accountable and liable for establishing a righteous paradigm shift in the earthly atmosphere to influence affirmative and constructive modifications, not altercations. You are given territory to rule. There should be a measure of peace that surpasses all understanding within your basis, foundation, or reason. You must be equipped to take territorial leadership within the inner city, urban community, professional business arenas, and governmental agencies as well as schools, churches, and your home.

God has not settled you in diverse communities or neighborhoods just to enjoy the best of life, but to be a living testimony to alcoholics; drug users; dysfunctional families, children, and spouse abusers; or even sexual predators. In spite of addiction and habitual behavior, the Lord is able to deliver or rescue anyone from anything. Only God can break the deception trying to gain assess to individual's minds and hearts, and bring enduring power to all unbelievers. You must be functional and operational to confer the godly authority and inborn ability to lead others to the throne of grace.

No matter what sort of transition you are involved in currently, travailing into your new season takes endurance, patience, and preparation. Change is designed as a process, not as a monotonous event. Moving to one's next dimension does not occur over night, but an effective changeover, conversion, or shift requires time. You must go through the process of elimination that is essential for you to learn lessons that will aid in redeveloping your inner strength required to possess the innovative place or guaranteed land. He will begin to extract foes one by one—all barriers, hindrances, impediments, obstructions, and obstacles that are challenging progression. The Spirit alters the unpleasant attitudes, foolish mind sets, and undesirable relationships, ridding all distractions that could jeopardize spiritual development—the strongholds escalating to monopolize aims, goals, and visions, God will use the various orchestrated conflicts and confrontations to assist with overcoming superficial fear and replace it with supernatural faith. You should remain thankful in the season of preparation and focus on optimistic outcomes with great expectation for what the Lord is training you to become. The Lord will remove the matters that would delay you and replace them with matter that will replenish drive and motivation. Transformation is not a private matter because while moving to the next dimension you will impact many people. Thank God for the peace that surpasses all understanding with wisdom, gratitude, and supplication for all material provision, refuge, and safety in the storms of life.

## PEACE AND THANKSGIVING

You must trust God to bring peace and thanksgiving in the midst of disorder, turmoil, and uproar. David wrote a wonderful song of laudation and thanksgiving in Psalm 100. It helps us perceive how to proclaim gratefulness unto the Lord over every condition and situation.

Everyone and everything on the earth is to express adoration and thanksgiving to the Creator: "Make a joyful noise unto the LORD, all ye lands" (Ps. 100:1). Helping, serving, and working with others with a servitude heart unto the Lord, with a spirit of gladness and contentment, is essential. Stewards of the Lord should never go before the Father with complaints, grumbling, and murmuring, but come with praise and worship oblation from the fruit of our lips. True worshipers esteem the Lord for all His goodness with a spirit of certainty and dependability, for we were created to offer Him glory, reverence, and tribute: "Serve the LORD with gladness: come before his presence with singing" (v. 2).

God will make allowance and concession for those who are poor in physical, mental, or spiritual health. He can dislocate calamity and upheaval of the present or impeding regret of the past, misfortune, or frustration caused by adventurous dangers, hazards, and perils. You are created in His likeness and given dominance over disturbing disappointment, upsetting grief, or sorrows of life. He is the Great Shepherd who will feed His sheep with anointed awareness, conception, intellect, perception, and wisdom. Have anticipation and expectation for you are His precious workmanship; and He will always take care of those who He loves. Although He uses the rod of correction to rebuke or scold by rectifying your defects and faults, He covers you with a shield of protection to safeguard you from the wiles of the roaring lion that is lurking around to devour your ambitions, hopes, and dreams.

Blessing and honor all belong to the Lord for He is worthy: "Know ye that the LORD he is God: it is he that hath made us, and not we ourselves; we are his people, and the sheep of his pasture" (v. 3). Even though you come into the sanctuary, the consecrated and holy place of prayer, conferring Him with appreciative and obsessive petition, He will not show up to your invitation if your heart is not set apart for His use. Children of the Most High God should know how to conduct themselves when they are requesting the glory of the Lord by invitation: "Enter into his gates with thanksgiving, and into his courts with praise: be thankful unto him, and bless his name" (v. 4). The Lord God is faithful, steadfast, and trustworthy in every way. He is full of mysterious love, even as He penalizes the obstinate with consist restraint. God's Word is without deceit or pretense, is forever, and has forbearance to all generations to come: "for the LORD is good; his mercy is everlasting; and his truth endureth to all generations" (v. 5).

Christ illustrates how a sinful woman interrupted a dinner party to anoint His feet with precious perfume. He told the host that her action sprang from gratitude for forgiveness (Luke 7:37–47). When He healed ten lepers only one, a Samaritan, returned to thank Him for the supernatural healing (17:11–19). Throughout the Old and New Testament it is emphasized that believers should be thankful for every individual provision and offer gratitude for God's saving grace. Those whom God has brought from death to life should understand the importance of thanksgiving.

Thanksgiving is a central component of prayer. Believers have retaining power enhanced with joy and peace; however, the Scriptures state that the redeemed are to give thanks for the essentials and rudiments provided by the Father. There will not be any glorification without prior visitation, no visitation without sanctification, or no sanctification with repentance. Therefore one cannot obtain exalting peace without all of these. Peace is necessary to avoid civil conflict and dismiss all signs of anxiety. The Spirit of peace can control actions, emotions, motivations, and thoughts. God's saving grace offers reassuring peace and complete security and well-being. God's peace includes prosperity, security, and tranquility.

> *Thank you, Lord, for abundance, for the immense contribution and supply of blissfulness, and for tranquility and wealth. Thank you, Lord, for hope, joy, and peace and the endurance, the ability to last, continue, or remain as the enemy brings severity, distress, and fatigue in my life. Thank you, Lord, for the tolerant, under unction of the Holy Spirit that will usher in the spirit of jubilation and silence. Thank you, Lord, for Your saving grace that rescued the profane from a sin-sick nature or state, releasing joy and peace. Thank you, Lord, for encouragement that gives hope, courage, and confidence to fill my spirit man with unchangeable joy and peace.*

There are promises of connectivity when we elect to obey God's commands even when disaster and calamity strikes. The Lord will ordain peace for those who trust in Him; abundant and overflowing peace and righteousness come in a refreshing wave. The good news pours out the contents of peace and salvation.

*Thank you, Lord, for joy and peace that will bring me back into godly order with the Word and Your will, which can disclose Your destination and purpose for me.*

The order, accompanied with joy, will give you peace to win the race and give you the endurance and strength to go on. We must thank God for the promissory note of redemption, where He erased the debt of sin and become responsible and obligated for all our defaults and demerits. The actual and practical concept of peace is both to attain fulfillment of full joy and healthy relationships with others. Eventually authentic peace can be found in God. Peace destroys the yoke of strife and restores joy when you can celebrate the uniqueness in others. Peace is not assured only to those who rest in the arms of the Master, but those who follow the commission of Christ and are led by the Holy Spirit. Peace is received by faith in Christ; this is what brings opposition to Satan and his work. Peace is another way of exposing what salvation implies—the saving grace plan which Christ's redemptive work will achieve for His disciples. Total well-being and inner rest of the spirit is linked to communion with God; all genuine peace is His gift.

Faith offers everlasting joy and peace; but salvation is the commonsense, biblical language used to identify the subjective change in a lifestyle, when by faith one has received the benefit of Christ's death, resurrection, and ascension. There are six appearances or categories of faith that is perceived in Scriptures: (1) doctrinal, (2) saving, (3) justifying, (4) indwelling, (5) daily, and (6) endowing. The peace of God escorts serenity and stillness of mind, freeing us from apprehension, nervousness, and trepidation. This is divinely bestowed in times of fretfulness, which exceeds our own discernment or observation of personal problems. It instills harmony and concordance created by God for His people; no matter what course of action occurs, you should maintain calmness. The Spirit provides a quiet and peaceable life that through intercessory prayer enables just governments to ensure the citizens a trouble-free residence from the fortress of evil or forces outside its borders. Your prayer also aids competent government in maintaining law and order within its own borders. In spite of every situation, remember joy does come in the morning, but not without peace.

## 12

## JOY COMES IN THE MORNING

*Then will I go unto the altar of God, unto God my exceeding
joy; yea upon the harp will I praise thee, O God my God.*

—Psalm 43:4

OW DOES ONE KNOW that joy will come in the morning? By the Word of God! Some may have experienced hours, days, weeks, months, or even years of burdens filled with oppressed anguish, remembrance, and pain. The measure of promised joy comes when one can comprehend the authority and power to obtain a level of maturity.

Joy and peace grows from a just life of faith due to God's goodness and mercy through the contentment and enjoyment that one displays in the things of God. Keep in mind that Jesus left His joy and peace to sustain us during the times when storms and raging winds of trouble begin to blow on our spiritual house. Regardless of circumstances, situations, or trials, there is always going to be a rainbow full of harmony and tranquility to assist you through life's daily challenges, obstacles, and stumbling blocks. Look to the hills, realizing that all your support comes from the Lord and there is nothing impossible for God. The rescue missions cannot take place if you are not in position to be rescued, if you are not ready to receive cheerfulness after an unanticipated or unexpected past, present, or future battle.

Our Father owns the cattle on the hills, therefore do not become consume with carnal desires, fleshly longings, and worldly urges, which can only lead you into foolish greed and prideful accomplishments while alluring you into the dark side. There is a path or side that is only concerned about their own selfish achievements, ambitions, and success—self-made individuals who gain everything without God or man's assistance. These individuals may never be willing to consider that material possessions cannot bring eternal bliss, sustaining contentment, or everlasting enjoyment until it is too late, when they are void of inner composure and serenity. Their mind is always racing trying to calculate how to acquire or attain the next undiscovered invention or product to make them more affluent or worldwide renowned. They are also looking for ways to have or take advantage of the unsuspected. Remember the Scripture asks us what the profit is if a man would gain the entire world and lose his soul (Mark 8:36).

God's joy and peace will release you from the world system. The illustration of the Samaritan woman at the well speaks of was a sinful woman, possibly an adulterous woman or a harlot or prostitute. She was detached from all the other women due to her immoral lifestyle, so she could only go to the well from dawn to early sunrise when the others weren't there. Dawn or early sunrise is the best time for a visitation from the Lord; His visitation was going to bring her interminable joy and incessant peace—a restored life. He told her all about her past, present, and future situation. She required cleansing from her corrupt moral fiber or makeup. When Jesus met her at the well, He offered her the living water of salvation that would not only deterge her mortal soul from the impurities of the flesh that she had been subjected to for many years, but also change the condition of heart, providing her with admirable principles, praiseworthy standards, and respectable values.

The Messiah would make accessible the living waters from His well of refinement and mercy, the fountain of truthfulness to bring revitalization and sanctification to her dead soul. She ran and left her water pot, representing her old nature, behind to share the good news with the town's people who would hear about this great Deliverer. Jesus discarded her misery, answered her desperation, and removed her embarrassment caused by internal obsessions and external desideration by giving an answer to her present state or condition.

First, the lust of the flesh is insatiable craving to pacify or fulfill a psychological and physical sense of necessity and give the inherit nature sensual gratification—man's eager craving for things of the world to provide tangible and pleasurable urges to the carnal desires. The Holy Spirit can give you sustaining power to choose freedom from fundamental and natural instinct. When you elect or select to choose things of the world, you ultimately exhibit rejection to the things of God.

> But put on the Lord Jesus Christ, and make no provision for the flesh, to fulfill its lusts.
>
> —Romans 13:14, nkjv

> Walk in the Spirit, and you shall not fulfill the lust of the flesh.
>
> —Galatians 5:16, nkjv

> Where do wars and fights come from among you?
> Do they not come from desires for pleasure that war
> in your members?
>
> —JAMES 4:1, NKJV

> Beloved, I beg you as sojourners and pilgrims, abstain
> from fleshly lusts which war against the soul.
>
> —1 PETER 2:11, NKJV

There must not be any alliances with any secular methods, routines, and techniques.

Second, the lust of the eyes possesses a yearning to comply or fulfill physical obsession with counterfeit imageries and uncontrolled metaphors posing irrational threats to the frame of mind, state of mind, or way of thinking. The lust of the eyes is a very dangerous and hazardous stronghold, since it is perplexed by controlling inner belief, judgment, opinion, and viewpoint. The eyes are a major and vital organ of sight in humans, needed for giving vision and voyage direction. The eyes can reveal artificial conception through projections that are played back to the former opinion of one's intelligence and outlook, which give delusion, false impression, and misapprehension to the mind storing sinful and lustful obsessions.

> And why do you look at the speck in your brother's
> eye, but do not consider the plank in your own eye?
>
> —MATTHEW 7:3, NKJV

> And if your eye causes you to sin, pluck it out and
> cast if from you. It is better for you to enter into life

with one eye, rather than having two eyes, to be cast
into hell fire.

—MATTHEW 18:9, NKJV

They are spots and blemishes, carousing in their
own deceptions while they feast with you, having
eyes full of adultery and that cannot cease from sin,
enticing unstable souls. They have a heart trained in
covetous practices, and are accursed children.

—2 PETER 2:13–14, NKJV

God's spiritual healing can remove the scales from the eyes,
providing undiscriminating visualization with perceptual foresight, hindsight, or insight.

Third, the pride of life is one's overestimated and overvalued
outlook about oneself, inflated with impudence and overconfi-
dence in how life is envisioned. It is disunited under the influence
or stronghold of the evil one, seeing life's rewarding as all about
getting things for one's self pleasure. The spirit of rapacious-
ness is a counterpart of this ungodly spirit. This individual is
condescending with arrogance, conceit, and loftiness because of
supernumerary desires for encompassing abundance of assets,
resources, and riches of this world, all without consulting God.
The person desires ownership of pertinent territory and is apt
to cheat, lie, or scam to attain others' property and material
possessions. Anyone who is encountering the influence of these
stronghold spirits will be capsized; their ship will sink.

At the end of the day, man has nothing to offer you but pipe
dreams and false hope. Put your assurance, confidence, and
trust in Jesus. God's nature is not to show an inattentive or
neglectful attitude as you come into His presence with a focused

JOY COMES IN THE MORNING

and ready posture along with a broken and contrite heart; He will answer your prayers. Do not expect a person to affirm or validate the inward working of conciliation or contentment that only comes from the anointing of God. The moral cheapening influences of this universe cannot give you something it does not have.

The limited power of this world system is not capable of incorporating genuine enjoyment, fulfillment, or pleasure. Even when Satan was in heaven, he was not complete with the joy and peace of God, regarding himself as supremacist in all things. He was full of abhorrent and obnoxious self-importance, which caused him to be permanently evicted from heaven (Isa. 14:12–15) and damned to the lake of fire in hell. This transparent biblical illustration shows the reader that Lucifer, Satan, was cast down from third heaven due to his deplorable misrepresentations and proceedings. He thought that he was greater than God. He was not satisfied with his heavenly position and desired more. The Bible teaches that unchaste leaders are lowered to satanic control and demonic influence; this world is directly under Satan's guidance, leadership, and subjection. The ruler, autocrat, or lord of this world will deteriorate along with its dehumanization and wickedness.

None of the characteristic traits of the evil one give off an illuminating spirit of joy, love, and peace. The spiritual personality of Christ gives a distinguished quality of joy and peace, with genuine quantity of love that comes through fasting and praying. The love of Jesus will give freedom from the world system of greediness and pretentiousness. The Holy Spirit will subrogate pride with humility—the state or quality of being meek and lowly, not inclined to anger or resentment, but absence of self-assertion. The Holy Spirit will replace lust with temperance, freeing from the redundant frame of mind or natural disposition to bring to proper continence and discipline, having much power to do things in moderation without conducting erratic action or deportment.

The highway of righteousness pilots us with surpassing joy and peace. Joy is the test of true righteousness when you are being tried during the midnight hour and the enemy of your soul is holding you hostage and will not allow you to seek the Lord before or by daybreak. The works of your tranquility will usher in the effective or operative assurance in knowing that all is going to work out for your good. After devastation and calamity leaves, restoration will come in to restore all things. The outpouring of the Spirit is linked with a more than sufficient supply of elements surrounding any foreign agents that will overshadow the valley and wilderness adventures as well as the mountaintop observations.

The fruit of the Spirit will led you to the path of goodness and uprightness. The test of time has proven that the more you go through, the greater the compensation; so remain in the fruitful field of gladness and solitude. This is where the anointing is held without limitations of joy and peace, providing breakthroughs in every circumstance or situation through God's saving grace and tender mercy. Daily you must learn how to pick up your cross and carry it, being able to reveal to the world that you are more than a conqueror if you are willing to stand up for equality and impartiality with integrity.

There is sureness and confidence that God hears the requests or cries of the people, supplying complete security and protection, which is given to those that love the enforced accountability and expected commands of respectability. All strife is resolved, and peace is reinstated. No matter how others may try to hold dictatorship over your life, allow the Creator to guide and direct your path of righteousness. Peace with God will involve contradiction to the aggressor and his work and workers and proclaims a deeper and more lasting sereneness in the fullness of sanction and seclusion from the presence of old nature. The Holy Spirit will usher you into the temple area that is separated from spiritual bondage from religious customs and traditional beliefs. Since the separation has been ripped in two by the purified sacrifice of Christ, it gives God's chosen and adopted stewards confidence in the purpose for which God allowed Jesus to travel thirty-two generations to become ruler of the entire universe.

This was the opportune moment to give humanity another choice in life which offered freedom from obsessive indulgences, criminal or moral offenses, miscellaneous transgressions, and vexing wrongdoings. God will furnish the means of support through focus on our profound joyous praise and triumphant victory with highlights of prominence. The former existence leads to permanent end of life and condemnation to an unhappy fate, since the sinful nature is bound up with bloodshed, hostility, insubordination, and unacceptability of God. The law brings condemnation since it points out and magnifies failures. You must no longer walk according to the flesh, but according to the Spirit. The kingdom of God is not of trivial matters, but righteousness, peace, and joy. There is no joy and peace to come until you are willing to extricate sin's defilement from every core or essence of your being, purging out your conscience with transparency, virtue, and wholesomeness.

As believers, there is hope and comfort in knowing that God's ordained message is that the nations everywhere will bow down and worship the sovereign God, for He is merciful and truthful. And His joy and peace lives forever; it is belongs to the realm of the supernatural. For the believer, the secular joys are common for the human existences which are dissimilar from spiritual ones. For instance, the joy of the harvest is used in Psalm 126:5-6 describes the final victory over one's adversaries. In other words, supernatural joys elevate secular happiness, as secular accomplishment and attainments are regarded as unexpected benefits from God.

To overcome the lusts of flesh, eyes, and world system, we have to gain victory over the sinful pattern in our standard of living or way of living. To do this you must submit yourself under the authority of God, because you have been born again and the Holy Spirit dwells within. This is not impossible, but is oftentimes challenging. Yet, there are two aspects that can occupy us in overcoming trials and taking back our joy and peace: (1) forsaking secular ideology and philosophy, and (2) upholding a committed and devoted lifestyle to the Lord. Christ died for your sins on an old rugged cross so you can be healed from all unrighteousness, and by His stripes you have healing power; not only physical healing, but also spiritual healing necessary to bring salvation to those who trust in Him. As aliens and strangers whose citizenship is in heaven, you must remain separated from the corruptible system of coercion, influence, manipulation, and persuasion of evil forces. We are no longer free to yield to destructive sinful desires, lusts, or urges, for these are things that keep man an enemy of God. The persecutions that you will have to face or undergo are divinely appointed or set to purify God's stewards. Never forget, certainty of salvation is a reason for fellowship with Jesus that brings continuous joy and peace.

# NOTES

## Chapter 1

### WHAT IS EXCEEDING JOY?

1. *World Book Encyclopedia* (Chicago, IL: World Book, Inc., 1985), s.v. "peace," 182–183.

## Chapter 2

### HOW DO I GET THIS THING CALLED JOY?

1. Edward E. Hindson, ed., *Zondervan KJV Study Bible* (Grand Rapids, MI: Zondervan, 2002).
2. Ibid.
3. Notes from Smith Wigglesworth, http://www.cai.org/bible-studies/notes-smith-wigglesworth (accessed August 1, 2008).

## Chapter 3

### WHO HAS TAKEN MY JOY?

1. *Holman Illustrated Bible Dictionary* (Nashville, TN: B & H Publishing Group, 2003), 621.

## Chapter 4

### WILL MY JOY SUSTAIN ITSELF?

1. *World Book Encylcopedia* (Chicago, IL: World Book, Inc., 1985), 346–351.
2. Ibid., 260–261, 400–401, 444, 960.

*Chapter 11*

## SALVATION BRINGS REASSURING JOY AND PEACE

1. *World Book Encyclopedia,* 183–184.
2. Earl D. Radmacher, *Salvation* (Nashville, TN: Thomas Nelson, Inc., 2000), 6.
3. Ibid., 7.
4. Silvia Charles, *Women in the Bible* (Tulsa, OK: Hensley Publishing, 2001), 113–114.

## TO CONTACT THE AUTHOR

kidsgrateful@yahoo.com